THE
ABUNDANT
LIFE

VOLUME 1

PRACTICAL THEOLOGY FOR
ABUNDANT LIVING

DARRELL J. AHRENS

The Abundant Life: Volume 1 – Practical Theology for Abundant Living

Copyright © 2023 by Darrell J. Ahrens

ISBN 978-1-62967-260-1
Library of Congress Control Number: 2023911708

WiseMediaGroup.com | Morro Bay, California

v23-7.25

OTHER BOOKS BY DARRELL J. AHRENS

Divine Love / Divine Intolerance

How secular progressive liberalism has corrupted the meaning of the word "Tolerance," and its devastating effects on Church, Government, Education, Society, and Culture.

Turn and Burn:
A Fighter Pilot's Memories and Confessions

The author's pride in being part of the fighter pilot community can be summed up by the final phrase of a poem about military aviators written by an unknown author that goes, "Because we flew, we envy no man on earth."

Ungodly, Unamerican, and Unhinged:
The New Radicalized Democratic Party

Evidence of political and spiritual corruption in the new, radicalized Democrat Party.

Acknowledgements

I dedicate this book to Jesus Christ, Son of God and Son of Man, my Lord, Savior, and Big Brother.

Gratitude

I am most grateful to my publisher Brian Schwartz for his understanding, patience, and superb talent in organizing my scribblings into a work of art.

66

Jesus said:

"I came that they might have life, and might have it abundantly."

John 10:10

Symbology of book cover to book's title "The Abundant Life."

The Image of Jesus reminds us that He is the author and source of *The Abundant Life* that belongs to those whose eyes are fixed on Him.

The flying birds remind us of the prophecy of Isaiah 40: "Those who hope in the Lord will renew their strength. They will soar on wings like eagles," which symbolizes the freedom we have with the Abundant Life in Christ.

The outstretched hands symbolize generosity, reminding us of the Apostle Paul's advice to his young protege Timothy in 1 Timothy 6: "Command them to do good, to be rich in good deeds, and to be generous and willing to share…so that they may take hold of the life that is truly life."

TABLE OF CONTENTS

INTRODUCTION

Some of you may remember the "Peanuts" cartoons which were so popular in the nation some years ago. In one of those cartoons, Lucy and Linus are looking out the window watching it rain. It was pouring, and had been for quite awhile. Lucy said, "Wow! Look at all that rain!" Then she became agitated and said, "What if it doesn't stop? What if it floods? What if it floods and covers the whole world?" Linus responded, "That will never happen because in the ninth chapter of Genesis, God promised Noah that there would never again be a flood that covered the whole world, and He gave us a sign of His promise - the rainbow." Lucy said, "Oh, I'm so relieved. You've taken a great load off my mind." And Linus said, "Good theology has a way of doing that!"

Linus was right. Good, sound theology not only has a way of taking a load off our minds, but it is the only sure foundation for life, for the abundant life. There is only one source, one location, for good, sound theology, and that is in the Word of God, Holy Scripture. And the more we know that Word, the more abundant life becomes. As the saying goes, "A Bible that is falling apart from use usually belongs to a person who is not falling apart."

Wise men of old, philosophers and seers, considered theology to be the "queen of the sciences." Why? Because everything since creation, including creation itself, is founded upon good, sound theology - that is, the order of creation established by a transcendent, immanent, present, personal God. It is this good, sound theology through which the Holy Spirit gives us knowledge and understanding of God's revelation and God's working in this world and in our lives. It is through this good, sound theology that the Holy Spirit brings us to saving faith in our Lord and Savior Jesus Christ. It is through this good, sound theology that the Holy Spirit trains us in true and godly discernment, the ability to distinguish between the true and the false, the good and the bad, the temporal and the eternal, the earthly and the heavenly.

Our Founding Fathers clearly understood this. In their brilliance, the vast majority of them were devout Christians with deep understanding of theology and its essential nature in building a nation unique and exceptional among all nations. They understood human nature and its sin, and that in a democratic republic government of the people, by the people, for the people, and a free society in which the people were to enjoy freedoms far beyond any society in the past, which they envisioned for America, it would be essential that both government and citizens acknowledge and willingly submit to a transcendent authority and a transcendent code of morality and ethics.

The Founders made it clear that they established this government and society on the foundation of Judeo-Christianity, the moral code of the Ten Commandments, and a government submissive to the people. George Washington, our first President, stated, "True religion" (and he was speaking of the Christian tradition) "affords the surest support to just government.....Of all the dispositions and habits which lead to political prosperity, religion and morality are indispensable supports.....Reason and experience both forbid us to expect that national morality can prevail in exclusion of religious principle." Time and time again, Washington insisted that religion and morality were the foundational pillars of free government and a democratic society, and that without them, neither free government or democracy could prevail.

John Adams, our second President, stated, "We have no government armed with power capable of contending with human passions unbridled by morality and religion. Avarice, ambition, revenge....would break the strongest cords of our Constitution as a whale goes through a net. Our Constitution was made only for a moral and religious people. It is wholly inadequate to the government of any other."

Thomas Jefferson, our third President, stated, "God, Who gave us life gave us liberty. And can the liberties of a nation be thought secure when we have removed their only firm basis, conviction in the minds of the people that these liberties are the Gift of God? That they are not to be violated but with His wrath?"

James Madison, our fourth President, stated, "We have staked the whole future of American civilization, not upon the power of government, far from it. We have staked the future of all of our political institutions upon the capacity of mankind for self-government; upon the capacity of each and all of us to govern ourselves, to control ourselves, to sustain ourselves, according to the Ten Commandments of God."

I could quote many, many other Founders involved in the birth of our nation, regarding their firm belief that the religion, theology, Ten Commandments, and morality, embodied in the Judeo-Christian tradition were foundational to the nation they were building, fundamental to the character of the nation, its institutions, culture, and society, and essential for the future strength, security, and success of that nation. The evidence is overwhelming, and to deny this is to blind oneself to reality and historical fact.

The abundant life built upon good, sound theology is also a well-governed life. Just as a poorly-governed nation and society eventually descends into confusion and chaos, so an individual poorly-governed life eventually results in disaster. The well governed life is not a life of sinless perfection; we are all sinners saved only by the grace of God in Christ our Savior. The well-governed life is one that determines to follow God, to seek His righteousness in Christ, and whose dominant influence in life is God's Word. And when one fails in this determination, the well-governed life confesses and repents of its sin, seeks God's forgiveness for the sake of our Savior Jesus Christ Who paid the full price for our sins on the cross and whose Blood just keeps cleansing us of sin, renewing us, and restoring us back into that well-governed life in the Father's love.

The Psalmist in Psalm one calls the person living the well-governed life "blessed." This does not mean that this person will not experience the hardships, trials, tribulations, and yes, even persecutions common to life in this sinful world. Jesus told us in His Word that just as He was mocked, reviled, and persecuted in this world, so His followers (that's us) would be. But He assures us that He will never leave us or forsake us, that He is right there with us in all conditions and circumstances of life, to strengthen us, support us, comfort us, and bear us up.

Just as a well-governed nation is organized to best serve, protect, and bless its citizens, so the well-governed life is organized to best serve, protect, and bless the person in all the circumstances, successes, failures, and hardships of this life. Do we want such a life? Do we want a life that overcomes all obstacles, trials, tribulations, and sheer frustrations that Satan, this world, and our sinful flesh throws at us, a life that bears much fruit for God's glory and our greatest good, a life that comes to its divinely directed fulfillment? We won't find the secret to such a life in some "how to" book written by some secular guru. We will only find this life when we are filled to the brim of our human capacity with the love of God, the fullness of God the Father; when we are at One in faith and obedience, praise and thanksgiving, with our Lord and Savior Jesus Christ Who is the Way, the Truth, and the Life; when we are totally submissive to the Holy Spirit, Who brings us to saving faith, and Who leads us, guides us, counsels us, sanctifies and sustains us in that faith.

And when such a life on this earth is ended, and the person goes to heaven into everlasting glory, God and people will say of it: "This was a life well-lived; this was a life with a lasting legacy; this was the well-governed life; this was the abundant life." It is my hope and prayer that the messages in this book might have some small part, or perhaps a greater than small part, in contributing to the readers' understanding of the abundant life. As Jesus said, He came and went to the cross, and rose again, so that we might have the new life, the blessed life, the well-governed life, the abundant life.

For His sake, and for your own sake, don't settle for anything less.

Darrell J. Ahrens

CHAPTER 1 - THE GOD OF THE BIBLE

"Satisfy us in the morning with your unfailing love, that we may sing for joy and be glad all our days. May the favor of the Lord our God rest upon us; establish the work of our hands for us - yes, establish the work of our hands."

Psalm 90: 14, 17

THE DIVINE LOVE AFFAIR

Text: Genesis 2: 2-17; Romans 6: 19-23; Mark 8: 1-13; John 5: 24-30.

Theme: God's Delight in His Creation.

Theme Statement: An aspect of God's love for us is His delight in His creation. God delights in you. His delight is evidenced by the fact that He created you for fellowship; He redeemed you to restore that fellowship when it was broken by sin; and He sanctifies you so that fellowship can continue throughout your life here on earth, and then in heaven for eternity. When He returns to take us to heaven with Him, we will know the fullness of that delight and rejoice in it forever.

Key Passage: Genesis 2:7. "The Lord God formed the man from the dust of the ground and breathed into his nostrils the breath of life, and man became a living being."

✝

God formed man out of the dust of the ground. I find it interesting that, in creating the heavens and the earth and all they contain, God simply spoke it all into being with His Word: "Let there be....!" But in creating man, His prize creation, He formed Him out of the dust of the ground. Why?

The word "formed" denotes a process of great complexity, great care, and accuracy. I think God thoroughly enjoyed Himself, took great pleasure and delight in forming the creature with whom He was to have the closest fellowship. The Apostle Paul in Ephesians 2:10 tell us that we are God's "workmanship." That word in the Greek also has the connotation of a "work of art." How about it? Do you feel like a work of art? You should! Because you are in the eyes of God Who formed you. And who are you to disagree with God?

Man's body is of the earth, but man also has a soul and a spirit. And we're told in Genesis 1:27 that "God created man in His image, in the

14

image of God He created him; male and female He created them." God breathed into the nostrils of this earthen body the breath of life, and man became a living being. With the breath of life, man received his soul with his nature, faculties, and intellect, and also his spirit, all of which in some way, through the miraculous, creative power of God, constitutes the image of God.

The image of God is intrinsic to man. Man would not be human without it. The image of God makes man, male and female, alone capable, through the Holy Spirit, of having a conscious, personal, relationship with the Creator. Through the Holy Spirit, man can know God and understand what God requires of him. The Holy Spirit communicates with man's spirit. All this, in some miraculous, mysterious way is related with the image of God residing in man. Although the image of God in man was marred by man's fall into sin, it was not extinguished. Otherwise, man would have ceased to be human.

Brennan Manning, in his book, The Signature of Jesus, speaks of God's delight in creating. He says: "Imagine God's great delight when God makes a person in HIs own image. Imagine His delight when He made you. God created you and gave you as His gift, not only to your parents, but to Himself." From the moment of your conception, God began a divine love affair with you. God invested you and me, and all His human creations, with an individual, personal nature. There are no two human beings perfectly alike. Each of us is God's masterpiece, God's one of a kind.

In the garden, God provided for all Adam's needs of body, soul, and spirit. For the fulfillment of the body, Adam had the food and drink God provided in the garden, including the tree of life and immortality. Then God provided a helpmate for Adam - Eve, and blessed them with the gift of sex and told them to be fruitful and multiply. For the fulfillment of the soul and its faculties, Adam had the indescribable beauty and majesty of the garden, along with the tasks God assigned him - to tend the garden and name all the animals, thus giving Adam the satisfaction of being productive and accomplishing important tasks. And for the fulfillment of the spirit, both Adam and Eve had the oneness of fellowship and covenant with their Creator and God whose image they bore.

Well, we all know the account of the fall into sin. They wanted to be like God, so they fell to the serpent's - the devil's - temptation and ate of the forbidden fruit of the tree of knowledge of good and evil. They lost their innocence and purity, were covered with sin, the original sin that we and every human being born since and to the end of time inherits from Adam. They were debarred from the garden and the tree of life, and the gift of immortality. They were spared from immediate death because they were to be the root of mankind, but their life from then on would be a dying life, for death was now inevitable.

The Apostle Paul, in our epistle reading, reminds the Roman Christians and us of the weakness of our natural selves because of our sinful nature which we inherited from Adam. It is so easy to deceive ourselves, to convince ourselves that something we want, but know in our hearts to be wrong, is actually right and good for us. And Satan is right there with us, just as he was with Adam and Eve, to help us in our self-deception, to convince us that our desires, addictions, wants, and lifestyles, although in direct contradiction to God's Word, will be acceptable to God because He loves us and wants us to be happy. This is pure evil coming from the father of lies and evil - Satan. God, not man, decides what is sin and what is not sin, and God has done this in His Word which stands forever. God tells us in His Word: "I am not a man who changes his mind," reminding us that what God's Word calls sin will remain as sin until the end of time when Christ returns and destroys sin and evil once for all and forever.

Paul tells the Roman Christians that, "just as they once offered the parts of their body in slavery to impurity and ever-increasing wickedness, so now offer them in slavery to righteousness, leading to holiness." Paul refers to sin as impurity and ever-increasing wickedness. There's a warning here for us humans who have a tendency to sometimes treat sin lightly, or with humor. First, all sin, as impurity, is filthy, abominable in the sight of God. God accepts us sinners, and is incredibly patient with us out of His love, and yes delight in us, but He never accepts our sins, just as He did not accept Adam and Eve's sin. He calls us to repentance so He can cleanse us, purify us in Christ's Blood and be reconciled to Him.

Second, sin as ever-increasing wickedness is like its father the devil, never satisfied with just a little corruption; it seeks ever-increasing wickedness and corruption until the person is totally corrupted. Like Jesus' example of the yeast that leavens the whole loaf, accommodating a little sin in one's life inevitably leads to more sin. I believe it was Francis Schaeffer who said: "Accommodation leads to accommodation, leads to accommodation."

Paul draws a parallel contrast. Slavery to sin results in no benefit whatsoever, only death. Slavery to God, however, results in freedom from sin, holiness, and eternal life. Are we really free from sin? Yes! Although we still sin because we still have a sinful nature inherited from Adam, we are no longer slaves to sin. Through Christ, we are free, forgiven, cleansed of all sin by His Blood, and His Blood just keeps on cleansing us of sin day after day after day until Christ returns and destroys sin once and for all, forever, and we are restored fully to the likeness of Christ and the image of God. The word slavery has a bad connotation, but slavery to God is true freedom.

Paul ends this passage with the powerful statement summarizing the contrast between slavery to sin and slavery to God. "For the wages of sin is death, but the gift of God is eternal life in Christ Jesus our Lord." Sin is personified here as a master who pays wages. When unbelievers finish their earthly existence, the sin-power pays them off with the wages that both Adam and Eve earned for them with their original sin, and the unforgivable sin which they earned for themselves, rejection of God's grace in Christ Jesus. These wages are the second death, final, eternal, and irrevocable death, the death of existence in hell and eternal separation from God.

But for you and I, and for all believers, there are no wages, only the gift of God which is eternal life in Christ Jesus our Lord. Whereas the first Adam earned original sin for us, the gift of forgiveness and eternal life was earned for us by the second Adam, the Christ, the Son of God and Son of Man. Ephesians 2:8 tells us: "For it is by grace you have been saved, through faith - and this not from yourselves, it is the gift of God - not by works, so that no one can boast." And this gracious gift of eternal life is ours already – now.

How do we know that this gracious gift of eternal life is ours already? Because Jesus says so. In John 5 Jesus says: "I tell you the truth, whoever hears my Word and believes Him who sent me, has eternal life...He has crossed over from death to life." "Crossed over from death to life!" That statement is packed with theology. It describes is six short words the whole plan of salvation. It describes the whole journey of the Christian in this life. It describes Jesus' mission to this earth as Son of God and Son of Man and the fulfillment of HIs mission - His crossing over from death to life. Because our crossing over from death to life is already a fact through faith, there is no delay when we close our eyes in transitory death in this life. We immediately are taken into the true, spiritual, heavenly life that goes on endlessly in glory into eternity. The Word we hear every Sunday, the Word we read and meditate on during the week, reminds us that we already have this life because the Word is the bearer of life. The Word is life because it is inseparable from the Living Word - Christ.

I emphasized God's love and delight in His creation - us. Does God still delight in us after the Fall? "Yes, and again yes!" But like a loving parent, this delight is sometimes tempered by frustration, and perhaps even anger, but a righteous anger. Our Gospel reading gives the account of the miraculous feeding of the four thousand. This was after the previous miracle of the feeding of the five thousand. Again Jesus expresses His compassion for the multitude because they had been with Him three days without food. And again the disciples respond: "But where in this remote place can anyone get enough bread to feed them?"

Did the disciples forget the previous miracle of feeding the five thousand? It doesn't specifically say that. But even if they remembered, they apparently had not understood the lesson they were to take from it - a lesson that we too have a tendency to forget.

Like the disciples, when we face a problem our first response is what can I do about it? How can I solve this? We forget that Jesus has promised to always be with us, that He is always able to supply the earthly, as well as the spiritual needs of those who trust Him, even in the remote areas and the desolate circumstances we encounter in our lives. Well, with seven loaves and a few small fish, Jesus again fed the multitude, the four thousand until they were satisfied. But it was in the aftermath of this second miraculous feeding that we encounter the clear frustration of Jesus with His disciples.

In the same chapter of Mark, right after the account of this miraculous feeding, the disciples were discussing how they had forgotten to replenish their stock of bread and were down to only one loaf. Jesus, aware of this, asked them: "Why are you talking about having no bread? Do you still not see or understand? Are your hearts hardened? Do you have eyes but fail to see and ears but fail to hear? And don't you remember? When I broke the five loaves for the five thousand, how many basketfuls of pieces did you pick up?" "Twelve," they replied. "And when I broke the seven loaves for the four thousand, how many basketfuls of pieces did you pick up?" They answered "seven." He said to them: "Do you still not understand?" Jesus clearly reveals His frustration and disappointment with the disciples' lack of awareness and understanding.

How about us? Do you think God has ever been frustrated with you? I don't want to think about the numerous times Jesus has been frustrated and disappointed with me. I can just imagine Him saying: "Darrell, do you still not understand the height, depth, and breath of my love for you, my delight in you, and that I want my love and delight to infuse you, to overwhelm you and fill every aspect of your life. Turn it all over to me; stop holding back; give it all to me, so I can give my all to you."

I mentioned before the love affair that God has with you and me and all our brothers and sisters in Christ. God's fervent desire is that His love affair be requited, that we have a love affair with Him. And what would such a love affair look like? A.W. Tozer, in his book, The Pursuit of God, tells us what that love affair looked like in the life of one servant of God named Frederick Faber. Faber felt a special kind of love for each member of the Godhead, Father, Son, and Holy Spirit. His love for the Person of Christ was so intense that it threatened to consume him. It burned within him as a sweet and holy madness and flowed from his lips like molten gold. In one of his sermons he said: "Wherever we turn, there is Jesus. He is the beginning, the middle, and the end of everything to us, our all in all."

So there it is - what a love affair with the Almighty would look like - a sweet and holy madness burning inside, with praise and worship flowing from the lips like molten gold. This world would think of such a person as a fool and insane. But to be called a fool for Christ is the highest compliment one can receive. To be counted worthy to suffer for Christ through persecution or physical disability as His witness in this world is the highest honor. To know Christ and Him crucified and risen above all else is the purest form of wisdom. And to be consumed by a holy madness for Christ is the highest form of sanity. God grant us such a love affair with HIm for Jesus' sake. Amen.

"The Lord your God is with you, He is mighty to save.

He will take great delight in you, He will quiet you with His love,

He will rejoice over you with singing."

Zephaniah 3:17

THE HEART OF GOD

Text: Matthew 27: 27-36; Luke 23: 32-43; John 19: 28-42

Theme: The cross shows us the heart of God.

> Theme Statement: The crucifixion of Christ can only be understood rightly if we look at it from Jesus' point of view - the view of God's forgiving love, the view of God's justice and mercy, the view of God's salvation and grace.

Key Passage: Luke 23: 34. Jesus said, "Father, forgive them, for they do not know what they are doing."

The Son of God as Son of Man, having been condemned by men, carries His cross to the place of execution. The beatings, the blows to the head and face, the terrible scourging, all the abuse throughout the night and morning, had taken their toll. Jesus broke down under the load of the heavy cross - broke down so completely that even his executioners saw that no amount of blows and cursing of theirs could make Him stagger on under that load. And so, the soldiers forced Simon, a Jew, to bear Jesus' cross. No Jew would willingly touch the cross, for to them, it was an accursed thing. And no Roman soldier would demean himself by carrying a cross for the condemned. So the soldiers caught a Jew, and probably thought it a good joke on this unsuspecting Jew, that he had to carry another Jew's cross.

They offer Jesus drugged wine to dull the agony, but Jesus refuses it. This was no act of mercy on the soldiers' part, but just the contrary. A drugged man would be easier to crucify, easier to handle. The Greek wording here indicates that Jesus was repeatedly urged to drink, and He repeatedly refused. Jesus was determined to go through the final ordeal with a clear mind and endure it all, without avoiding a single agony. If He had taken that drugged wine, He could not have spoken as He did on the cross and made His death what it was. And so, they crucified Him!

"A cross outlined against the sky;

For our sin Christ will atone.

The Holy One is lifted high,

To win for us a throne."

The cross of Christ is the center of the world's history. The Incarnation of Christ, and the crucifixion and resurrection of Christ together form the pivot round which all the events of the ages revolve. And if you want to know God, really know God, you must look to the cross, for it is the cross that shows us the heart of God.

How do we see the heart of God in the cross of Christ? For one thing, in the cross we see the justice and mercy of God; we see the conjunction of God's justice and mercy. God is a supremely just God, and His perfect justice demands that sin be paid for. Only man makes light of sin; only man in his foolishness and ignorance scoffs and laughs at sin and fails to recognize it for the terrible thing it is. All sin is an affront to God, rebellion against His will and Word, and all sin demands a payment. Scripture tells us, "The wages of sin is death." God's just nature demands payment for sin. The Psalmist tells us that righteousness and justice are the foundation of God's throne. The Apostle Paul tells us that, in the cross, God demonstrated His justice. In the cross, we see God's justice against sin. But in the cross, we also see God's incredible mercy in giving His Son to suffer the full effects of that justice for us.

Yes, God is supremely just, but God is also infinitely merciful. What right does man have to expect God to be merciful to him? None whatsoever! Yet the prophet Micah tells us that "God delights to show mercy." And in Titus 3:5 we are told, "God saved us, not because of righteous things we had done, but because of His mercy." And God, in His unspeakable mercy, knowing that we, in our sinful state, could never satisfy the demands of His perfect justice and reestablish fellowship between God and man, gave His only begotten Son to take on our humanity, and while remaining fully Son of God, become also fully Son of Man, except without sin, to take our place, to be the payment for our sins, the perfect sacrifice for our sins, to suffer the full demands of justice for our sins. In the cross, we see God's supreme justice and His infinite mercy, and in that justice and mercy, we see the heart of God.

In the cross of Christ, we also see humility and sacrifice. We see the terrible nature of the sacrifice required in order for us to be redeemed, free from the bondage of Satan, sin, death, and hell. God made Himself, in the Person of His Son, the sacrifice in our place because only the suffering and death of the Son of God as the sinless Son of Man, the GodMan, the Lamb of God without spot or blemish, was sufficient to satisfy the demands of God's justice. And so, Jesus humbled Himself to take on our humanity; humbled Himself to accept the worst humiliation that was rightly ours; humbled Himself to suffer the torture that was rightly ours to suffer; humbled Himself to have His Body broken and His Blood shed when He was nailed to the cross, when it was rightly our bodies that should have been broken and our blood that should have been shed; and finally humbled Himself to die the death that was rightfully ours to die.

In his first epistle, the Apostle Peter tells us, "For you know that it was not with perishable things such as silver or gold that you were redeemed, but with the precious Blood of Christ." When we look at Jesus on the cross, we should sink down into the dust in humility and sorrow for our sins which He bore for us. Yet, how often we fail to humble ourselves beneath that cross. In the cross, we see God's humility and sacrifice, and in that humility and sacrifice, we see the heart of God.

In the cross, we see salvation and grace. There is no salvation apart from Christ and His cross. And the cross of Christ is the ultimate expression of God's grace. In Acts 4:12 we are told: "Salvation is found in no one else, for there is no other name under heaven given to man by which we must be saved." And in Romans 3:23-24, we are told: "All have sinned and fall short of the glory of God, and are justified freely by His grace through the redemption (salvation) that came by Jesus Christ." The writer to the Hebrews, chapter 12 verse 15, warns us: "See to it that no one misses the grace of God and that no bitter root grows up to cause trouble and defile many." Satan has no defense against God's grace; he has no defense against the cross. He knows that the salvation Christ won for us on the cross removes us from his dominion. Don't let Satan cause you to doubt your salvation which you have through faith in Christ. Don't let Satan sow bitter roots of pride or animosity towards others in your heart. Don't miss the grace of God. Look to the cross. In the cross, we clearly see God's gift of salvation; we clearly see God's amazing grace. And in that salvation and grace, we see the heart of God.

In the cross, we see power. The cross is Gospel; Gospel is the cross. And in Romans 1:16 we are told: "The Gospel is the power of God for the salvation of everyone who believes." And in 1Corinthians 1:18 we are told: "The message of the cross is foolishness to those who are perishing, but to us who are being saved, it is the power of God." Power which causes Satan and all the demons of hell to cower in fear and trembling. Power which removes the stain and guilt of sin. Power which gives eternal life and takes the sting out of death for everyone who believes. Power that will cause every knee to bow to the One Who suffered and died on that cross, and Who rose again. Power that will cause every tongue to confess that Jesus Christ is Lord, to the glory of God the Father. In the cross, we see the ultimate power, and in that power, we see the heart of God.

In the cross, we see the ultimate expression of love - God's agape love which is a sacrificial and forgiving love. In 1John 4:10 we're told: "This is love, not that we loved God, but that He loved us, and sent His Son as an atoning sacrifice for our sins." Some of Jesus' first words, hanging from that cross in agony, were: "Father, forgive them, for they

Yet, throughout history, man has attempted to build a bridge of his own that will bring him to God and God's favor. And it is all futile, futile for man to try and lift himself out of the mire and filth of his sin by his own strength, ability, and knowledge. The one and only bridge to God is the cross of Jesus Christ. Without the cross, man can never know God, for it is the Blood Jesus shed on the cross that cleanses us, and keeps cleansing us, of our sins, and makes knowing God, really knowing God, possible. The Blood of Christ alone purchased for us the new life, new life for today, and new life for eternity.

Centuries ago on the south coast of China, high on a hill overlooking the harbor of Macao, Portuguese settlers built an enormous cathedral that they believed would weather time. They placed a massive bronze cross on the front wall of the cathedral that stood high into the sky. Sometime later, a typhoon came and swept away man's handiwork. All of that cathedral was pushed down the hill and into the ocean as wreckage, except for the front wall and the bronze cross that stood high defying storm and weather. Centuries later, there was a shipwreck beyond that harbor. One of the survivors was hanging onto wreckage from the ship, moving up and down in the ocean waves, disoriented, frightened, not knowing where land was. But as he would come up on the crest of a wave, he could see that cross standing in the distance. His name was Sir John Bowring. He made it to land, lived to tell the story and wrote a beautiful hymn:

"In the cross of Christ I glory," When the woes of life o'er take me,

Towering o'er the wrecks of time; Hopes deceive, and fears annoy,

All the light of sacred story Never shall the cross forsake me;

Gathers round its head sublime. Lo! It glows with peace and joy.

God grant that we glory in the cross of Christ, for there we see the heart of God. Amen.

CHAPTER 2 - SALVATION THEOLOGY

"For God did not send His Son into the world to condemn the world, but in order that the world might be saved through Him. Whoever believes in Him is not condemned, but whoever does not believe is condemned already, because he has not believed in the Name of the only Son of God.

John 3: 17-18

For God so loved the world that he gave his one and only Son, that whoever believes in him shall not perish but have eternal life.
John 3:16

WHAT CHILD IS THIS?

Text: Judges 13: 2-7; Philippians 2: 5-11; Luke 1: 26-38.

Theme: The Wonder of the Incarnation.

Theme Summary: God is a God of the impossible. Just one example of this is God bringing forth some of the most important men in Scripture from mothers who had been barren. The greatest Child of a miraculous birth however, the Son of Man, would come not from a barren womb, but from the most unlikely womb of a young virgin, Mary. What Child is this? Jesus Christ, the Incarnate Son of God, taking on our flesh.

Key Passage: Luke 1: 35, 37. The angel answered, "The Holy Spirit will come upon you, and the power of the Most High will overshadow you. So the Holy One to be born will be called the Son of God....For nothing is impossible with God."

✝

O ur God delights in doing the impossible for His people. One of the many examples of this in Scripture is God bringing forth some of the most important men in the Bible from women who had been barren. The mothers of Isaac, Jacob, Joseph, Samson, Samuel, and John the Baptist had all been barren before God miraculously opened their wombs.

Our Old Testament passage tells us of Samson, one of the Judges. Samson gives us a picture of Christ in two ways. First, his birth was announced by an angel. Jesus' birth was announced by an angel. Second, Samson was born to free the Israelites from the oppression of the Philistines, and so he did for a time through great feats of human strength and power. Jesus, Son of God, was born Son of Man to free us from the oppression of sin, death, satan, and hell, and so He did, not just for a time, but once for all forever. And He did so in sharp contrast to Samson, by humbling Himself, choosing to be mocked, tortured, and spat upon for our sakes, choosing to take the world's sins, our sins, on His back in the shape of a cross, and on that cross, sacrifice His Body and His Blood to wash us clean of the filth of sins and free us from the condemnation and damnation of hell.

Yes, God brought some of His greatest servants into this life through wombs that were once barren. But the greatest Child of a miraculous birth, the Son of Man, would come not from a barren womb, but from the unlikely womb of a young virgin, Mary. This birth, the Incarnation of our Lord, along with the bodily Resurrection of our Lord, are the two greatest miracles of the ages, and constitute the centerpieces of Christianity. Without the Incarnation and the Resurrection there is no Christian faith.

It is a tragedy that, as we approach each Christmas season, thousands upon thousands of people will trade the supreme riches of a Christ Christmas for the rags of a secular Christmas. Even committed Christians can get caught up in the lure of a worldly Christmas. At such times, it would be good to remember the theme of the Church's Advent season, which is to remind us "What Child is This?" It is the most important question a person can ask, for how one answers that question will determine to a great extent one's life here on earth, and to a full extent one's eternal destiny - the glories of heaven or the fires of hell. Let us consider the question together.

In our Gospel passage, the angel connects the story of Mary with that of Elizabeth because they belong together. The angel tells Mary about Elizabeth's miraculous conception and the length of her pregnancy - "in the sixth month." It is the same angel - Gabriel - that was sent to Zacharias to announce John the Baptist's birth.

We're told twice that Mary was a virgin. Luke, under the inspiration of the Holy Spirit, obviously intends to stress this fact. Both Mary and the man to whom she was pledged to be married were descendants of David. It was vital for Jews and later Jewish Christians to know that Mary, the mother of Jesus, and Joseph, the legal but not biological father of Jesus, were of the house of David.

31

Gabriel tells Mary in the clearest and simplest way about God's intent for her. One, she shall conceive. Two, she shall give birth to a Son. And three, that Son's name shall be Jesus, which means the One through Whom God brings salvation. Gabriel goes on to say, "He shall be great and will be called the Son of the Most High," in other words, the Son of God. "Most High" designates God in His supreme exaltation and majesty. Gabriel says that God will give this Child the throne of his father David. Any gift of the Father to Jesus is, of course, made to Jesus' human nature, to the Son of Man, since Jesus, as Son of God, co-equal with the Father and Holy Spirit, has all things.

Finally, Gabriel says that this Child "will reign over the house of Jacob forever; His kingdom will never end." The house of Jacob denotes all His descendants, not merely the Jewish nation as such, but the spiritual descendants on through the ages, believing Jews and Gentiles alike. So it is now, and so it will be forever, just as the angel foretold.

Mary is perplexed. The last thing she dreamt of was becoming the mother of the Messiah, the Son of God and Son of Man. She is willing, but how will this be since she is a virgin and knows not a man? Mary's question does not contain any indication of doubt or unbelief, just perplexity. The angel ends Mary's perplexity, and Gabriel's answer to Mary answers the question of the entire Church as to how the Savior, Son of God, could be born as Son of Man to a virgin. And so we confess, "conceived by the Holy Spirit, born of the Virgin Mary." Gabriel tells her, "The Holy Spirit will come upon you, and the power of the Moat High will overshadow you." The power of the Most High would envelop her. And so, we have the Incarnation, the Son of God taking on human flesh, and while remaining fully the divine Son of God, becoming also fully Son of Man, although without the original sin that all humans inherited from Adam.

This says it all. Farther than this the miracle could not be revealed, for the human mind could not follow farther. Beyond this we cannot go, for all else is impenetrable to human intellect. And we would do well to remember that even an ordinary human conception is, in spite of all our science, to a great extent, a great mystery. We'll have to wait until we are with the Lord to know completely. The divine record presents the facts and no more. Gabriel concludes his comments with, "For nothing is impossible with God." On this assurance, Mary can rest her faith. And we too. Mary's final reply is brief, yet beautiful and spiritually perfect. Mary expresses her will that what the angel has said to her may come to pass. This is holy submission, mighty confidence, blessed readiness. And all this in one so young! And so, the Son of God takes up residence in the womb of a young virgin for nine months to become fully human as well as fully divine.

The Apostle Paul, in our epistle reading, and through the inspiration of the Holy Spirit, gives us a statement of pure doctrine concerning the facts, the realities, of the Son of God coming to us as the Son of Man, the realities of the Incarnation. In order for God's plan of redemption to work, it was absolutely necessary for the Son of God to take on our humanity in all aspects except without sin. Both the humiliation and the exaltation of Jesus Christ as Savior deal with His human nature. The divine nature, the Son of God, cannot suffer and die, cannot be humiliated or exalted, for He is immutable, unchanging. Only the Son of Man could suffer, die, be humiliated, be exalted.

As we consider the question, "What Child is This?" It is important that we understand, at least as much as human intellect enables us to, what the Incarnation consisted of. Paul tells us that "Christ Jesus, Who being in very nature God, did not consider equality with God something to be grasped…". The Greek word for nature is "morphe," meaning form, substance. Christ Jesus, in both form and very substance, was and is God. But instead of grasping, coveting equality with God, He made Himself nothing, humbled Himself with a self-sacrificing humility and love for His human creation.

Paul tells us that Christ Jesus "took the very nature of a servant, being made in human likeness." Again, that word nature, the Greek "morphe," the very form and substance of a servant made in human likeness. This is the Incarnation, the Son of God taking on our humanity and becoming the GodMan. In form and substance fully divine; in form and substance fully human without sin. Paul then goes on to say that our Lord further humbled Himself and became obedient unto death - even death on a cross. This is also referred to as His taking on the form of a slave. Paul speaks of two humblings - the first when Christ took on our humanity, being made in human likeness,the Incarnation, and the second, after being made in human likeness, taking on the form of a slave and becoming obedient unto death. It is a mistake to think that Christ taking on the form of a slave was part of His incarnation. The two are separate humblings on the part of our Lord.

In the Incarnation, the human nature which Christ Jesus assumed was made partaker of the divine nature, of all that belonged to the divine nature of Christ. The human nature did not become divine, but partook of the divine. Hence, the GodMan. The two natures, although two, cannot be divided. There is no sharp line of separation of the two. Think of the Trinity - three Persons, yet indivisible as One God. Jesus, in HIs humanity as Son of Man, possessed all His divine attributes as Son of God. There was no exchange involved in the Incarnation. Christ did not exchange one iota of His divinity to take on our humanity. Both Christ's divine nature and His human nature are immutable, unchanging, and remain so today and forever.

There were times during Jesus' ministry when His divine nature shone through His human nature - the miracles, the transfiguration, His words and acts on the cross where even the centurion said, "Surely this was the Son of God," His resurrection and ascension. And John testifies in John 1:14, "We beheld His glory, glory as of the only Begotten from the Father." Although all this glory dwelt in His human nature, Jesus used it only to the degree needed for His office and mission.

Jesus taking on the form of a slave is also referred to as His emptying Himself, making Himself nothing, emphasizing the voluntary nature of it. He considered not Himself, but us, you and me, and all mankind. He considered only the mission given Him by the Father, and for which He took on our human nature and then took on the form of a slave. He emptied Himself in order to fill us, that we might be made the righteousness of God in Him. But after His resurrection, and our salvation achieved, the form of a slave was dropped, and Christ's human nature took on a glorified form, reflecting all that His deity has bestowed on His human nature at the Incarnation.

Jesus had to accomplish the Father's plan for our redemption as both Son of God and Son of Man, with the full weight of both His deity and His humanity. In His humanity, He bore the humiliation, the suffering, and the dying. But even in His suffering and dying, He had to be the mighty God in order by His death to conquer death, hell, and satan, to raise up again the Temple of His Body, to take up His life again. He is not only the Second Adam as man, but the Lord from Heaven - truly the GodMan.

Men have tinkered with the fact of the Incarnation over the centuries to try and make it at least somewhat reasonable, but all their tinkering leaves them with the same seeming impossibility. They refuse to admit that there are some things known only to God, and some things possible only to God. Paul sees and accepts the mystery as the fact it is, and we Christians accept it as the fact it is. And they who say that only the human Christ was on the cross, thereby separating the divine nature from the human nature, destroy the efficacy, the sufficiency of the cross. Luther said, "If I permit myself to be persuaded that only Christ's human nature suffered for me, then Christ is to me a poor Savior, then He Himself indeed needs a Savior."

The entire sufficiency and effectiveness of Jesus' suffering and death for us lies in His Godhead dwelling in His human nature bodily. And this dwelling of His Godhead in His human nature began at His conception in the womb of the Virgin Mary by the Holy Spirit, and was consummated at His birth in Bethlehem.

And so, the question, "What Child is This?" He is the Logos, the Living Word of God! What Child is This?" He is my Savior, your Savior, the only Savior through Whom men must be saved! What Child is This?" He is the Way, the Truth, and the Life! What Child is This?" He is Jesus Whom God exalted to the highest place, and before Whom one day every knee will bow, in heaven and on earth and under the earth, and every tongue confess that Jesus Christ is Lord, to the glory of God the Father.

Even so, come Lord Jesus! Amen.

GREAT SINNERS; GREATER SAVIOR

Text: Exodus 20: 12-24; Matthew 15: 1-20.

Theme: The absolute sin of sin; the absolute mediation of Christ.

Theme Statement: In our Old Testament passage, we have God's awesome display of His power and majesty when giving the Law to the Israelites on Mt. Sinai. Surely this display served to impress on the people the power of the Law to condemn. The people, realizing they needed a mediator between them and God asked Moses to be their mediator. In our Gospel passage, Jesus made it clear that sin originates from the heart and thus defiles both our physical nature and spiritual nature. Thus, we too need a mediator to stand in the breach between God and us, intercede for us, present our requests to God, and give us God's Word. God has provided us that Mediator, the only perfect Mediator, His sinless Son Who as Son of Man gave His Body and Blood as the perfect sacrifice for our sin, reconciles us to God, and restores our oneness with God. Thus, the lessons these passages give us for our Christian journey are 1. The absolute sin of sin, and 2. The absolute salvation through the sacrifice and mediation of Christ our Lord and Savior.

Key Passage: Matthew 15: 19. "For out of the heart come evil thoughts, murder, adultery, sexual immorality, theft, false testimony, slander."

†

Our reading from Exodus begins with reference to the last six of the Ten Commandments, commonly called the laws of the second table. They include honoring parents, forbidding murder, adultery, stealing, false testimony, and coveting. Just as the first four commandments emphasize our duty to God, so these six commandments emphasize our duty to ourselves and to one another, reminding us of what Jesus called the second great commandment, "Thou shalt love thy neighbor as thyself." As the first four commandments remind us that true faith in God is an essential branch of true righteousness, the last six remind us that true righteousness towards others is an essential branch of true faith. To see our face In the mirror of the law, and to recognize our hopeless condition of sinful disobedience to God and sin against our neighbor is certainly a vital part of our Christian journey, and absolutely essential to opening our hearts to receive the grace of God.

The Law was given to the Israelites, we're told, with an extraordinary and terrifying demonstration of God's power, majesty, and sovereignty. God was establishing a covenant with His people, the Covenant of the Law, and perhaps the thunderings, lightnings, the mountain covered in smoke, the trumpet blast, were all meant to impress upon the people, and us, the power of that Law to condemn to hell, and to persuade them to live in holy fear of God's judgment against sin. In fact, Moses told them that God was testing them so that the fear of God would be with them to keep them from sinning. Perhaps also, this fearsome display of power would prepare them to eagerly anticipate the comforts of the Gospel which promised a Savior. For in God's time, the Covenant of the Law would be replaced with the Covenant of Grace as we're told in John 1:17 - "For the Law was given through Moses; grace and truth came through Jesus Christ?"

We're told that the people trembled in fear and told Moses, "You speak to us and we will listen, but do not have God speak to us or we will die." And here we have another important lesson for our Christian journey - the people realized they could not go into the presence of God alone. They needed a mediator, someone to stand in the breach between them and God and mediate their requests to God and God's Word to them. God granted their request and gave Moses as their mediator. And so, in our Old Testament passage, we have two truths that bear directly on our life of Christian faith. These are 1. The absolute and fearsome power of the Law to condemn and cast into hell, all reflected by the thunderings, lightnings, and the mountain smoking, and 2. Our hopeless condition due to sin and our absolute need for a mediator between us and God. I'll say more about this later. And that brings us to our Gospel passage.

The Pharisees and teachers of the law criticized Jesus that His disciples did not follow the "tradition of the elders," in this instance not washing their hands before eating. The "tradition of the elders" was the entire body of rules, some 600 of them, handed down orally that supplemented the Law given at Sinai, and regulated conduct down to the smallest details. The tradition for washing was considered essential, not for sanitary reasons, but for fear that the hands had brushed against a Gentile or something belonging to a Gentile, thus rendering the person ceremonially unclean. The divine Levitical Law given in Scripture required no such washing in any way. Jesus and His disciples observed the Levitical Law given in Scripture, the Torah, but disregarded the rabbinical tradition. Why? Not because human customs as such are to be disregarded, but because, in practice, "the tradition" was placed above the canon - the Word of God - and considered by the Pharisees as binding the conscience even more than the actual written law of God. Jesus gives a clear example of this in vv. 3-6.

Jesus confronts them with their hypocrisy, their transgressing the law, the commandment of God, for the sake of their tradition, by referring them to the commandment to "honor your father and mother...." which includes caring for them in their old age. He tells them, "But in your tradition, you say, 'whatever help you might have otherwise received from me is Corban,' that is, a gift devoted to God." Thus, the person is not required to honor father and mother with it, but can continue to keep it for himself as long as he wants. "You hypocrites!" Jesus tells them, "Isaiah was right when he prophesied about you: 'These people honor Me with their lips, but their hearts are far from Me.'"

The Law given by God considered honoring parents so important that anyone who cursed his parents was to be put to death. Jesus showed how they had in effect nullified the commandment and He condemned their action as hypocritical, for though it may appear to be spiritual, it actually was used to serve their own sinful human agenda and personal desires. And here we have another lesson for our

Christian journey, and that is to be totally honest when we look into the mirror of the law and avoid any effort to modify God's Word, even so slightly, in order to satisfy a human desire, agenda or tradition. Just as those Pharisees were setting aside the commandment of God for the sake of their tradition, and claiming they were right to do so, so today many people, including some officials of the church, government, our educational institutions, set aside the commandments of God for the sake of modern, human, cultural traditions.

A former high official in a previous Democrat administration insisted that God's Word must be brought up to 21st century standards concerning abortion, gay marriage, and what constitutes a family. We have recently had government officials insist that abortion must be allowed for any reason and right up to the moment of birth. Many of these people claim to be Christian, and for their motive they claim a twisted, skewed, human version of love, and thereby deceive many people. But to sanction and approve of peoples' actions that, if not repented of, will put them in danger of hell is not love but hate, and the most dangerous form of hate. One can only wonder: Have they never read Psalm 139, which clearly identifies God as the Source, Creator, and Sovereign of life from conception on, and that God creates each person in His own image? Are they ignorant of God's Word that identifies God as the Institutor of marriage - one man and one woman? Are they ignorant of the fact that God is the designer of the family - one man, one woman, children? Cultural traditions may change, but God does not change, and God's Word does not change for God and His Word cannot be separated.

Just as the Pharisees elevated the tradition of the elders above God's commandments, these modern day Pharisees elevate cultural traditions and so called modern human rights, which in effect are nothing more than wicked desires and sinful passions, above God's Word. How must we Christians respond to these modern day Pharisees? Just as Jesus did to those He faced. He nullified and wiped out their appeal to the "tradition of the elders" by facing them with the Word of God which they had set aside. We must face the modern day Pharisees with the truth and power of God's Word over and over again, and warn them of the condemnation of the law and invite them to repent and receive anew the Gospel, God's forgiveness and grace and reconciliation through Christ.

In our passage, Jesus then goes on to elevate the law to a new standard. He tells the Pharisees and His disciples that it is not what goes into a man's mouth that makes him unclean, but what comes out of his mouth is what makes him unclean. When His disciples ask Him to explain, He says, "Whatever enters the mouth goes into the stomach and then out of the body. But the things that come out of the mouth come from the heart, and these make a man unclean. For out of the heart come evil thoughts, murder, adultery, sexual immorality, theft, false testimony, slander. These are what make a man unclean.

When Jesus identified the heart as where sin originates, He elevated the law from the purely legalistic standard to the spiritual standard. What Jesus is telling them is that defilement is not just physical, but moral and spiritual. Jesus had expounded on this moral and spiritual aspect in His Sermon on the Mount when He said, "I tell you that anyone who looks at another lustfully has already committed adultery in his heart." "I say to you, whoever is angry with his brother, wishing him harm, has committed murder in his heart and is subject to judgment."

When the law was considered only in a legalistic way - that is, to violate the law meant actually committing the act - it was possible for a person to deceive himself, thinking he was clean. Remember the account of the rich, young ruler, who came to Jesus and said, "Teacher, what must I do to inherit eternal life?" Jesus said to him, "You know the law and the commandments." The man said, "All these I have kept from my youth on." He was speaking legalistically, convinced he was clean of sin. But when Jesus invited him to sell all his belongings, give to the poor, and come follow Him, the man went away subdued. Jesus had shown him that he was not clean spiritually. The sin of idolatry resided in his heart, his wealth being his idol.

I'm sure there are those today who would dare say they have kept the commandments, never having murdered, committed adultery, stolen, etc. etc. They are speaking in a legalistic, physical sense, not in the spiritual sense involving the heart which Jesus emphasized. Sin originates inside the person, namely in the heart, the seat of all thought, emotion, and volition. And defilement occurs not only when the sinful contents of the heart spill out in words and action; defilement is there before they even start to come out. Sin arising in the heart already defiles the person.

Who among all humanity can say, "I have never had a lustful thought." Who among all humanity can say, "I have never entertained a murderous or harmful thought against another person." Who among all humanity can say, "I have never told a lie, never slandered another person, never coveted what someone else had." There is only One Who can claim such purity and sinless perfection - the Godman Jesus Christ. And that brings us back to our discussion of mediator.

The Israelites knew that to approach God on their own merits meant certain death because of their sin and defilement. They recognized their need of a mediator. And so it is with us! God designated Moses as their mediator even though Moses too was sinful and not perfect. But God the Father has given us Christians the only perfect Mediator - His Son, Jesus Christ the Messiah - Who with His perfect, sinless life, and with His Body and Blood given and poured out for us on the cross for the forgiveness of our sins has cleared the way for us to approach God the Father freely and at all times in His Son's Name. Jesus intercedes for us, closes the breach between God and us caused by sin with His Blood, reconciles us to the Father and restores us into oneness with Him. 1 Timothy 2: 5-6 tells us: "For there is one God and one Mediator between God and men, the Man Christ Jesus Who gave Himself as a ransom for all men."

And so, what from our Scripture passages do we take with us on our Christian journey and beyond? First, a full awareness of the absolute sin of sin and the fearsome power of the Law to condemn absolutely.

Second, a warning to be on our guard against modern day Pharisees who replace the Word of God with human and cultural traditions. Third, the realization that the defilement of sin is not just physical, but spiritual; that sin originates in the heart, that the heart is deceitful, and that we must always use God's Word as the judge of whether or not what our heart is telling us is true or not, and whether it conforms to God's will.

And finally, and most importantly, we take with us the comforting knowledge, the blessed certainty, that we have a Mediator given us by the Father Himself, His Son, the Godman, Who ransomed us from sin, death, satan, and hell with His Body and Blood, which just keeps cleansing us from sin until He returns to take us into glory.

We are great sinners, but we have a greater Savior. Christ is our living hope. Christ is our Mediator Christ is our victory. Christ is our Lord and Savior. And Christ is our joy. Amen.

IT IS FINISHED

Text: Leviticus 16:3,5,6-8,15-22; Hebrews 9:11-15;
            John 19:28-30.

Theme: Mission Accomplished.

Theme Statement: With His shout, "It is finished!" Jesus announced His full accomplishment of the mission given Him by the Father, the redemption of the world, and for which He left His throne on high and took on our humanity, became sin and a curse for us although He was sinless, suffered the full and terrible punishment for our sins, and was obedient unto death, even death on a cross. Jesus' life and death was the fulfillment of God's promise of a Savior to Adam and Eve, the fulfillment of the Abrahamic covenant, the Mosaic covenant, and the Davidic covenant, the fulfillment of all those animal sacrifices, and the fulfillment of all those ancient and Old Testament prophecies concerning the Messiah. No wonder Jesus shouted from the cross, "It is finished." It is finished indeed!

Key Passage: John 19:30. "When He had received the drink, Jesus said, 'It is finished.' With that, He bowed His head and gave up His spirit."

There are two profound statements that can be considered as the most important statements made during the history of this world and humanity. The first statement is, "Let there be light," which ushered in the creation, the heavens and the earth and the seas and all they contain, and all life, plant, animal, and human. The second profound statement is, "It is finished," which ushered in the redemption of humanity and God's creation. Underlying both statements is the amazing grace, the everlasting love, and the incomprehensible mercy and compassion of a just, benevolent, and awesome God.

We're told in our Gospel passage that after Jesus received the drink He requested, and knowing that all was completed and that death was imminent, He cried out, "It is finished." And according to Matthew and Mark, it was a loud cry, a cry of victory. In the Greek, it is "*Tetelestai*," the perfect tense emphasizing a completed state, denoting an action brought to its termination, done once for all time, leaving nothing undone, an action that stands finished forever. Let us consider what was completed, the profound nature and extent of what was "finished."

Some think Jesus was referring to only His suffering being finished. Certainly, His suffering, passion, and the malice, torture, and enmity of His persecutors was finished. But His cry cannot mean only that. Certainly, the will of the Father for His Son to fulfill the law and the prophets, to redeem creation, to suffer the full and terrible punishment for our sins was completed, finished. All that happened, all that Jesus did, went exactly according to the will and Word of the Father. Jesus had said, "I have come to do the Father's will. My food, my meat and drink, is to do the will of the Father."

He had prayed to His Father in Gethsemane, "Your will be done." Now He can shout, "Your will is done." "It is finished!"

Certainly, Jesus' cry was a cry of victory over Satan and a fulfillment of God's promise to Adam and Eve in the Garden after they had sinned, that He would send a Savior Who would crush Satan's head and Satan would strike His heel. Certainly, Jesus' cry was a fulfillment of the Abrahamic Covenant in which God promised Abraham that all peoples on earth would be blessed through Abraham's seed, the Messiah.

Certainly, Jesus' cry was a cry of finish, of completion, of the Mosaic Covenant with its law and its countless ceremonial animal sacrifices for sin. It was a cry of finish for the Day of Atonement described in our reading from Leviticus. The High Priest would enter the most Holy Place, the Holy of Holies of the Tabernacle and later the Temple, where the Ark of the Covenant was located, the Presence of God, only on one day of the year - on Yom Kippur - the Day of Atonement, and he would enter alone, and he must not enter without blood.

Two goats were chosen by lot - one lot for the Lord as a sacrifice for the peoples' sins, and one lot for the scapegoat to remove the sins of the people far from them. The High Priest would enter the Holy of Holies room behind the curtain twice on that day, once with a bull's blood for the cleansing of his household and himself as high priest to enable him to act for the people, and then with the blood of the goat chosen by lot for the Lord as a sacrifice for the people. He would sprinkle the blood of this sacrifice on the atonement cover of the Ark and in front of it to atone for the sins of the whole community of Israel. Then, outside the Holy of Holies, he would take the goat chosen by lot as the scapegoat, lay his hands on its head and put all the sins and wickedness of the people on its head. Then the goat was to be taken to a solitary place in the desert and released.

Here we have a type, a picture, of sins being forgiven through sacrifice, and sins being removed by the scapegoat. And it is all a picture of Christ. The entire Day of Atonement was a picture of Christ. And all those myriads, countless, animal sacrifices commanded by the Mosaic law and covenant were pictures of Christ and fulfilled in Christ on the cross. Christ is both our sacrifice - it is His Blood that cleanses us from sin and guilt - and our scapegoat - it is His sacrifice that removes our sins from us, as David said in his psalm, as far as the east is from the west. With the cry of Jesus, "It is finished," the ceremonial laws and sacrifices of the Mosaic covenant were finished.

All those animal sacrifices could not bring completeness. The blood of animals cannot save. God used them to point to the one sacrifice of Jesus that would save and indeed bring completeness. And thus, through the Holy Spirit, the Israelites believed in that coming, ultimate sacrifice, the Christ, and by faith obtained pardon and forgiveness from their sins and guilt. All those sacrifices foreshadowed the Christ, the Messiah. The Christ had come, and now the Mosaic covenant makes way for a better hope, the hope of all mankind, the New Covenant in Christ's Blood.

This is made clear in our reading from Hebrews, which presents Christ as both our High Priest and our sacrifice. We're told that Christ went through the greater and more perfect tabernacle that is not man-made, not a part of this creation. As our High Priest, He entered the heavenly Sanctuary, and He did not enter it by means of the blood of goats and calves, but He entered it once for all by His own Blood, having obtained eternal redemption for mankind. Only the Blood of Christ, Who offered Himself unblemished to God can cleanse us from sin and cleanse our conscience from acts that lead to death. Christ, our High Priest, offering the only sacrifice that cleanses, and Christ, our Savior, the Sacrifice Himself.

When the sacrifice of Jesus on Calvary was complete, when He entered the heavenly Sanctuary with His expiating Blood, the full payment of His Blood for our sins, all that the earthly tabernacle, the earthly temple, with its Holy Place and Holy of Holies foreshadowed had come to pass and was fulfilled, finished. A full satisfaction is made to the justice of God against sin. The full punishment for sin required by God's just nature is paid. The condemnation of the law, for all God's faithful in Christ, is finished because Jesus fulfilled every requirement of the law for us.

In Christ, the way to the heavenly Sanctuary is made manifest at last. In the heavenly Sanctuary, there is no more a Holy Place and a Holy of Holies with a veil between them. The veil, the curtain, is rent in two; the wall of partition between God and man because of sin is removed. Because Christ entered the heavenly Sanctuary with His Blood, we will forever be in the Presence of God with nothing to separate us or come between us. We're told in our epistle that because Christ died as a ransom to set us free from the sins committed under the first covenant, the old covenant of the law, that He is now the Mediator of a new covenant - the Covenant of Grace - and that those who are called -

that's you and me and all our brothers and sisters in Christ - may receive the promised eternal inheritance.

Only Christ, our Mediator, the One Who intercedes for us to the Father, the One Who mediates between God and us on the basis of His Blood, can give us this eternal inheritance. 1Timothy 2:5 tells us, "For there is one God and one Mediator between God and men, the man Christ Jesus Who gave Himself as a ransom for all men."

Why only one Mediator, the Christ? Because it was He Who delivered the fatal blow to the power of Satan; it was He Who ended the bondage of transgression and sin; it was He Who opened a fountain of grace that shall ever flow; it was He Who laid the foundation of peace with God and joy that shall never fail; and it was He Who clothes us with an everlasting righteousness, His righteousness.

In Daniel 9:24, the angel Gabriel revealed to the prophet Daniel six purposes to be fulfilled by the Messiah - to finish transgressions, to put an end to sin, to atone for wickedness, to bring in everlasting righteousness, to seal up vision and prophecy, and to anoint the most holy. In Christ, all these are fulfilled. And not only those, but all the other Old Testament prophecies concerning the Messiah, including of course those in Isaiah describing the Suffering Servant.

There is one other covenant fulfilled in Christ as a result of His death and resurrection, and that is the Davidic Covenant. God promised David that the Messiah would come from his seed, that his house and his kingdom would endure forever before God, and that his throne would be established forever. And so it was - Christ the Son of God born as the Son of man in the lineage of David; Christ as the Son of David, the King of kings and the Lord of lords whose kingdom is eternal.

Christian theology is blood theology. The price of our salvation was paid in full with our Lord's Blood once and for all. "It is finished." *Tetelestai!* But the grand result of that Blood sacrifice goes on and on and on because the Blood of Christ just keeps on cleansing us from sin and guilt, and it will keep doing so until we say, "It is finished," and leave this life for our life with Christ in glory.

And so, all this is complete, finished - the Abrahamic Covenant, the Mosaic Covenant, the Davidic Covenant, the ancient Old Testament prophecies, the defeat of sin, death, Satan, and hell, the accomplishment of the Father's will and work of redemption, forgiveness, salvation, renewal, reconciliation with God, and the opening of the Sanctuary of heaven - all this complete and contained in those three words **"It is Finished."**

In Christ, everything is brought to completeness. In Christ, all becomes complete and right according to the Father's will and the Spirit's design. Christ our Savior; Christ our sacrifice; Christ our scapegoat; Christ our High Priest; Christ our Mediator. Only He offers that completeness to us, to all mankind, the completeness He purchased for us on the cross. The entire past, present, and future rest on the Lamb slain from the foundation of the world.

The sufferings and agonies of His human soul and body are finished. The storm is over and He is going to Paradise, entering upon the joy and glory set before Him by the Father. The work is done, the battle is over, the victory won. And Jesus announces this to His Father: "It is finished." He announces it to the world and to Satan: "It is finished." And He announces it to us, to you and me: "It is finished." And it is for us to hear since His whole suffering, passion, and death, were for us. He bore your sins and my sins, and His shout of victory is our victory through faith in Him. He says to us, and to all mankind, "Your redemption from sin and death is complete. Accept your redemption from my holy hands nailed to the cross for you, and enter into a new life with Me - a life of freedom from the bondage of sin, freedom from an accusing conscience once at war with God; a life of peace with God in Christ, a peace that passes all understanding.

After His monumental declaration "It is finished," Jesus commits His spirit to the Father, bows His head and gives up His spirit. As His suffering was voluntary, so His death was voluntary. The bowing of

His head also showed His submission to the Father's will and His obedience to death, even death on a cross. Certainly Jesus' death was one of peace and joy. His cry of victory attests to that. With the hard, bitter, agonizing work of redemption all done, Jesus goes to the Father. Like a tired, exhausted. Child He lays His head to rest in His Father's arms. It is finished! It is finished indeed! Amen.

THE SUPREME AGONY

Text: Psalm 22:1-18; 2Corinthians 5:21; Galatians 3:13; Matthew 27:45-54.

Theme: Forsaken by the Father.

Theme Statement: During those three hours of darkness, the Father turned away from the Son. A wall of separation had risen between the Father and the Son, namely, the world's and yours and my sin, and the curse of sin, now placed on Jesus. During those terrible hours, the sinless Son of God and Son of man was made to be sin for us, and a Holy God cannot have communion with sin. The Father forsaking the Son for a time was necessary for Jesus to suffer the full punishment for our sin. But then, the darkness would lift, the Father would turn back to the Son, and, Jesus knowing this, could confidently and joyfully commit His soul into the Father's hands.

Key Passage: Matthew 27: 46. "About the ninth hour Jesus cried out in a loud voice, 'Eloi, Eloi, lama sabachthani?' - which means, 'My God, my God, why have You forsaken Me?'"

The first great miraculous sign at the crucifixion of Jesus was the strange darkness that covered all the land from the sixth Jewish hour - our noon - until the ninth hour - our 3:00 p.m. The darkness fell when the sun was normally at its zenith, shining with intense light, and it lasted three hours into the afternoon. Some claim that this was a natural eclipse of the sun, but all astronomical science denies that since a natural eclipse of the sun cannot take place when the moon is almost full, and this was such a time. There is only one conclusion: This darkness was wholly miraculous, exactly like the other signs that followed after Jesus died - the shaking of the earth, the splitting of the rocks, a number of holy people raised from the dead, and the curtain in the temple being torn in two from top to bottom.

What was the meaning, the significance, of this darkness? Those hours of darkness signified judgment. Darkness and judgment go together as we see in numerous Scripture passages. The judgment associated with this darkness took place during the darkness itself; it took place on the cross itself; it took place in the Person of the dying Savior Himself. And, at the climax of this darkness and judgment, at about the ninth hour, Jesus shouted with a loud voice: "My God, my God, why have You forsaken Me?" The words are from Psalm 22. In this Psalm, David desperately cries out to God for help during one of his periods of intense suffering: "My God, my God, why have You forsaken me?" And on the cross, his descendant Jesus, Son of David, the Messiah, cries out to God in His intense suffering with the same words. Only the Holy Spirit, the Spirit of prophecy, could have inspired David in his suffering to write a Psalm that describes prophetically the suffering Messiah and His crucifixion in such amazing detail, and to place at the beginning of that Psalm the supreme cry of agony of our Lord on the cross.

The physical suffering of the cross, as terrible as it was, did not cause that loud cry of Jesus. There was a greater agony, a supreme agony, that brought out this cry. And that supreme agony was that for those three hours of darkness, Jesus, the Son of God and Son of man, was forsaken by God the Father. In the Garden of Gethsemane, God the Father heard the prayers of Jesus and strengthened Him for the terrible ordeal of the cross. On the cross, God the Father turned away from Him during those three hours of darkness.

Why? If God does not forsake the repentant sinner in the hour of death, how could He forsake His sinless Son when death was coming for Him? You would think that the crown of thorns digging into His scalp, the spit, the beatings, the floggings that turned His back into raw flesh, and then being nailed to a cross and left hanging in unspeakable agony would be sufficient, more than sufficient, for our redemption. But it wasn't! One more agony Christ had to suffer to complete our redemption, being forsaken by the Father for a time, the "supreme agony."

52

2 Corinthians 5:21 tells us that "God made Him Who had no sin to be sin for us, so that in Him we might become the righteousness of God." Galatians 3:13 tells us that "Christ redeemed us from the curse of the law by becoming a curse for us, for it is written: Cursed is everyone who is hung on a tree." All the ugliness, all the filth, all the curse of sin, from Adam's and Eve's sin in the Garden to the last sin committed by man before Christ's return, was laid on the pure, holy, and sinless Jesus while He hung on that cross. Sin is anathema to a holy, just, pure, God. God accepts and communes with sinners, but not with sin. When God the Father saw His Son covered with all the world's sin and curse, He turned away from Him.

And it was necessary that He do so in order for Jesus to taste the full wrath of God against sin, to empty the cup of God's wrath against sin down to its last dregs, to endure the full penalty for our sin, to pay the full and terrible price for our salvation during those three hours of darkness. In Gethsemane, Jesus wrestled with Himself and brought Himself to do the Father's will; on the cross, during those three hours forsaken by the Father, Jesus simply endures the unspeakable agony. During those three hours, Jesus no longer had the comfort of Oneness with God as Father, for a wall of separation had risen between the Father and the Son, namely the world's sin and curse now placed upon the Son of God as Son of Man.

Jesus thirsts for God the Father, but God the Father has removed Himself. It is not the Son that has left the Father, but the Father the Son. The Son of God as Son of Man cries for God, and God makes no reply. Judicially speaking, when Jesus became sin and a curse for us, the Father had to turn from Him in order for God's justice to be fulfilled, which was an essential requirement for our full salvation. What it meant for God the Father to forsake, to abandon, Jesus His Son for that awful time, no human being can know or comprehend. Certainly, the Father suffered with the Son during that time.

Jesus cries "My God, my God, why have You forsaken Me?" Notice that He addresses the Father as "My God," and not as "My Father."

But was not Jesus fully divine, God Himself, co-equal with the Father and the Holy Spirit? Yes! Yes! And being fully divine, was not Jesus all-knowing? Yes! Yes! Then did He not know the reason for the Father's forsaking Him, that it was necessary for His mission - our salvation - and that it was only temporary? No! He did not know that, for if He did, His cry of agony would have been meaningless. Here we have a great mystery!

We know that Jesus' divine nature and human nature cannot be separated. Yet the two are distinct. Both the Son of God and Son of Man hung on that cross. And today, at the right hand of the Father in glory, Jesus remains fully divine and fully human. But during His ministry and sacrifice on this earth, certain aspects of His divine nature were, so to speak, set aside. He still had them as fully God, but did not use them. It was in His human nature that Jesus had to live the sinless life for us. It was in His human nature that Jesus could experience our humanity in its fullest, except without sin, experience our trials, our tribulations, sufferings, joys, needs, disappointments in their fullest, in other words experience everything we go through., including our temptations. And it was in His human nature that Jesus had to suffer the punishment we deserved and die the death that was ours.

In His divine nature, as Son of God, God was Jesus' Father. In His human nature, as Son of Man, God the Father was Jesus' God. Thus, His cry, "My God, my God…", and not "My Father, my Father." And, in His human nature, His all-knowing divine attribute was limited for a time, keeping from Him the purpose of God's forsaking Him during that time. Thus, His cry, "My God, my God, why have You forsaken Me?" was genuine and revealed an agony greater than all the physical torture he was experiencing. It was the apex of His suffering; it was indeed the "supreme agony."

Consider also this: Jesus had to suffer both the powers of human wickedness and and the powers of spiritual wickedness in order to pay the full price for our sin. His human torturers had done their worst to cause Him physical agony. I wonder if Jesus, being the Living Word of

God, and suffering the torment of His human torturers, remembered the words of Job In his sufferings when he said: "God has turned me over to evil men, and thrown me into the clutches of the wicked." In addition to this human wickedness and darkness, the powers of spiritual wickedness and darkness were let loose to do their worst. Certainly the religious leaders reflected this spiritual wickedness and darkness, but there was more, much more.

Ephesians 6:12 tells us: "For our struggle is not against flesh and blood, but against the rulers, against the authorities, against the powers of this dark world and against the spiritual forces of evil in the heavenly realms." Certainly Satan and his demons, whom Jesus had conquered during His earthly ministry, whom He was conquering now on the cross, and whom He would totally and eternally conquer with His resurrection, did their worst to tempt and agonize Him while He hung on that cross.

Satan probably tempted Jesus on the cross just as he had in the wilderness - "If you are the Son of God," prove it by turning these stones to bread, by leaping from the temple. Only now it would have been - "If You are the Son of God, prove it by coming down from the cross; if You are the Son of God, where is your Father, why is He allowing this to happen to you?" And just as he had tempted Jesus with all the kingdoms of this world if He would only bend the knee and worship him, I'm sure he whispered in Jesus' ear: "Turn to me, and I'll get you off this cross." What is ironic is that Jesus, with His divine power, could have come down from that cross anytime He wanted, could have called upon legions of angels to destroy His torturers, but if He had, our redemption would not have been accomplished. And that is what Satan wanted, to prevent our redemption at all costs.

We don't know of all Satan's activities during the crucifixion of Jesus, but we can be certain that, just as he worked through the human powers of darkness to cause Jesus the greatest physical torment, so he worked through the spiritual powers of darkness to cause Jesus the greatest spiritual torment.

Even though God the Father turned from Jesus and left Him for a time, Jesus cries out to Him and holds fast to Him as His God. "My God, my God..." Here we see the divine perfection of Jesus. Even though He was made sin and a curse for us, even while suffering the worst that human wickedness and spiritual wickedness could do to Him, even while suffering the "supreme agony" of being forsaken by the Father, Jesus did not sin by turning from the Father. He remained the Lamb of God without blemish to the very end. In those hours, the full punishment and penalty for our sins was suffered, the full cost of our salvation was paid, and our bondage to sin, death, and Satan was broken, broken for good and for eternity.

And when that was done, the darkness lifted, the sun shone, and God the Father turned again to Jesus His Son. And Jesus knew it. As Son of man, Jesus knew again the blessed love of His God, and as Son of God, Jesus knew again the blessed Oneness with His Father. And knowing this, with the time of death near, He confidently and joyfully committed Himself to the Father with the words: "Father, into Your hands I commit my Spirit!" Jesus had to suffer the "supreme agony" of being forsaken by the Father for a time to secure our salvation. And it is an agony that all those who reject Christ, who reject God's grace through Christ, will suffer at the last judgment. But it is a suffering, an agony, that you and I and all who are in Christ by faith, will never experience. Jesus assures us: "I will never leave you; I will never forsake you." His suffering and death were personal, personal for you and for me.

We confess Christ died - that is history. We confess Christ died for sinners - that is Christianity. We confess Christ died for me - that is salvation. Hallelujah! Amen!

THE DEATH OF DEATH

Text: Job 19:25-27; 1Peter 1:3-9; Matthew 28:1-10

Theme: Easter is Christ Triumphant; Easter is Life.

Theme Statement: Christianity alone gives the absolute assurance of forgiveness of sins, reconciliation with God, and a blessed life eternal, and that assurance rests solidly upon the fact of Easter.

Key Passage: Matthew 28: 5-6. The angel said to the women, "Do not be afraid, for I know that you are looking for Jesus, Who was crucified. He is not here; He has risen, just as He said."

May it please God, in His infinite mercy and grace, to open our hearts and the hearts of countless other people in all parts of the world, to the message of our risen Lord and Savior, and may it bring many to saving faith, strengthen God's people in the faith, and give us hope and courage and assurance for the days and years ahead, until we join our resurrected Lord Who lives forevermore. Amen.

Christ is risen! He is risen indeed, Hallelujah! Our Lord brought His great work of redemption to its completion on Calvary, where He bore the sin and guilt of all humanity. He endured the worst humiliation, anguish, agony, that Satan, all the demons of hell, and His human enemies could lay upon Him. His Body was broken for you and me and all humanity; His Blood poured out for you and me and all humanity. The work of redemption was finished. Jesus Himself said so on the cross with His triumphant cry, "It is finished!" Yet it remained for God the Father to give His clear and unmistakable stamp of approval for the great work of His Son. So, on the third day, Jesus was raised from the dead. The resurrection was the Father's "Amen" to His Son's statement, "It is finished!" Our Savior burst the bonds of death and came forth from the tomb, the living and victorious Christ. Easter was the day that death died. Easter was the death of death.

Easter sets Christianity apart from all other beliefs, apart from all the religions of this world. No other belief system has the absolute assurance of the grace of God and life eternal that Christianity gives. And that assurance, our faith itself, rests on the solid, unshakable, undeniable, fact of the resurrection of our Lord Jesus, Who three days after His crucifixion, took up His life again in His glorified state. All who alter the fact of the resurrection in any way, or deny it, no longer deserve the Christian name. Those who deny the bodily resurrection of Christ face a great stumbling block, that being the absence of Jesus' dead body and the necessity of accounting for what became of it. They can resort only to explanations that are fanciful and ridiculous to the highest degree, and which can easily be refuted. The historical and physical evidence for Christ's resurrection is overwhelming, and is infallible proof for the authenticity of the Gospel accounts. But of far more importance than the historical and physical proofs of the resurrection is the fact that we have God's Word on it. Whatever the world may do about it, whatever people's attitudes may be towards it, however those who do not accept it may deny it, the stubborn fact remains unchanged - Jesus is the Living Lord; Christ is risen! Scripture tells us that "He is declared to be the Son of God with power, by the resurrection from the dead."

The resurrection of Jesus validated His every claim He made while on this earth. He claimed to be not only the Son of Man but the Son of God. He said that "He and the Father were One." His every act, His every Word bears the eternal Truth and infinite value of One Who was and is the Son of God Himself, as the Nicene Creed says in the second article: "....begotten of His Father from all eternity, God of God, Light of Light, Very God of Very God, begotten, not made, being of the same Substance of the Father, by Whom all things were made..." The resurrection was the supreme test. If He could not keep His promise to rise bodily again, our faith would have been meaningless, in vain. But He kept that promise; He rose from the dead.

The resurrection of Jesus gives meaning and fulfillment to every promise given by Christ, to every promise given by God in Holy Scripture. When He says to us: "Lo, I am with you always, even to the end of the world," we need never again feel lonely, lost, or afraid, because this is the promise of our Living Savior. When He says to us: "Come to Me, all you that labor and are heavy laden with burden, and I will give you rest," we can come to Him with confidence because this is the promise of our Living Savior. When He says to us: "I have prepared a place for you in heaven where you will share in My glory and blessedness, and know joy and delight far beyond anything you can imagine here on earth," we know that that is true for it is the promise of our Living Savior. We can hold to His promises with absolute trust and assurance because as the Living Savior, He is King of kings and Lord of lords, and has been given all authority in heaven and on earth and under the earth. "Every knee shall bow and every tongue confess that Jesus Christ is Lord to the glory of God the Father." His promises are sure; He means what He says, and He will most assuredly do what He has promised.

All who are in Christ by faith are the redeemed of God. Christ has redeemed us with His Blood, sealed our redemption with His resurrection, and made us righteous by the Holy Spirit. We are His through faith, and being His, we are also the Father's because Christ and the Father are One. And when we sin, as we do because we still have our sinful nature, the Father is ready to forgive us when we confess and repent, because Christ paid the price in full for our sin on the cross. We are no longer under the power of sin to condemn us because Christ has freed us from the power of sin and death. "O death, where is your sting? O grave, where is your victory?" We still die, but death cannot hold us. For those in Christ, death is merely passing through the veil into the glorious presence of Christ Himself. His resurrection assures us of our own resurrection. We are told in 2Timothy1:10 that "the grace of God was given to us in Christ Jesus before the beginning of time, but it has now been revealed through the appearing of our Savior, Christ Jesus, Who has destroyed death and has brought life and immortality to light through the Gospel." The great Easter message is the death of death. And those in Christ who have passed through that veil of death live, and they now rest in God and Christ in indescribable glory, and we will be reunited with them in that glory.

There was once a dear old Scotch lady who wanted so much to go to the city of Edinburgh, but for years she could not be persuaded to take the train because of her great dread of a tunnel through which she would have to pass. One day circumstances arose which forced her to go. Her fear was great and her agitation increased as the train drew near the dreaded tunnel. But before the tunnel was actually reached, the old lady, worn out with excitement and dread, dropped peacefully off to sleep. When she awoke, she discovered that the tunnel she had dreaded had been passed. The resurrection of Jesus assures us that we have nothing to fear from the tunnel of death, and that we shall awake in the full brilliance of our Lord's presence. The joy of knowing that our sins are atoned for, and that in Christ we are heirs of the Kingdom of Heaven, is the joy of every person who receives Christ through faith. It is the joy of Easter.

Easter brings peace to our hearts and lives, the peace that passes all understanding, the peace that the world cannot give. Jesus said: "In the world you will have trials and tribulation, but be of good cheer - I have overcome the world." And through faith in Him, we share in His victory because in Him we are sons and daughters of the Father in Heaven and brothers and sisters of our Savior the Son of God and Son of Man.

Easter means that heaven and earth are joined, for Christ our Savior is risen and God is reconciled to His human family. This is the supreme Easter truth. Easter means Christ's return from the violence and agony of the cross; His return from death and imprisonment in the tomb. Easter means Christ triumphant over all that Satan, sin, death, and man could do to Him. Easter means Christ in His Kingly splendor, Christ in His serene glory, Christ in His exaltation as King of kings and Lord of lords. Easter means that we need no longer fear the powers of this world and of hell itself that would try to restrict, deny, or strangle the life that is ours in Him.

Christ defeated death in order that life in Him might never end. And that is the life we want, isn't it? Life that never ends. Whether we put it in words or not, our constant hope and thought is life, more life, always more and more life. We want that life that never ends in ourselves, in our loved ones, in our friends, the life that cannot be diminished, the life that expands, the abundant life. And that life is only to be found in the risen Christ. As the Apostle Paul said, so we can say: "For to me, to live is Christ." That, my brothers and sisters, is Easter.

A pastor was once writing an Easter sermon, and when he was halfway through, the thought of the risen Lord broke in upon him as it had never done before. "Christ is alive!" he said to himself - "alive forevermore." He paused, and then repeated, "He is alive this very minute, living as certainly as I myself am." He arose, repeating as he walked, "Christ is living!" At first, it seemed strange, and then it came to him as a sudden burst of glory - "Christ is now living!" It was like a new discovery, although he thought he had believed it before. Then he said, "I must get this across to my people. I shall preach about it again and again until they realize it as I do now." For months after, and in every sermon, the Living Christ was the dominant theme, and there and then began the custom of singing in that church an Easter hymn on every Sunday morning.

Have we laid hold of the fact that we have a Living Lord and Savior, One Who ever lives to make intercession for us to the Father and to act for us in every time of need? Have we laid hold of the height, depth, breadth, of God the Father's love for us, for you and me, in giving His Beloved Son to be the sacrifice for our sins? Have we laid hold of Jesus' love for us in suffering so horribly so that we might be cleansed of sin and reconciled to the Father? Have we laid hold of the awesome nature of the event when we celebrate the resurrection of our Lord and Savior, and what it means to us who are followers of Christ? Death, with all the power of Satan behind it, could not hold Jesus in the tomb. When

Jesus left that tomb, death died, and when death died, it lost its power to hold us in the grave. When death died, we were given new life, abundant life, eternal life in Christ to the glory of God the Father.

Oh, may each of us grow in knowledge and understanding of the full meaning of Easter, of our Lord's resurrection, not just once a year on Easter Sunday, but every day of our lives. Because Christ has risen from the dead, every morning can be Easter to you and me, every day a day of resurrection. And may our hearts overflow with gratitude to our merciful and loving God for His amazing grace, thanking and praising Him that we have a living Savior. And because He lives, we too shall live. Amen.

CHAPTER 3 – FELLOWSHIP WITH GOD

"Yet I am always with You; You hold me by my right hand. You guide me with your counsel, and afterward You will take me into glory. Whom have I in heaven but You? And earth has nothing I desire besides You. My flesh and my heart may fail, but God is the strength of my heart and my portion forever."

Psalm 73: 23-26

THE GOD-SHAPED VACUUM

Text:　　　Isaiah 40: 6-8;　Titus 3: 4-7;　John 3: 1-6

Theme:　　The necessity of being "born again."

Theme Statement: There is a God-shaped vacuum in every human heart that can only be filled by God Himself through Jesus Christ. Education can't fill it. Wealth can't fill it. Power, prestige and fame can't fill it. The religion of humanism can't fill it. The only way to fill that vacuum, as Jesus made clear to Nicodemus, is to be born again of water and the Spirit, to have a spiritual rebirth, to be regenerated and renewed into a life of faith in Christ. The Holy Spirit gives us that new birth which is essential to enter the Kingdom of God.

Key Passage: John 3: 5-6. Jesus answered, "I tell you the truth, no one can enter the Kingdom of God unless he is born of water and the Spirit. Flesh gives birth to flesh, but the Spirit gives birth to spirit."

†

St. Augustine said, "O God, You have made us for Yourself, and our hearts are restless until they find their rest in You." Pascal, a genius in mathematics and experimental physics, said it this way: "There is a God-shaped vacuum in the heart which cannot be filled by any created thing, but only by God, made known through Jesus Christ." Many people today are desperately trying to fill the vacuum in their lives and hearts. The tragedy is that they are trying to fill that vacuum with things that don't bring lasting fulfillment. Nicodemus had a vacuum in his heart he wanted desperately to fill. Let's consider this man Nicodemus, what we can learn from him and apply to our lives.

If ever a person seemed to have it all, a person no one would suspect of having a vacuum in their heart, it would have been Nicodemus. First of all, he was one of the most highly educated men in all Israel. He was a Pharisee, a top scholar, a Rabbi, and one of the Scribes, the lawyers of Israel. He was an expert in the Law, the Torah, the Old Testament

Scriptures. Jesus Himself referred to Nicodemus as Israel's teacher. The fact that Nicodemus came to Jesus shows the great impression Jesus had made on him, how deeply Jesus affected his heart.

He came to Jesus at night, for it was risky for him to do so. He was convinced that Jesus came from God as a teacher, a prophet. He said that no one could perform the miracles Jesus did unless God was with him. In fact, he addressed Jesus as Rabbi -Teacher- which shows his humility. He had seen the glory of God in Jesus' teachings and miracles. The question in Nicodemus' mind was whether Jesus was the coming Messiah Who all of Israel desperately waited for, the Messiah Who would save them, Who would fill the vacuum in their lives and lift them out of their bondage. Nicodemus, as a scholar of the Scriptures, should have known that everything prophesied about the Messiah pointed to Jesus as the One. Yet, in spite of all his education and learning, the question remained in Nicodemus' mind, "Is He the Messiah, the One to come?" For the answer, he knew that he had to go to Jesus.

Some people try to fill the vacuum in their heart and life with education. They believe that education is the road to happiness, prosperity, fulfillment. Now, education is good, it's absolutely necessary, both in a secular sense and a spiritual sense. Scripture tells us we are to study, learn and grow in knowledge and wisdom. But we need to remember, as Isaiah tells us, that the wisdom of man is not to be trusted, for it is as grass compared to the Word of God that stands forever. One lesson we learn from Nicodemus is that there are people who have extensive knowledge of Scripture, but they don't know Christ, and that not even the highest education, in and of itself, can fill the God-shaped vacuum in one's heart and life.

Some people think wealth is the answer. Wealth will bring them happiness, fulfillment, security, and fill that vacuum. And so, they work themselves to a frazzle, their schedules leaving time for little else than work in order to accumulate wealth. A Texas land baron once took his friend out to his porch to show him the view. Waving his arm toward the horizon, he said, "Everything you see belongs to me. Those oil wells on the horizon - they're mine. That golden grain on the hills - that's mine. All those cattle in the valley - mine, all mine. Twenty-five years ago, I had nothing. But now I own everything you see." His friend hesitated a moment, then pointed towards heaven and asked his host, "And what do you own up there?"

Nicodemus had wealth. He undoubtedly had a fine home with servants and all the material comforts. We know he was wealthy because we're told in John 19 that he bought seventy-five pounds of myrrh and aloes to prepare the body of Jesus for burial after he and Joseph of Arimathea took it down from the cross. Those spices were used in royal burials because they were so expensive, and they would have cost Nicodemus a huge sum. And yet, all his wealth could not satisfy his greatest need - his need for the answer to the question, "Who is this Jesus?" Another lesson we learn from Nicodemus is that no amount of wealth can fill the God-shaped vacuum in one's heart and life.

Some people think that power, prestige, fame can fill that vacuum and bring them fulfillment. And yet, we read and hear of many famous celebrities who resort to drugs, alcohol, promiscuous sex in a desperate search for satisfaction and fulfillment. Isaiah tells us that all the power and glory of man is like grass, here today, gone tomorrow. Nicodemus was a man of power, prestige and authority, a top celebrity of his day. He was a member of the Sanhedrin, the ruling council of all Israel. His position was similar to that of a United States Senator today. Yet, all his power, prestige and authority could not satisfy his greatest need - his need for the answer to the question, "Who is this Jesus?" And so, another lesson we learn from Nicodemus is that all the power, prestige, and fame this world offers cannot fill the God-shaped vacuum in one's heart and life.

Finally, many people turn to religion in their search for satisfaction and fulfillment. And many find that much of the religion today does not bring the satisfaction, fulfillment and wholeness they desperately crave. Religion, to a great extent, has become so generalized, so accommodating to culture and society, that many believe, but they are not sure what they believe. As one person put it, "The church in America may be a rock, but even rocks are subject to erosion" - the erosion of doctrinal clarity and content, the erosion of Biblical precision, the erosion of theological truth by human philosophy, feelings and sentiments. Isaiah tell us that the wisdom of man is like grass, and only the Word of God stands forever.

Nicodemus was religious - was he ever! He was a Pharisee, one of the most revered and respected religious leaders in all Israel. And yet, his being religious, his conformance to the rules, laws and demands of his religion, did not meet his greatest need, his need to know "Who is this Jesus?" A final lesson we learn from Nicodemus is that religion itself, or simply being religious, cannot fill the God-shaped vacuum in one's heart and life.

So, what can and does fill that God-shaped vacuum? Jesus answered that question for Nicodemus and for all people. Jesus zeroed in on the greatest need of Nicodemus and all people - the need to be born again, the need for an entirely new birth. In Greek, it also means to be "born from above." This confused Nicodemus, and he asked, "How can a man be born again when he is old? Surely he can't enter again into his mother's womb and be born." Nicodemus isn't giving some smart-aleck answer to Jesus or refuting Jesus' words. His question simply indicates his difficulty in understanding Jesus' words. He perceives that Jesus means some other, far higher kind of birth, and he is asking "how?"

Jesus knew that Nicodemus' questions were sincere. He makes it clear to him that the rebirth He is speaking of is a Spirit (capital "S") rebirth. Jesus says, "I tell you the truth, no one can enter the Kingdom of God unless he is born of water and the Spirit." Water symbolizes the purification, the cleansing from sin that the new birth gives, and Spirit identifies the One Who gives this new birth - the Holy Spirit. "Flesh gives birth to flesh, but the Spirit gives birth to spirit," Jesus says. Imagine Nicodemus' surprise at his hearing that his being a Jew did not assure him a part in the Kingdom, that his being a Pharisee, a member of the Sanhedrim, availed him nothing, that he is not yet in the Kingdom, and that unless he receives the new birth, he shall not see the Kingdom. Nicodemus' religious life had emphasized works, works, works. Now he is hearing Jesus telling him new birth, new birth, new birth by the Spirit through the washing of regeneration, becoming a new creation.

And then Jesus goes on to tell Nicodemus to whom the Holy Spirit gives this new birth - to all who believe in Him; to all who receive Him as Lord and Savior. He speaks to Nicodemus those words we all know, or should know. "For God so loved the world that He gave His one and only Son, that whoever believes in Him shall not perish, but have eternal life."

Jesus' word on the new birth shatters once and for all any idea that man's attainments, the merits of human deeds, or one's status or station in life are passports into the Kingdom of God. There is only one passport into the Kingdom of God, and that is the new birth, for only the new birth creates the true spiritual life, the regenerated life, the renewed life, the life of true, saving faith, the life of salvation. The new birth and all that comes with it, by the grace of God, comes to all who have genuinely received and acknowledged Jesus Christ as Lord and Savior, and committed themselves to Him. The spiritual rebirth, the regenerated life, the renewed life of faith in Christ is the only thing that can fill that vacuum of the heart. Why? Because it is a God-shaped vacuum, and God has ordained that it can only be truly filled with Christ through the Holy Spirit. Without Christ, we remain strangers to God, and the vacuum is never filled.

This is precisely the point Jesus was making to Nicodemus. Changes were going on in Nicodemus' heart, that vacuum was being filled. The Holy Spirit was producing these changes, the Holy Spirit had led him to Jesus. Only the Holy Spirit gives new birth, a new nature, a new life of faith. It speaks highly of Nicodemus that he was open and receptive to the Holy Spirit's working, that he allowed Jesus to teach and lead him forward. Nicodemus had come to find out if Jesus was the Messiah. He got his answer - the vacuum was filled and his restless heart calmed.

All of us, if we genuinely believe in Jesus Christ as our Lord and Savior, have received the new birth, the regenerated and renewed life. But it's so easy to let the cares, demands, pressures and pleasures of this life take priority over our greatest need - to grow and mature in that new birth, that life of faith. Let's remember the example of Nicodemus. Though highly educated, he recognized his ignorance apart from Christ; though he was wealthy, he recognized his poverty apart from Christ; and though he was powerful, he recognized his helplessness apart from Christ. And he brought his ignorance, poverty, and helplessness to Jesus, because he knew that only Jesus had the answers he was seeking, only Jesus could fill the vacuum in his heart. And in the same way, only Jesus has the answers we are seeking in our lives, and only Jesus can fill the vacuum in our heart. But He can't fill a closed heart. God grant that we open our hearts to Him completely and allow Him to fill them to overflowing. Amen.

THE GREATEST JOY

Text: 2 Samuel 6: 12-23; Philippians 4: 4-7; Luke 1: 39-45.

Theme: The Joy only those in Christ have.

Theme Statement: Scripture tells us to rejoice in the Lord always. Those in Christ through faith have the greatest reason to rejoice - the assurance of salvation, the forgiveness of sins, the indwelling of the Holy Spirit, and the eternal joy in the presence of our Lord in heaven. Only the presence of God through Christ gives this joy. In our readings, we have examples of the Greatest Joy of King David and John the Baptist who, when experiencing the presence of our Lord, leaped and jumped, and David danced, in the ecstasy of this Greatest Joy. May the joy we experience in our fellowship with our Lord be our Greatest Joy.

Key Passage: Philippians 4: 4."Rejoice in the Lord always. I say it again: Rejoice!"

✝

In his great writing entitled *Orthodoxy*, G.K. Chesterton writes about Jesus and why he, Chesterton, became a Christian. He was once an avowed atheist, who fought Christianity with all his might. He said that there was a mystique about Jesus that no one understood and was to an extent hidden from all people. It was something that was too great for the Lord to show entirely when He walked the earth. The human mind couldn't comprehend it. "Then" Chesterton said, "as I have studied and restudied the life of Jesus, I have discovered that the great mystique partially hidden was His great joy." Christianity without joy is a betrayal of our Lord. We are a forgiven, redeemed, people, who belong to the faithful flock on the way to heaven. We are people who have every reason under heaven, and especially when we get to heaven, to have great joy, the Greatest Joy.

Our epistle reading tells us, "Rejoice in the Lord always!" And the Apostle Paul repeats it for emphasis, "I will say it again: Rejoice!" The purest joy is to fill the Christian life. Why? Because of Christ! Because we have the assurance of salvation, the forgiveness of sins, the true righteousness, the indwelling of the Holy Spirit, the living hope of the blessed resurrection, and the eternal joy in heaven in the presence of our Lord. Paul wrote this as a prisoner. And just as nothing ever dimmed his spiritual joy, nothing is ever to dim our spiritual joy.

The joy of the Christian is genuine, not a bit of it artificial like the joys of the world. And because the Christian joy is genuine, Paul tells us that we need not be anxious about anything. We are to cast all our anxieties on our Lord because He cares for us. In joy, we are to bring everything by prayer and petition to God, and not shrink from asking. In what better hands can any trouble of ours rest than in God's hands. And our prayers are to be accompanied with thanksgiving, and thus offered with joy, for a thankful heart is a joyful heart. Finally, Paul tells us that the blessed result of rejoicing in the Lord and leaving everything in God's hands by means of prayer with thanksgiving is the peace of God which passes all understanding. God creates and bestows this peace, and, like a sentry, it will guard our hearts and minds in Christ Jesus, lest anything disturb them.

In our readings, we have the examples of two great men of God who rejoiced in the Lord, and the profound joy they experienced in the presence of God. First, we have the account of David bringing the Ark of the Covenant to Jerusalem. After David became king, he made the city of Jerusalem his stronghold. The Ark of God had been stored in the home of Obed-edom, and God had richly blessed the household of Obed-edom and everything he had because of the Ark. And so, we're told, David and company went down and brought up the Ark of God to the city of David with rejoicing.

David sacrificed burnt offerings and peace offerings in joy and thanksgiving to God. And then we're told that David danced before the Lord with all his might as they brought up the Ark with shouts of joy and the sound of trumpets. David, the great soldier, statesman, and king, caught up in spiritual ecstasy and great joy over the Ark which

God had set apart for His presence on earth, leaped and danced with all his might. This is the only reference in Scripture to a man, much less a king, dancing.

David is so full of joy over God's presence among them that he does not hesitate to humble himself and make a fool of himself to show his devotion to the Lord. Also, David had laid aside his imperial purple attire and put on a plain linen ephod, a garment worn by those who served before the Lord at His sanctuary. The attitude of David, whom God had called "a man after His own heart," was that, as God's chosen king, he would do all to support the grandeur and authority of his royal position. But in acts of devotion to the Lord, he would lay aside all trappings of royalty, humble himself to the dust before the Lord, and join in with the humblest services done in honor of the Lord.

Arriving in Jerusalem, they set the Ark in the midst of the tabernacle or tent that David had prepared for it. And then, he blessed the people in the Name of the Lord Almighty, gave each person a loaf of bread, a cake of dates, and a cake of raisins, and sent them home. The gifts were probably tokens of his joy and gratitude to God, and his love for the people of God.

We're told that when David and company were entering Jerusalem, and Michal, his wife and daughter of Saul, saw him leaping and dancing, she despised him in her heart. When he got home, she scolded him for his dancing and leaping and for setting aside his royal garments for a linen ephod. As far as she was concerned, David had made a fool of himself before the people, which I'm sure embarrassed her, and she didn't hesitate to tell him so.

David's response to his wife's scolding was that it was before the Lord, and to the glory of God, that he had leaped and danced, that he would continue to celebrate before the Lord and become even more undignified than this, even more of a fool than this, in his celebration and devotion before the Lord, and be humiliated in his own eyes. And David told her that the response of the common people, whose reproach she feared, would be to esteem him and honor him so much the more for his pious acts in devotion to the Lord.

There are many like Michal today who mock Christians for their worship and devotion to God, for their exuberant expressions of joy in Christ their Savior. Their attitude is, "go ahead and have your worship services, your celebrations, your joy feasts, but keep them private and to yourself, and don't make any public confession or demonstration or celebration of your faith. Our response to them should be like David's response to Michal. God's punishment to Michal for her insolence and unjust criticism of David for his joyful expression of devotion to God was that she would be childless, barren, to the day of her death, a disgrace in Hebrew society.

A few lessons we can take from this account. 1. We should be very, very careful in censuring or criticizing the worship of others that confess and honor Christ, but may not conform with our sentiments, tradition, or practice. 2. The more we are criticized or vilified for expressing and witnessing our faith, the more resolute we should be in it, in living it, witnessing it, never fearing reproach, and remembering that those who honor God, He will honor. And 3. To be thought of as a fool for God by the secular masses is the highest honor they can give you.

In our Gospel reading, we're told about someone else who rejoiced and experienced the greatest joy in the presence of the Lord. Sometime after the angel Gabriel's annunciation to Mary, Mary hurried to go visit her relative Elizabeth, who was six months pregnant. Her desire to see Elizabeth was strong, which is understandable. The profound nature of what these two women shared in the redemptive plan of God must have given them a closeness of relationship we can only imagine. Mary stayed with Elizabeth for about three months before she returned home.

We're told that when Elizabeth heard Mary's greeting, the baby in her womb leaped and Elizabeth was filled with the Holy Spirit. The baby in Elizabeth's womb was, of course, John the Baptist, the one prophesied to be the messenger of the Christ, the one whose ministry would prepare the way for the Christ , the one who would one day point out Jesus to his disciples and say, "Behold, the Lamb of God Who takes away the sin of the world."

The presence of his Lord in the womb of Mary caused the baby John to leap for joy in the womb of Elizabeth. With this joyful leaping in the womb by John, the word of the angel to his father Zechariah concerning him was fulfilled when the angel said, "He will be filled with the Holy Spirit from his mother's womb." The unborn messenger of Christ felt his Master's Presence, and was himself filled with the Holy Spirit, and the Spirit then filled also his mother.

As a child of God, Elizabeth was already filled with the Spirit Who moved her to faith and faithfulness. But the filling of which Luke now speaks was a charismatic filling, enabling her to speak as she did. Only through the Spirit's revelation could Elizabeth have had the knowledge she now expressed. Without having heard about the angel's visit to Mary, now at the sound of her greeting, as in a flash by the Spirit's revelation, all is perfectly clear to her.

We're told that Elizabeth speaks in a loud voice? Why? Because of her exuberant joy. And that joy centers on the child in Mary's womb. "Blessed are you among women" denotes a continuous state of being blessed, her blessedness, of course, the fact that God chose her to be the mother of His Son. Elizabeth's question, "Why am I so favored that the mother of my Lord should come to me?" voices her feeling of unworthiness that she should be so honored. The astonishing thing is the clarity and assurance of Elizabeth's recognition of Mary as the mother of her Lord. Elizabeth speaks as if she herself had heard the angel's words. Again, the revelation of the Holy Spirit.

Elizabeth's beatitude to Mary addresses her faith. "Blessed is she who has believed that what the Lord has said to her will be accomplished." "What the Lord has said," includes all the angel's prophecies about the Person, nature, and work of Mary's Son. For Mary to hear Elizabeth speak in this astonishing way, to declare that all the prophecies concerning her Son would be fulfilled, must have been a mighty uplift to her faith and comfort for her soul. For Mary certainly knew that Elizabeth spoke through the Holy Spirit's revelation and inspiration.

And so, we have two examples of the Greatest Joy, the presence of God, experienced by two of the greatest servants of God. David experienced that Greatest Joy through the Ark of God which bore the presence of God. John the Baptist experienced that Greatest Joy through the womb of Mary which bore the very Person of God. Considering the Presence in the Ark, and the Person in the womb, we can say that the purpose of the Ark of God was fulfilled by the womb of Mary.

Finally, let us consider the joy that Jesus brings to us, to you and me, to all humankind, not only during Christmas and Easter seasons, which unfortunately too many people do, but every day through every season of life. The joy of a Savior, the joy of a living hope, the joy of being loved by our God and Savior with an unconditional love beyond our comprehension, the joy of being uplifted when we are heavy hearted and oppressed, the joy of forgiveness, the joy of salvation, the joy of having our Lord's Presence with us now in His Word and Sacraments, and the joy of knowing that He will come again for a final time to take us to be with Him in eternal glory where we will experience that Greatest Joy forever and ever.

And if that makes you want to leap and dance and shout for joy to the Lord, why go ahead. Care not what others think or say, and treat their jaunts, rebukes, and criticism as praise. Remember that to be thought of as a fool for the Lord is the greatest of honors. And so, "Rejoice in the Lord always. I say it again, Rejoice!" Amen.

SERVANTHOOD, THE PATH TO GREATNESS

Text: Esther 4:12-16; Matthew 20:17-28.

Theme: The suffering, anxiety, joy, and blessings of servanthood.

Theme Statement: During His ministry on earth, Jesus emphasized to His disciples the central place of servanthood in His Kingdom. It is the only path to greatness, not the false greatness of self-pride, fame, notoriety, but the true greatness of humility, strength, and walking with God. Scripture is filled with examples of true servanthood, that of Jesus, of course being the ultimate example. In the Old Testament, the book of Esther contains a beautiful example of servanthood. Esther was the only one who could appeal to the king to save her people from the evil Haman who had devised a plot to murder all the Jews. But to do this, meant almost certain death. Esther prayed that God would calm her great fear and make the king receptive to her request. And so He did. The Jews were saved, Haman the plotter executed, and Esther honored by the king. In her great fear and anxiety, Esther had no one to turn to except God. Jesus, in His Passion, suffering, and death, had no one to turn to except God his Father. And so it is with us as we live out our lives of servanthood. There are times when God is our only recourse.

Key Passage: Matthew 20:27,28. "Whoever wants to become great among you must be your servant, and whoever wants to be first, must be your slave - just as the Son of Man did not come to be served, but to serve, and to give His life as a ransom for many."

Let us consider the theme of servanthood. Jesus had a lot to say about servanthood, and Scripture is filled with examples of true servanthood, Jesus 'example of course, being the ultimate. In the Old Testament, the book of Esther gives us a beautiful example of servanthood. Our passage in Esther is taken from the prayer of

Mordecai, one of the captive Jews of Persia, who prays on behalf of his cousin Esther, who faces a terrible crisis. Esther was the queen of Persia, chosen by King Xerxes as his wife. The king did not know she was a Jew, since Mordecai had advised her not to tell him.

The king's primary assistant was a man named Haman who hated the Jews intensely. Through lies and deception, He convinced the king to issue a decree naming a certain day when all the other people in Persia were to annihilate all the Jews - young and old, women and children, and to plunder their goods. When Mordecai heard of this, he appealed to Esther to serve her people by going into the king's presence to beg for mercy and plead with him for her people. But to do this entailed great danger for it was law that any man or woman, including the queen, who went into the king's presence without being summoned by him was to be put to death. The only exception was if the king extended the gold scepter to them, thus sparing their life. Esther informed Mordecai of this and of her great fear.

Mordecai told her, "Who knows but that you have come to royal position for such a time as this." Esther had no one to turn to except the Lord. Mordecai prayed for her and God's deliverance as we read. And Esther fled to the Lord, praying, "Help me, who am alone and have no helper but You....give me courage, turn the king's heart, save us from the hands of evildoers and save me from my fear."

Esther went into the king's presence and the Lord was with her. The king extended his gold scepter and asked her for her request. Esther told him of all Haman's lies to the king in getting the king to agree to his plot to kill all her people, admitting that she was a Jew. The king ordered Haman to be put to death, gave to Mordecai Haman's office and estates at Esther's request, and issued another edict to all the provinces giving the Jews authority to destroy anyone who attacked them. The tables were turned, the Jews got the upper hand, and destroyed all their enemies.

Esther, in her servanthood, gives us a picture of Christ. She was the only one who could save her people. Jesus, as the GodMan, was the only one who could save us from sin, death, and hell. Esther experienced great fear and anxiety over what she considered her certain death in serving her people. Jesus, in His humanity, experienced fear, anxiety, and anguish over the extreme suffering and agony of His certain death in serving and saving humanity. Esther, in prayer, fled to the Lord Who alone could help her and save her from her fear. Jesus, in prayer, fled to His Father, Who alone could relieve His fear and strengthen Him for the sacrifice only He could make. God honored Esther for her courage and obedience in serving Him and her people. And God honored His Son's courage and obedience by accepting His sacrifice as full payment for mankind's sins, raising Him from the dead, and exalting Him as King of kings and Lord of lords.

As I mentioned at the beginning, Jesus had a lot to say about servanthood. During the three years of seminary training Jesus gave His disciples, He emphasized servanthood time and time again. And He, of course, was their role model, and ours, of servanthood. In our Gospel reading, Jesus and His disciples and other followers are on their way to Jerusalem. The time was drawing near for the supreme sacrifice of servanthood, the cross. One can never say that Jesus didn't try to prepare His disciples for His death. At least three times He spoke of His death to them. Now He takes them aside, privately, and tells them plainly what will occur.

Whereas before He spoke of deliverance into the hands of men, He now gives specifics - first deliverance to the chief priests and teachers of the law, the Sanhedrim, who would condemn Him to death, then deliverance to the Romans, who would carry out the death sentence. Jesus, here and elsewhere, described His Passion - being mocked, beaten, spit-upon, scourged, crucified. Then, He sets against this black background the glorious light and assurance of His Resurrection.

Jesus wanted His disciples to be fully aware of His coming Passion and death to avoid confusion and panic on their part. He wanted them to understand that this was the culmination of His mission on earth - a mission of atonement and redemption, and not the establishment of a kingdom on earth as they expected. But I think there was another reason. When we face a major crisis in life, suffering, sorrow, and loss, we want, we need, the comfort, support, and prayers of family and friends. I think Jesus, in His human nature, also needed and wanted comfort, support, and prayers from His disciples who were His family. Did He not tell them in Gethsemane to "watch and pray" with Him before they promptly fell asleep?

Well, Jesus' words of His coming passion again went right over their heads, and as our passage shows, they were still thinking of His Kingdom as an outward earthly kingdom and its glory. We're told that "then the mother of James and John, whose name was Salome, came to Jesus with her sons with a request for a favor." That word "then" identifies her coming to Jesus after He spoke of His Passion. Jesus asks her what she wants. Her answer: "that one of these two sons of mine sit at your right and the other at your left in your kingdom." Did James and John put their mother up to this? Probably! After all, who can refuse a mother's request?

Salome wants her sons to have the highest places in His kingdom. Jesus tells her, "You don't know what you are asking." Then He asks James and John, "Can you drink the cup I am going to drink?" What cup? The cup of His passion, suffering, and death which He had just described. That word "drink" in the Greek, "piein", means to drink completely, empty the cup He Himself is about to drink. Jesus is telling them that the way to greatness in His kingdom is not as they think, by mere decree, but by way of suffering and servanthood. Do they realize that? Their all too ready reply, "We are able!" reveals that they do not. Patiently, Jesus tells them, "You will indeed drink from my cup." They may not realize what that cup meant now, but they would come to realize its full meaning.

Here Jesus identifies the sufferings of His followers, past, present, and future, endured for His sake and the Gospel's, with His own sufferings, the only distinction being that the suffering of Jesus was redemptive and atoning for humanity, while the suffering of His followers is a confessional suffering. We're told in Romans 8:17: "Now if we are children, then we are heirs - heirs of God and co-heirs with Christ, if indeed we share in His sufferings in order that we may also share in His glory." Think what it would have meant to Jesus if James and John, instead of requesting seats of glory, would have told Him: "Lord, we want to go through this with you; we want to share in your sufferings and passion." Come to think of it, as a co-heir with Christ, have I ever prayed, "Lord, grant that I may share in your sufferings." I can't remember ever asking that. Can you? As far as the seats of glory at Jesus' right and left in the Kingdom, Jesus says they are not His to grant; they belong to those for whom they have been prepared by the Father.

Despite the fault of Salome's request for her sons, it is worth noting that her wish, in a purified form, has been made by many a mother, praying that her son might turn to Christ and serve Him in His Church. Monica, the mother of Saint Augustine, is a classic example. For years, decades, she prayed that her wayward son would leave his wanton lifestyle, turn to the Lord in faith, and serve Him in His Church. Finally, her prayer was answered, and her son, Augustine, became one of the most important bishops and theologians of the Christian Church. Augustine said of James' and John's request to sit at Jesus' right and left: "They sought the exaltation, but did not see the step to exaltation, the cup of suffering." Luther found something noteworthy in their request: He said, "Jesus treated the presumptuous pride of the Pharisees with severity, but the ambition of these disciples He treats with gentleness, for it springs from faith and needs only to be purified."

We're told that the other disciples, when they heard about James' and John's request, were indignant that they had tried to secure those seats for themselves, showing themselves no better than the two. In fact, not long before this, Peter had said to Jesus: "We have left everything to follow you! What then will there be for us?" It shows where their mindset was. Apparently there was no one in that group with the presence of mind to say, "Wait a minute guys! Our Lord just told us what awaits Him in Jerusalem - suffering, mocking, scourging, crucifixion, and here we are jockeying for positions of greatness in His Kingdom."

They were degrading the Kingdom of Heaven to the level of worldly kingdoms, and following a wrong principle in regard to greatness. So Jesus intervenes. He turns the incident into a great and profound lesson for all His disciples, including you and me, a lesson of true greatness and the path to that greatness - servanthood. In the worldly kingdoms, rulers oppress their subjects with power and authority to establish and maintain greatness. "Not so with you," Jesus emphasizes. In the Kingdom of God, "Whoever wants to become great among you must be your servant, and whoever wants to be first must be your slave." The path to greatness in the Kingdom, in the Church, is by being a servant to others - "doulos" in the Greek, the humblest and lowest of servants. And service to God's people is service to God.

Greatness is measured by blessed service to God's people, and whether one is rewarded or exalted for this service makes no difference. Jesus promises rewards for those who serve Him, but we do not serve with reward as our motive. We serve with love as our motive, love for Him Who gave His Body and Blood, Who gave His all for us, and love for our neighbor. And then, with the words "just as," Jesus casts a flood of light and meaning on what He has told them about servanthood. He says, "just as the Son of Man did not come to be served, but to serve, and to give His life as a ransom for many." Jesus gives them and us the ultimate example of servanthood - Himself. He Who was man, and yet far more than man- God's Incarnate Son - infinitely great, all-powerful, could have compelled all men to be His "douloi," His servants, but He came "not to be served, but to serve", and His supreme service was "to give His life as a ransom for many."

"To give!" The act is voluntary. And He gives His life, not only on Calvary, but His whole life, from His Incarnation, His Nativity, His Ministry, to Calvary. From His perfect, sinless life He lived for us, to the beaten, bloody, crucified life He gave up for us on the cross, it was all the ransom for our sin, the payment for our release from the bondage of sin, the payment for our release from the guilt and penalty of sin, a payment in expiation, in substitution for the payment we owed but could not make. Only the Son of God as Son of Man could make that payment. Luther described the ransom as follows: "He...purchased and won me from all sin, from death, and from the power of the devil, not with gold or silver, but with His holy, precious blood, and with His innocent suffering and death."

Servanthood can be lonely at times, when serving God and others brings criticism, loss of friends, and persecution from worldly sources. Esther found that, in her servanthood, she had no one to turn to but God. Jesus found, in His ultimate servanthood, that He had no one to turn to but His Father. Perhaps there have been times in your life when there was no one to turn to but God. But that's o.k. As the saying goes, "One person and God make a majority." David understood this. In Psalm 73, he says: "Yet I am always with You; You hold me by my right hand. You guide me with your counsel, and afterward You will take me to glory. Whom have I in heaven but You? And earth has nothing I desire besides You. My flesh and my heart may fail, but God is the strength of my heart and my portion forever."

Servanthood is both the path to greatness and the path to the only legacy of life that has lasting meaning. We are told to love God with all our heart, mind, soul, and spirit, and to love our neighbor as ourselves. Well, love entails service. Just as faith and obedience are inseparable, so are love and service inseparable. And those whose lives are shaped by that faith and obedience and that love and service, will receive that lasting legacy when they hear their Lord and Savior say, "Well done, good and faithful servant." God grant that to us all, in Jesus' Name. Amen.

WARTS AND ALL

Text: Jeremiah 18: 1-4;   Hebrews 4: 14-16;
          Mark 1: 40-42;   2: 15-17

Theme: God's acceptance of us as we are.

Theme Statement: God, in His grace, accepts us as we are - warts and all - and in His mercy, changes us for His purpose and our highest good. God, through the Holy Spirit, is continually at work forming and shaping us to remove the blemishes in our lives that dim His image.

Key Passage: Hebrews 4:15. "For we do not have a high priest who is unable to sympathize with our weaknesses, but we have One Who has been tempted in every way, just as we are — yet was without sin."

I have some quirks, idiosyncrasies, that can be frustrating. They drive my wife up the wall at times. For instance, I have a thing for turning off lights. I can't stand it if lights are left on in a room that is not being used. My wife will turn on a light, leave the room for a few minutes intending to come back, and find that the light has been turned off. Then there's the matter of locking doors. I will check to insure they are locked even when she tells me she has done it. Another thing that really gets to her is when we get into the car and I jiggle the emergency brake up and down a half-dozen times to insure its off. "Alright, already, it's off! Let's go," she will say.

We all have our idiosyncrasies. I'll bet you are thinking of yours, or those of your loved ones, right now. They are generally harmless and can even be humorous. But there are times when even harmless idiosyncrasies, quirks, habits, can grow in proportion to where they seriously affect our attitude, personality, and our relationships with family, friends, and most important, God. A little insecurity grows into a phobia or aversion; a questioning nature becomes one of doubt and suspicion; a little temper grows into anger or abuse; a little envy becomes rampant jealousy; a tendency to stretch the truth just a little becomes outright lying; a frugal nature becomes a stingy and greedy one, and so on. At that point, they cease to be humorous idiosyncrasies, quirks, and become major warts in our lives, blemishes that dim, or perhaps even hide, the image of God that should shine through every Christian, warts that inhibit us from being everything God wants us to be, and doing all He wants us to do.

I'm so thankful for the Holy Spirit, and I marvel at His patience. For you see, an important ministry of the Holy Spirit is our sanctification - that is, forming and shaping us into the image of Christ and bringing us to spiritual maturity. And an important part of that is removing the warts in our lives. You see, our loving God accepts us and loves us just as we are, warts and all, but He won't leave us just as we are.

Our passage in Jeremiah gives us a picture of the merciful goodness and determination of God to form and shape us into the person He created us to be, and which is our highest good. We are the clay, with all our warts and blemishes, flaws and weaknesses. Unless God, the Potter, works in us and upon us, we simply lie helpless only to waste away. Without God, we can no more attain a worthy end in life than the clay can become a shapely vessel without the potter.

Just as the potter has a purpose for the clay, God has a purpose for every life. The potter forms the vessels of clay. God forms the vessels of our characters, our souls, our lives. God's first priority in forming us is not what we are to do, but what we are to be. And what we are to be is His beloved children through faith in His Son Jesus Christ as our Lord and Savior. One of the ministries of the Holy Spirit is to urge us, prompt us, bring us to that saving faith. That's justification. Once justified, the Holy Spirit begins the work of sanctification - that is, forming and shaping us more and more into the image of Christ, which is a lifetime process. Through sanctification, we can be used more and more for God's purposes, just as the clay is of service after the potter has done his work with it. Like the potter who presses, stretches, and forms the clay until the blemishes are removed, God presses, stretches, and shapes our lives on one side and another through the circumstances of our lives until one wart after another is removed or smoothed out. And through it all, God steadily and patiently works out His purposes for us and our highest good as individuals, a community of believers, a church.

Now we as clay can either submit to the potter's hand or resist and refuse to be formed and shaped. If we submit to the Lord's hand, God breathes His Spirit into us and sustains us every moment in all situations by His indwelling Spirit, and forms us into something far more wonderful than we can imagine for ourselves. If we submit, He will work in us both to will and to do. On the other hand, if the clay resists or refuses to be formed, it must be broken up and refashioned. So with us! We have a free-will and can be stubborn, rebellious to God's perfect will for us, and we must be broken for our own good. Our lives are disturbed, disrupted, shaken up so that God can again begin to fashion us and form us for His desired purpose and our greatest good. God's discipline can be as hard and uncomfortable, or as gentle and easy, as we make it. And God, through His infinite patience and gracious perseverance can use the disappointments, destructive events, failures, and disruptions that we bring upon ourselves through our resistance, our insistence on having our own way, to shape us and effect His great purpose and secure the true and lasting blessedness of His precious children.

In our Epistle passage, which is one of my favorites, the writer to the Hebrews reminds us that we have a High Priest - Jesus, our Savior and Lord - Who is able to sympathize with our weaknesses because He was tempted in every way we are, yet was without sin. Think of that! You have the sympathy of the Son of God as the Son of Man Himself! In taking on our humanity, He took upon Himself all our warts and weaknesses, all our sins, and defeated them by living the perfect, sinless life. When the warts, weaknesses, and temptations of life assailed Jesus, they found no sin with which they could connect. There was not even the resemblance of sin in Him. The clay that was Jesus Christ in His human body was absolutely perfect. And then, after living the perfect, sinless, life, He paid the price for our warts and sins in our place by taking them to the cross, making it possible through His sacrifice for us to be cleansed of them, forgiven for them, and be rid of their power over us once and for all. And because He did this, because we have a great High Priest, Jesus, Who can sympathize with us, and Who paid in full the price for our sins, we can approach the throne of grace with confidence in order to receive mercy and find grace for our need. The compassion of Jesus for our weaknesses, our warts so to speak, is to me one of the deepest, richest, and most comforting of all His Savior qualities.

The sympathy and compassion of Jesus for us is shown in all His miracles of healing. In the healing of the leper, in one of our passages, we are told that Jesus was filled with compassion. He felt pain at the sight of the man's suffering. Luke, in his account of the healing, states that the man was "full of leprosy." His terrible disease was in an advanced stage. He was accounted as one dead, and thus unclean. We can marvel both at the leper's boldness and courage in publicly approaching Jesus, and at his faith and confidence that Jesus could heal him, remove this horrible, devastating, wart in his life. Jesus reached out His hand and touched the leper and healed him.

To touch a leper was not only considered a dangerous and gross act, but it made one ceremonially unclean according to the law. You can be assured that none of the religious leaders would have done so. They would have looked with disgust and horror on the man's flesh that was eaten away, at the raw sores spreading over his body. Jesus touched him, and not only restored the man's body completely, but also restored his dignity with that touch. The lesson for us is that there are no warts in our lives, no weaknesses, that Jesus won't touch and heal if we ask Him to, if we will only come to Him like that leper in humility and faith. He not only accepts us - warts and all - but He sympathizes with us, feels deep compassion for us, and wants to restore us to wholeness.

Do we sympathize with those around us who are burdened with major warts and weaknesses in their lives? Do we help them, extend the grace of God in Christ to them? Or do we avoid them, criticize them, ostracize them in our self-pride and self-righteousness? It is a human tendency to point out the warts and weaknesses and failures of others, but to ignore one's own. Like Jesus said, we point to the splinter in our brother's or sister's eye, and ignore the two-by-four in our own eye. I'll bet each of us could identify a wart or two of our own right now. But if we were asked to identify our spouse's warts, we could probably come up with a list stretching across the room.

Well, God may not ask us to touch a leper, but He may very well ask us to reach out and touch someone with compassion and His saving grace who we would rather have nothing to do with, whose person and deeds we find offensive. He has a way of testing us like that. A wretched woman found in the slums of New York was taken to a Christian mission. She was dressed in rags, covered with vermin, thoroughly offensive in appearance and attitude. The pastor's wife sat with her, told her of God's love. With a growl, the woman said, "What do I care about the love of a God in heaven? No one has ever loved me down here." The pastor's wife told her that she loved her and longed for her salvation. The woman snapped, "You say you love me! People who love each other show affection; they kiss each other and put their arms around each other. You would never kiss a thing like me." The challenge hit the pastor's wife at a weak spot because she was a prim and proper woman. Still, without hesitation, she threw her arms around the woman and kissed her. The woman threw herself to the floor, crying and asking God for mercy. She later became a wonderful Christian. The pastor's wife showed the sympathy and compassion of Jesus for that woman with all her warts.

The sympathy and compassion of Jesus for the peoples' warts and weaknesses was deeply resented by the religious leaders, and they hated Him for it. In our other Gospel reading, we are told of a dinner with many tax-collectors and sinners present, notorious sinners who had an abundance of warts and weaknesses. And who was right there in the midst of them? Jesus and His disciples! The religious leaders asked why He ate with them, for they were considered the dregs of society.

To eat with a person was considered a sign of friendship, and the scribes and Pharisees shunned such people as outcasts. Jesus' answer that a physician is for the sick, not the healthy, both gave His reason for socializing with them and served as a rebuke to the religious leaders.

Why was Jesus there? He accepted those sinners, warts and all, that He might free them from their sins, remove their warts and fashion them for the lives God willed for them. This was no mere social gathering. Here too, just as in the healing of the leper, Jesus was fulfilling the role of the potter, refashioning the clay. His great mission was to seek and to save the lost.

If Jesus was physically present today, where would we find Him? Would He be in the churches? Certainly, if those churches were faithful to God's Word. Would He be in our homes? Certainly, if we have invited Him to be there as Master. But you know where else I think we would find Him? Down on the wrong side of town, the ghetto, ministering to the drunks, the drug addicts, the prostitutes. The Great Physician would be curing the sick, removing warts, refashioning the clay. Would we resent our Lord associating with such people like those religious leaders resented Jesus for doing so? Many Christians would. We Christians can sometimes be a bit self-righteous, like those religious leaders in Jesus' day, and feel superior to all those miserable sinners around us. We can sometimes think of ourselves as less guilty than the other person who is involved in things we think we would never involve ourselves in. We can sometimes be like the man who told his friend that he took exception to the Scripture that says "there is no difference; all have sinned and fall short of the glory of God." He was convinced that he was better than most, and he said, "I don't like that teaching." His friend responded: "Well, let's make a concession in your case. Let's say that there are superior sinners, and there are inferior sinners. You are a superior sinner." The man dropped the argument.

What matters most in life is not that we know God, but the fact that He knows us - you and me and all our brothers and sisters. We know Him only because He first knew us. And He loves us just as we are -

warts and all. But praise Him, He won't leave us as we are. Don't ever let Satan convince you that, because of your warts and weaknesses and failures, that God has abandoned you. God is continually at work, forming, shaping us, working to remove those warts that blemish our lives and inhibit His purpose for us. You are never out of His mind. There is no moment when His eyes are off you. There is no moment when His care falters. God went to the greatest expense for you; there is no higher expense than the cross. God splurged His love and mercy and glory on you, and He continues to do so.

Karl Barth, probably the most well-known Lutheran theologian of the 20th century, was once asked: "What is the greatest theological insight you have experienced?" The person asking the question undoubtedly expected a complex theological reply. The great theologian's immediate answer was: "Jesus loves me, this I know, for the Bible tells me so," a child's nursery song.

It's as simple as that. And as profound as that. God has a love affair with you and me, and God's love is the only lasting reality, in this world and for eternity. Revel in His love; rejoice in His love; and respond to His love, to the honor and glory of His Name. Amen.

CHAPTER 4 - DISCIPLESHIP

"We wait in hope for the Lord; He is our help and our shield. In Him our hearts rejoice, for we trust in His Holy Name. May your unfailing love rest upon us O Lord, even as we put our hope in You."

Psalm 33:20-22

WHO IS MY MASTER?

Text: Isaiah 49: 8-16; Romans 1: 8-17; Matthew 6: 24-34

Theme: The central and most important question in life.

Theme Statement: We all have a master in our lives, whether we realize it or not. This master will determine our priorities in life, and our priorities in life will reveal just who or what is our master. Every individual must make a choice as to their master, and this choice will shape both their life in this world and in the life to come. Jesus says: "No one can serve two masters;...You cannot serve both God and money." In other words, you cannot serve both God and the things of this world. And so, the central and most important question in life is "Who is my master; who do I serve above all others; to whom do I give my utmost loyalty and devotion? Is it the Living God, my Creator and Redeemer, or is it the world and its riches and possessions?"

Key Passage: Matthew 6:24. "No one can serve two masters. Either he will hate the one and love the other, or he will be devoted to the one and despise the other. You cannot serve both God and money."

✝

"**N**o one can serve two masters. Either he will hate the one and love the other, or he will be devoted to the one and despise the other. You cannot serve both God and money." The thought that underlies this word of Jesus is that no man is his own master. Liberal psychology, liberal philosophy, elevates the human being as his own master. Scripture calls this foolishness. We all have a master in our lives, whether we realize it or not. That master will determine our priorities in life, and (now hear this) our priorities in life will reveal just who or what is our master.

Jesus says, "You cannot serve both God and money." The word money here is taken from the Aramaic "mammon," and includes wealth, property, possessions, anything in which one puts their trust.

Everyone must make a choice as to their master, and this choice will shape both their lives in this world and determine where they will spend eternity. So it all boils down to the central and most important question in life: "Who or what is my master; who or what do I love above all else; who or what do I serve above all others; who or what am I devoted to above all else?" "Is it the Living God, my Creator and Redeemer; or is it a false god, an idol, the world's riches and possessions?"

Jesus says that a person who is foolish enough to try and serve two masters will suffer serious spiritual and emotional turmoil - hating the one and loving the other, holding to the one and despising the other, being torn between the two. We all experience that turmoil at times, torn between giving priority to God or giving priority to our worldly needs, especially during hard times. Many today are experiencing severe stress, worry, and turmoil due to current economic circumstances. Others live with the stress of physical, emotional and mental disability. Millions live with the worry of what tomorrow will bring, or whether they will even make it through tomorrow.

Yet, Jesus goes on to say: "Do not worry about your life, what you will eat or drink, or about your body, what you will wear. Is not life more important than food, and the body more important than clothes?" Many would say, "Wait a minute, Jesus! I'm about to lose my house; I've lost my job; I'm behind on my bills; and I'm in debt up to my eyebrows. And You're telling me not to worry." And Jesus says, "Yes, that's exactly what I'm telling you!" But Jesus, it's hard not to worry when my life is going to pieces around me.

That word worry, in the Greek "merimna," is also translated as anxiety. Jesus is not saying, "Ignore your troubles, your problems, your needs." He is saying, "don't let those problems, troubles, no matter how serious, become your master. Don't let them overwhelm you. Don't let them cause you to doubt your true Master, and turn you away from your highest priority - God's perfect will and purpose for you. Don't let them erode your trust in His promise to work out all your problems and troubles to His glory and your highest good."

Worry affects the spiritual, emotional, and physical health of a person. Worry and anxiety leads to discouragement, and discouragement can lead to doubt, unbelief, and being torn between trusting God first and foremost, or trusting this world first and foremost for a solution for our problems; in other words trying to serve two masters.

C.S.Lewis tells a story about Satan meeting with all his demons to discuss strategies for drawing Christians away from their Lord and Master. He lists the weapons in his arsenal that have proven effective - money, sex, sickness, fame, pride, ego, broken relationships, and on and on. He said that all these were useful, but there was a weapon more effective than all of them - a weapon he could not do without - and that weapon was discouragement. Discouragement can weaken a Christian faith more than all the others, discouragement that sprouts from planting the seeds of worry, anxiety, doubt and panic.

Discouragement can cause the Christian to doubt whether God hears their prayers, whether God knows their desperate condition, whether God even cares. Satan uses discouragement to try and get the Christian to doubt or forget God's Word like that in Proverbs 3:5-6: "Trust in the Lord with all your heart and lean not on your own understanding; in all your ways acknowledge Him, and He will make your paths straight." Or His Word in Psalm 119 where the Psalmist prays: "I am laid low in the dust; preserve my life according to Your Word...my soul is weary with sorrow; strengthen me according to Your Word." Or Jesus' words in Matthew 11:28: "Come to Me, all you who are weary and burdened, and I will give you rest." Or Jesus' promise to never leave or forsake us. Satan knows that if he can overwhelm the Christian with worldly concerns, worries, and anxiety, doubts and discouragement, there is the chance that these things will take priority in his life and become his master even without his realizing it. It is so easy in this hectic life to try to serve two masters - our Lord and this world. One of these must take priority.

Jesus emphasizes the Father's love for us with His examples of the birds and the lilies - the birds who do not sow and reap and store away, and yet the Heavenly Father feeds them - and the lilies that do not labor or spin, and yet the Heavenly Father dresses them in splendor greater than Solomon was dressed in all his royal glory. Yet, God is not a father to the birds and lilies; He is a Father to us, His children in Christ Jesus. Jesus says, "Are you not much more valuable than the birds and lilies?" In other words, will God nourish the birds and forget His children? Will God clothe the lilies and not clothe His children? Of course not, Jesus says. Jesus also emphasizes the futility of worry and anxiety when He says: "Who of you by worrying can add a single hour to his life?" Worry and anxiety usually shortens life instead of lengthening it.

Jesus is not giving us permission for sloth and laziness which are condemned in the Bible. He is not saying, "Kick back, forget your problems, let God take of it." He is saying "Don't let worry, anxiety, cripple you. Don't let satan use discouragement to plant doubt in your mind that your Lord and Master will keep His promise to guide you through all the trials and troubles and problems of your life. The Apostle Paul tells us the same thing in Philippians 4:6 where he says: "Do not be anxious about anything, but in everything, by prayer and petition, with thanksgiving, present your requests to God." Yes, it's hard to give thanks when everything is falling apart around you, but it is so important that we do so, for in doing so, we show our hope and trust in our true Master. And the Apostle Peter tells us in 1Peter 5:7, "Cast all your anxiety on Him because He cares for you."

Jesus emphasizes this care that the Heavenly Father has for you and me and all His children when He says: "Your Heavenly Father knows your needs, even before you ask Him." We human beings tend to confuse needs and wants. Our wants can easily become needs in our minds and become our master. I think the source of much of the worry and anxiety in life is our wants and not our needs. Many today are facing a stark choice between wants and needs.

The United States Public Health Service, some time ago, issued a statement about the tendency of worry to weaken and shorten life, which agrees with what Jesus said. The statement reads: "No bird ever tried to build more nests than its neighbor. No fox ever fretted because it had only one hole in which to hide. No squirrel ever died of anxiety, lest it should not lay up enough for two winters instead of one, and no dog ever lost any sleep over the fact that it had not enough bones laid aside for the declining years." How true! Worry, anxiety, wreaks havoc. It makes us ineffective and inefficient and weakens us for the long haul.

Jesus gives us the cure for worry and anxiety. He says: "Seek first the Kingdom of God and His righteousness, and all these things will be given to you as well." Jesus does not say "Seek the Kingdom and nothing more." He says, "Seek first the Kingdom." Again, it all comes down to priorities, who is the master of our life. Is our Master He Who met our greatest need by going to the cross for us and paying the terrible price for our sins with His Body and Blood; He Who gives Life, Who has redeemed us and calls us His own; He Who has given us eternal life and made us heirs with Christ; He Who knows our needs better than we ourselves and Who promises to meet all our needs? Or is our master our wants, our possessions, and the things of this world? The Apostle Paul said that he counted all worldly gain and accomplishments as rubbish compared to the surpassing greatness of knowing Christ Jesus his Lord. Material provision is important, but the first motive, the first priority, must be seeking God's Kingdom, His righteousness, His will for our lives. He who seeks the Kingdom first will seek all other things from the Father in the right way - by humble and submissive prayer, without placing a false value on all those other things. To those who seek in such a way, Christ's promise will be fulfilled - "these will all be supplied to you."

We Christians have a great advantage in overcoming the troubles and problems of this life. We have not only our Master, the Lord, but we have our fellow believers to help, comfort, and strengthen us through our troubles and problems. Just as Paul, in our Epistle reading, longed to go to Rome to impart to those Roman Christians a spiritual blessing, to strengthen them in the faith, and that he and they might be mutually encouraged and comforted through each others faith, so we as members of the Body of Christ are to be a spiritual blessing to each other, strengthen each other in the faith, and be mutually encouraged and comforted through each others' faith - at all times, and especially during times of trouble and problems, and anxiety which this life brings to each of us.

So why can't a person compromise and serve two masters? Because their commands are in opposition. God says, "Give Me your heart!" The world, mammon, says, "No, give it to me!" God says, "Be content with such things you have!" The world, mammon, says, "No, grasp all that you can." Satan, the world and mammon say, "God has forgotten you!" God says, "I will never forget you!" And that brings us to our final passage, the one from Isaiah, a passage of immense comfort to those who are being overwhelmed by the troubles, trials, and anxieties in life.

The condition of Israel as a nation at the time was desperate and the people could see no solution. They felt that God had forgotten them. Have you ever felt that God had forgotten you? God, through Isaiah, tells them "No! No! I have not forgotten you! Those who hope in Me will not be disappointed." And He drives the point home by saying: "Can a mother forget the baby at her breast and have no compassion on the child she has borne?" Then God goes even farther and says: "But even though a mother could forget her child, I will not forget you." David, in Psalm 27:10, expresses his faith that God won't forget him. He says, "Though my father and mother forsake me, the Lord will receive me." And then, this amazing expression of God's love when He says: "See, I have engraved you on the palms of My hands." I love that expression. Figuratively speaking, we could say that God's palms are tattooed with the names of His children, and your name and mine are among them.

Some see an application of this verse to the terrible wounds in Christ's hands when He was nailed to the cross. Whenever our Lord looks at those wounds, He also sees the names engraved on the palms of His hands, your name, my name, the names of all believers, and He remembers those for whom He suffered and died. And our names are indelibly engraved on the palms of our Lord and Master for all eternity.

Do not let Satan discourage you no matter what troubles and problems come into your life. Don't let him make your passage through this world more dark and unpleasant by filling you with anxiety, by tempting you to serve two masters. Christ is our only Master, for all the gifts of God the Father - His grace, salvation, blessing, and provision for all our needs - pass through Christ to us, and all our petitions and prayers and thanksgiving pass through Christ to God the Father.

When Satan tempts us to think that God has forgotten us, God grant, for Jesus sake, that we, in the good times, the bad times, and at all times, come right back at him and reply boldly, in faith and in the power of the Holy Spirit: "My Lord and Master cannot, will not, forget me, for He has purchased me and won me with His Body and Blood, and He has my name engraved in the palm of His hand." What a Master we have! What a Master! Amen.

OUT WITH THE OLD; IN WITH THE NEW

Text: Acts:11: 1-18; Revelation 21: 1-6; John 13: 31-35.

Theme: New Man, New Creation, New Commandment.

Theme Statement: We are all unfinished products spiritually. Our faith in Jesus Christ as Lord and Savior makes us new creations; however, in this life we do not have the consummated newness we will receive when the Lord returns. We have a glimpse of that consummated newness when we come together for worship and the Lord's Supper, when we have our private devotions and prayer, when we are cleansed of our sins for our Savior's sake. Not only are we unfinished products, but heaven and earth will also experience a cosmic renewal, a newness, a consummation, when our Lord returns. We are totally dependent on the salvation of Christ and His Blood for our daily cleansing and renewal, and we seek His strength and the leading of the Holy Spirit to obey the new commandment the Lord gave His disciples and us - to love one another as He has loved us. This love, the sacrificial love of Jesus is the ultimate standard for love. In the power of this love, man can say, "Out with the Old Man with his sin, self-pride, and rebellion, and In with the New Man with his faith, humility, and love.

Key Passage: Revelation 21: 5-6. And He Who was seated on the Throne said, "Behold, I am making all things new...Write this down for these words are trustworthy and true. It is done! I am the Alpha and the Omega, the beginning and the end."

$$\dagger$$

S t. Augustine once said, "Our soul was created by God and exists for God and is therefore never quiet until it rests in God." And the Apostle Paul tells us in 1Corinthians 15, "Just as we have borne the image of the man of dust (the first Adam), so we shall also bear the image of the Man of Heaven (the Christ)." And Jesus said, "Behold, I am making all things new."

We are all unfinished creations, and in this life, we are going through a finishing process. That process started when the Holy Spirit brought us to saving faith in our Lord and Savior Jesus Christ. That's justification. We are justified by faith. The finishing process continues throughout life as the Holy Spirit forms and shapes us into who and what God created us to be. That's sanctification. Justification is complete when we come to faith in Christ. Sanctification, however, is only complete when we go to be with the Lord, when we enter that perfect rest in God that Augustine refers to, and when we clearly and fully bear that image of Jesus Christ that Paul refers to, and when we completely become that new creation that Jesus spoke of.

Our Scripture passages have a common theme of newness, and I would like to address three aspects of that newness: The new man, the new heaven and earth, and the new commandment. First, the new man. Our reading from Acts tells of God's creating a new man, the Roman Cornelius. To get the full story, we need to consider the background given in the passages previous to our reading. We are told that Cornelius, a Roman centurion and a Gentile, was a devout man who feared God with all his household, who gave alms generously to the people, and who prayed continually to God. Yet Cornelius, spiritual as he was, lacked that true spirituality that is only in Christ and through faith in Christ. God sent an angel to him who told him to send men to Joppa to bring one Simon who is called Peter to him.

At the same time, God gave Peter a vision of a great sheet descending from heaven filled with all kinds of animals and reptiles and birds, and a voice told him, "Rise, Peter, kill and eat." But Peter said, "By no means, Lord, for I have never eaten anything that is common or unclean." Peter shrank from the idea of eating non-kosher food in violation of Mosaic regulation. And the voice said, "What God has made clean, do not call unclean." The sheet disappeared back into heaven. While Peter was wondering what it all meant, the men sent by Cornelius arrived. They told Peter of the angel that appeared to their master and instructed him to send for Peter.

When Peter and six companions arrived at the house of Cornelius where his entire household, relatives, and friends were gathered, Peter understood the vision. He told Cornelius, "You yourselves know how unlawful it is for a Jew to associate with or visit anyone of another nation, but God has shown me that I should not call any person common or unclean." Peter preached the Gospel to Cornelius and all those with him, and while he was preaching, the Holy Spirit descended upon them. And Peter and his six companions, Jewish Christians, were amazed that the Holy Spirit was poured out even on Gentiles. And Peter commanded that they be baptized in the Name of Jesus Christ. Cornelius, his family and relatives, were made new that day, justified by faith in Christ. And for them, the finishing process, sanctification, had begun.

Peter was criticized by the Jewish Christians in Jerusalem for going to, and eating with, the uncircumcised Gentiles and for baptizing them and receiving them into the Church. Apparently, they didn't stop to consider that God had sent an angel to Cornelius, and apparently that angel didn't fear being contaminated by entering a Gentile's house. This was a new thing, a revolutionary thing. But when Peter informed them of the vision, how God Himself impelled him to go, how God had given those Gentiles the Holy Spirit just as He had given it to them, they fell silent and glorified God saying, "Then to the Gentiles also God has granted repentance that leads to life." It is interesting to note that Jesus was criticized by the Pharisees for eating with sinners and tax collectors; now Peter is initially criticized for eating with uncircumcised Gentiles.

God, in sending Peter to Cornelius, was doing a new thing, namely teaching those Jewish Christians that circumcision and the legal ordnances of Moses had nothing to do with salvation, but only the Word of the Gospel and faith in Jesus Christ as Lord and Savior. God was telling Peter and those Jews to stop making distinction between Jew and Gentile. In Christ, they are one. So, how does this apply to us today?

We Christians need to be careful to avoid that attitude of the Pharisees who thought they were better, holier, than those sinners and tax collectors, that attitude of those Jewish Christians who thought they were superior to the Gentiles. It's so easy to fall into that holier-than-thou attitude towards others, not only unbelievers, but even towards other Christians. Their worship styles, their rituals, their traditions are different from ours; therefore, they must be inferior. That's pride, sinful pride. The only distinction we are to make in the Church is between those who are faithful to God's Word and to their Lord Jesus Christ, and those who are not. Those who are faithful are members of the Body of Christ, and in the Body of Christ there is no distinction between Jew and Gentile, between black and white, red or yellow, tan or brown, because all are one, all are new creations, made new in Christ Who makes all things new.

God not only makes His human creation new; He makes His material creation new. Our reading from Revelation tells us of a new heaven and a new earth. Just as man was corrupted by sin and had to be made new in Christ, so creation itself is corrupted by sin and has to be made new in Christ. Paul, in Romans 8, speaks of creation itself waiting eagerly with longing and groaning to be set free from its bondage to corruption and obtain the freedom of the glory of the children of God. With the new heaven and earth, the old separation of the highest heaven of God, of angels, and of saints who have gone before us, and our present heaven and earth is forever ended. God's highest heaven and the new heaven and earth are joined and made one. It is a creative act of God - a new creation, but not like the creation in Genesis 1.

This is expressed in beautiful symbolic language. The holy city, the new Jerusalem, coming down out of heaven from God, as a bride adorned for her husband. And what does this symbolize? The loud voice from the Throne tells us: "Behold, the dwelling place of God is with man." The great blessing of the new heaven and earth will be that restored mankind will again behold God face-to-face and live in His immediate presence. This is the final consummation of all God's plans

102

for His people - the closest union and communion between the faithful and God, a holy fellowship which God Himself initiates and which lasts to all eternity.

Then follows a description of blessings that flow from this most holy fellowship. No more tears, for there will be nothing in this new creation to call forth tears. No more death, mourning, crying, pain, suffering - all abolished. The former things have passed away. God dwelling with man is the ultimate fulfillment of the Name of Jesus - Immanuel - which means "God with us."

"Behold, I am making all things new." This is Christ exercising all authority in heaven and on earth, authority given Him by the Father. Then He says, "It is done." What is done? All God's revelation from the first to the last letter; all history from start to finish; the consummation of all God's saving work. It is done; it is reality! And then Jesus signs His Name to it all. He says, "I am the Alpha and the Omega, the beginning and the end." Jesus tells John to write it all down for us - the readers - to increase the longing of our hope by this strongest assurance, to increase our courage and endurance by this divine certainty. Jesus says that to the thirsty He will give from the spring of the water of life. And without payment on our part, because He paid for it with His Body and Blood on the cross.

In this life, we drink of His grace, and we thirst for the glory. And Jesus promises that our thirst will be fully quenched. Our loved ones in heaven are in God's glory, but they too await the consummation of that glory when they will accompany their Lord at His glorious Second Coming.

It is Jesus that makes us new creations just as He made Cornelius and his household new creations. It is Jesus that creates the new heaven and new earth that He revealed to John in his vision. And what is the dominant characteristic, the dominant quality, the power behind these new creations? That too is new. And Jesus reveals it in our Gospel passage where He tells His disciples, "A new commandment I give you, that you love one another; just as I have loved you, you also are to love one another."

The love of Christ is the power that makes His followers new creations; it is the love of Christ that makes the new heaven and new earth. It is the love that drove Him to the cross to free man, to free creation, from the bondage to Satan, sin, and damnation. Jesus brought a new love into the world, a perfect, sacrificial love. The love that the world gives is a counterfeit love, whereas the love of Jesus is a genuine, holy, all-encompassing love. And Jesus says that we are to love one another with this love, just as He loves us. This love is only made possible through oneness with Christ through faith and through the power of the Holy Spirit.

Jesus tells His disciples that, when His visible Presence is taken from them, they will still have each other, and ought to be the more closely attached to each other, loving each other as Jesus loved them. This applies to us just as to them. When a loved one is taken from us, when their visible presence is no longer with us, we still have our brothers and sisters in Christ to love us as Jesus loves them. That love of Jesus and our fellow believers is our comfort and strength and assurance during our times of grief and mourning.

Jesus says, "By this all people will know that you are My disciples, if you have love for one another." Where this love exists, it is bound to show itself, and others will see and realize its presence, be affected by it, and if possible, be drawn into this community of love. It is the love that grows out of Christ's love for us, that flows out of Christ's love, and that grows as our faith in Christ grows. The Apostle Paul, in Colossians tells us, "Put on the love of Christ which binds every thing together in perfect harmony." And in Romans, Paul tells us, "So now faith, hope, and love abide, these three; but the greatest of these is love."

Our loved ones in heaven know this love in its fullness. For us, this love cannot reach that perfection as long as the sinful flesh dwells in us, but as faith grows and as sinful flesh is overcome, more and more this love unfolds, until it reaches its full perfection and glory when we join our Lord and our loved ones in glory.

So, in the Word for today, we see the new man, the new creation, the new love, and it is all in Christ and the power of His love. And in the power of His love, we can cry out, "Out with the Old; In with the New." "Out with the old man with his sin and pride and rebellion; and in with the new man with his faith, humility, and love." We can cry out, "Out with the old creation with its sin, wickedness, and corruption; and in with the new creation with its glory, majesty, and righteousness. So let it be, Lord Jesus. Amen.

CROSSING THRESHOLDS

Text: Genesis 12: 1-4; Ephesians 4: 11-16;
        Matthew 7: 21, 24-27.

Theme: Being doers of the Word, not just hearers.

Theme Statement: Walking with God and receiving the blessings of the Christian life requires that we cross thresholds of faith and service that He places before us.

Key Passage: Matthew 7:21. "Not everyone who says to Me, 'Lord, Lord,' will enter the kingdom of heaven, but only he who does the will of my Father who is in heaven."

✝

There is a saying that goes like this: "One must learn by doing the thing. For though you think you know it, you have no certainty until you try...At that moment, you cross a threshold." That statement has great application to life, including our spiritual life. Life is a continuous process of crossing thresholds, of growing, maturing, learning by doing the thing, experiencing the thing. Some thresholds take only a relatively small step to cross. Others require us to make a giant leap. But with all of them, we learn by doing.

We cross the first threshold kicking and screaming as we are forced to leave the safety, security, and comfort of the womb and enter this world of trial, tribulation and suffering. The first day of school is a threshold for both children and parents. And then there is marriage and parenting. Marriage is a giant leap across a threshold into the unknown. You can only learn marriage by doing it, and that's a lifetime job. You can only learn parenting by doing it. Would you accept advice from a marriage counselor who had never been married, or from one who was successful in marriage, who had learned by doing it? Would you accept advice on raising your children from one who had never had children, or one who was successful in parenting, one who had learned by doing it?

There are so many thresholds to cross from which we learn - thresholds of success and failure, pain, sickness, and disability, joy and sorrow, and on and on. The most important threshold we cross in this life is the threshold of faith, faith in Jesus Christ as Savior and Lord. It is the one threshold that irrevocably determines success or failure of this life, the final outcome of this life, and the location of the life to come. Crossing that threshold of faith brings life; failure to cross brings spiritual death and eternal loss. We cannot cross that threshold of faith by our own will and power, but only by the grace of God and in the power of the Holy Spirit. We are totally dependent on God's grace and power. Crossing that threshold of faith means giving our Lord priority in our life, holding nothing back, giving Him sovereignty over every aspect of our life. And that is why many refuse to cross that threshold of faith.

Once we cross that most important initial threshold of faith, we find the strength to cross other thresholds of faith. The Apostle Paul knew this. He said, "I can do all things through Christ Who strengthens me!" And God told him: "My strength is made perfect in your weakness." It is in God's strength that we find strength to cross the thresholds of life. If we are in Christ through faith, we are God's children, sons and daughters of the Most High, and our Abba Father has promised that no evil will permanently harm or defeat us, and He will protect and hold us in the palm of His hand.

Two men stood by a fence watching some boys playing in a field. One said to the other, "Watch this!" He called to one of the boys "Come here!" The boy came, the man lifted him up, put him on top of that fence, backed off, held out his hands and told the boy "jump!" The boy looked at the space separating them, hesitated only an instant and jumped. The man caught him, gave him a hug, and sent him back to play. He then called another boy, set him on top that fence, backed off, and told him to jump. The boy looked at the space that separated them, became fearful, and refused to jump. The man assured the boy that he would catch him, that the boy could trust him, but the boy refused to jump. The man lifted the boy down from the fence and sent him off to play. The man asked his friend, "Why did the first boy jump and the second boy refuse to jump?" His friend said, "Perhaps the first boy was braver." The man said "No!" His friend said, "Perhaps the second boy was more cautious and less foolhardy." The man said "No!" Then the man told his friend, "The first boy who jumped is my son. The other boy is someone else's son who does not know me." And there was the difference. The first boy had assurance in his father's ability to catch him, but he had something more. He had trust; he trusted that his father would not let him fall. And he acted on that trust. The second boy, although he might have believed in the ability of the man to catch him, lacked the trust of the son. And so, he would not put his belief into action. He just couldn't bring himself to cross that threshold. God stands before us, His sons and daughters, with open arms, urging us to put our faith into action, cross the thresholds He places before us, and trust Him to not let us fall.

The Psalmist tells us that "the steps of a man are ordered by the Lord." Often those steps ordered by the Lord takes us to thresholds we would rather not cross. One thing about thresholds - once you cross them, there's usually no going back. And that means that there is fear involved - the fear of the unknown, the fear of uncertainty, insecurity, vulnerability, and loss of control. I'll bet Abraham felt that fear of uncertainty, the fear of the unknown. He and Sarah had a good life in Haran, with many possessions and servants. And he was seventy-five years old, and Sarah sixty-five, a time to retire and enjoy the fruits of their labors. But the Lord had different plans for them. He told Abraham: "Leave your country, your people and your father's household, and go to the land I will show you." Talk about a threshold! But God never calls us to cross a threshold without a promise. So it was with Abraham. God promised, "I will make you into a great nation and I will bless you; I will make your name great, and you will be a blessing. I will bless those who bless you, and whoever curses you, I will curse; and all people on earth will be blessed through you."

We're told that Abraham left as the Lord had told him. No argument, no excuses. He could have said, "I want to stay here Lord. It's comfortable here, safe, and I'm happy and secure here." Or at least he could have asked the Lord where he was going. But he didn't. His faith was manifested by prompt obedience in crossing that threshold. And God kept His promise to him. Abraham is the human spiritual father of all Christians, whether Jew or Gentile, and through his seed, the Messiah would come, and all peoples on earth were and are blessed through him.

Speaking of the Messiah, when we consider the life of Jesus on this earth, we can clearly see giant thresholds He had to cross. The first was the threshold of humiliation. Only the Son of God taking on our humanity, being both fully God and fully man, except without sin, could be the acceptable sacrifice for our sin and purchase our salvation and redemption with His Body and Blood. And Jesus said, "Yes, Father, according to your will, I will cross the threshold of humiliation. I will leave the glory I have with You and take up residence in the womb of a young virgin for the sake of our human creation."

Then there was the threshold of a life of poverty. The Lord and owner of all the riches of this world, during His time on this earth, had no material goods to speak of. He Himself said, "The foxes have holes and the birds have nests, but the Son of Man has nowhere to lay His head." And Jesus said, "Yes, Father, according to your will, I will cross that threshold of poverty for the sake of our human creation."

Then there was the threshold of being hated, reviled, ridiculed, and rejected by the people and religious leaders. The Apostle John tells us, "He came to His own, and His own did not receive Him, yet to all who did receive Him, who believed in His Name, He gave the right to become children of God." And Jesus said, "Yes, Father, according to your will, I will cross that threshold of hatred, ridicule, and rejection for the sake of our human creation."

Finally, our Lord came to the terrible threshold of the cross, the threshold of supreme agony and a horrifying death. In His humanity, He didn't want to cross that threshold. He hesitated just as we do when faced with a threshold we don't want to cross. He asked the Father to take it from Him, but He also said, "Not my will, but yours be done." It was the Father's will that Jesus cross that threshold, that He go to the cross for you and me and all mankind. And Jesus said, "Yes, Father, I will cross that threshold of agony on the cross for the sake of our human creation." And so He did! But then, there was another threshold Jesus crossed after He crossed the threshold of the cross. And that was the threshold of resurrection, exaltation, and the glory that awaited Him in the presence of the Father and all the hosts of heaven.

Our Epistle passage mentions some thresholds. It says that God calls some to be apostles, some to be prophets, some to be evangelists, some to be pastors and teachers. And the Church, the Body of Christ, is to be built up by them, right? No! No! They are not to do all the work. As we read on, we're told that they are to prepare God's people, that's you and me, for works of service, to cross thresholds of service that God calls each of us to. They are to train God's people in the work of the Church so the people can learn by doing. And for what purpose? So the Body of Christ may be built up, that we all reach unity in the faith, in the knowledge of the Son of God, that we become mature in the faith, attaining to the whole measure of the fullness of Christ. And hear this - "as each part does its work." "Each part." That's you and me. "Attaining the whole measure of the fullness of Christ" should be the goal of every Christian and congregation. One does not attain to the whole measure of the fullness of Christ without crossing the thresholds of faith and life our Lord leads us to and urges us to cross.

I think that God expends a lot of time, effort, loving patience, and yes, frustration, in trying to get us Christians to cross thresholds. He has plans for each of us, what He created us to be and what He wants us to do for His glory and our highest good, both as individuals and as a congregation, a community of saints. Every member of a congregation should be involved, both in faithful attendance of worship services and in the work of the church, striving to attain to the whole measure of the fullness of Christ. And know this! There is no work done for Christ and His Church that is too small in God's eyes. Jesus Himself said, "Truly I say to you, whoever so much as gives a cup of cold water to one of my little ones, he shall not lose his reward." What threshold is God calling you to cross in faith and service to Him? Do not fear! Reach out in trust, take Jesus' outstretched hand, and let Him lead you across.

One learns by doing, by crossing thresholds of faith. Jesus talks about doing in our Gospel reading. He says, "Not everyone who says to Me, 'Lord, Lord,' will enter the kingdom of heaven, but only he who does the will of my Father who is in heaven." True discipleship is found not just in words, not even in being religious. True discipleship is the obedience of faith, putting faith into action, doing the will of the Father in the Name of Jesus, and through the power of the Holy Spirit. We are saved by faith, not by works, but as the Apostle James said, "Faith without works is dead." Faith must be dynamic, not static.

We learn by doing the thing. There is a marvelous unity between knowing and doing. Knowing Christ as Lord and Savior should result in doing the Father's will, and doing the Father's will increases our knowledge of the Father's will. There is a saying that goes, "I hear, I forget; I see, I understand; I do, I remember."

Jesus describes the wise person who built his house on the rock of hearing His words and putting them into practice, and the foolish man who hears His words, but does not put them into practice. The wise man's faith was an active faith. An active faith is a house built on rock, indestructible, withstanding the ravages of time, the attacks of satan, and the trials and tribulations of this world. The foolish man's faith was an idle faith, and an idle faith is a paralyzed faith, a house built on sand, susceptible to the ravages of time and vulnerable to the attacks of satan and this world.

As we face the thresholds of faith and life, there will be times when we stumble and fall, when we fail to do what God would have us do. But the Blood of Christ covers our failures too. God forgives and He takes us by the hand and leads us past those failures. And know this! Failure in a faithful attempt to do a work for God and His Church is not failure in God's eyes. God can turn even our failures into success to His glory and our benefit. Often, it is through failure and affliction that we learn great lessons of life and discover the reality of God's grace and presence.

There is a final threshold that we have no choice but to cross. And that is mortal death unless we are still here when the Lord returns. It can be frightening, but as Christians we need not fear it. "O death, where is your sting? O grave, where is your victory? Thanks be to God Who gives us the victory through our Lord Jesus Christ." During the French revolution, a Catholic bishop was sentenced to death. In his prison cell, there was a small window in the shape of a cross. The guards later discovered that, while awaiting his execution, the bishop had scratched some words into the wall at each point of the cross. At the top, he had scratched the word "height." At the bottom, he had scratched the word "depth." To the left, he had scratched the word "width." And to the right, he had scratched the word "breadth." The height, depth, and breadth of Christ's love had sustained that bishop as he crossed the threshold of death. And Jesus will reach out to bring us across that threshold of our death also, to bring us across into the glory and the unspeakable wonder of His presence where there are no more thresholds to cross, but only perfect peace and inexpressible joy forevermore.

Well, crossing thresholds can be frightening, but it can also be exciting, fulfilling, and bring God's richest blessings. Jesus came to give us life, the abundant life, the fullness of life. And we can only experience that fullness of life, that abundant life, when we give Him control over every aspect of that life. Jesus said, "I am the Way, the Truth, and the Life!" He created our life; He redeemed our life from sin, death, and hell by His suffering, death, and resurrection, and He promises to be with us throughout this life and help us cross every threshold we face. Do not fear the thresholds, no matter how intimidating or challenging they may be, but face them with the attitude of St. Paul who said, "I can do all things through Christ Who strengthens me!" Satan will tempt you with fear and insecurity, and try to convince you that you cannot do the thing. Tell him to get away from you and go back to hell where he belongs, and then, like that boy in the story who jumped, jump into your Heavenly Father's arms, for He most certainly will be there to catch you and strengthen you for the threshold you have just crossed.

All of us can cross thresholds with praise and thanksgiving to God, and with joy and confidence from the promise God gives us in Isaiah 58:11, a passage very appropriate for us here in Phoenix. It reads, "The Lord will guide you always; He will satisfy your needs in a sun-scorched land and will strengthen your frame. You will be like a well-watered garden, like a spring whose waters never fail." O that each of us, as individual children of God, and as a community of faith, might be a well-watered garden, a spring whose waters never fail, to all who God would have us witness to and minister to. O God Holy Spirit, lead each of us to the thresholds You would have us cross in order to accomplish that. For Jesus' sake. Amen.

GUARDING THE FAITH

Text: Acts 15: 1-12; Galatians 2: 1-10; Matthew 16: 13-19

Theme: Steadfastness in the faith and in the Word.

Theme Statement: Since the foundation of the Church, it has had to guard against heretics and heresies, false teachers and false teachings. Our passage in Acts gives an early example of this when some of the Jewish Christians insisted that Gentile Christians had to be circumcised and follow the law and customs of Moses, in addition to faith, in order to be saved.   Our reading in Galatians tells of Paul having to contend with these false teachers who were misleading the Christians in Galatia. In both instances, the Apostles and Paul stood steadfast and immovable in the faith, and in doing so, they guarded the faith. How do we guard the faith today against enemies of the Church? Just as they, and faithful Christians down through the centuries have done, by holding fast to the confession of Peter when Jesus asked His disciples, "Who do you say that I am?" Peter's answer, "You are the Christ, the Son of the living God!" is also our confession. By remaining steadfast, immovable, in this confession, and in the Word of God given to us by Jesus, the Prophets, and the Apostles through the Holy Spirit, we remain impregnable to all false teaching and, as Jesus said, the very gates of hell will not prevail against us.

Key Passage: Matthew 16: 16.   Simon answered, "You are the Christ, the Son of the living God."

The Christian Church is under attack today as never before, with Christians being persecuted throughout the world.   But perhaps the greatest danger is not from outward persecution, but from heretics and secular progressives both within and outside the Church who insist that certain doctrines, beliefs, and teachings of the Church must be revised, updated, compromised, in order to conform to cultural and societal standards of morality accepted today. In other words, they insist that it is not the Church which is to shape culture, but culture which is to shape the Church.

This is nothing new. Since the foundation of the Church, it has had to guard the faith against false teachers and false teachings. Our passage in Acts gives an early example of this. Some of the Jewish Christians insisted that Gentile Christians had to be circumcised and required to obey the law of Moses and its customs and traditions, in addition to faith, in order to be saved. This greatly disturbed the Christians at Antioch, many of whom were Gentiles. These Judaizers, they were called, were emphasizing law instead of Gospel. It is important to understand that they were believers in Christ, members of the church at Jerusalem, but they erred in a most dangerous way.

When the New Covenant, resting wholly on Jesus' blood, His death and resurrection, was established, circumcision and the legal system of the Old Covenant, with all its animal sacrifices, was at an end. The Mosaic system, the Old Covenant, was replaced by the New Covenant, the New Testament. It was hard for these Jewish Christians to realize and accept this truth, and that is understandable. They had previously been Pharisees, members of that Jewish sect most strict in adhering to all the law of Moses, as well as the additional 613 commandments they had added to that law. They thought that the Gospel was incomplete without circumcision and the law of Moses.

Paul, Barnabas, and some others from Antioch were sent to Jerusalem to confer with the Apostles and elders there about this question. Peter, after much discussion, addressed the convention. He spoke with authority, not only as an Apostle, but one who had witnessed what God had done among the Gentiles. It was him who God had sent to the Gentile Cornelius, his family and household, to present the Gospel to them. They believed, were baptized, and received the Holy Spirit. God made it clear to Peter that salvation through Christ, apart from the law, was available to Gentiles as well as Jews.

Peter reminds them all of this. Then he tells those Judaizers that they were testing God by putting on the Gentiles a yoke that neither they nor their fathers have been able to bear. The way of salvation was one - through faith in Christ - for both Jew and Gentile, and not through the law and traditions of Moses. Even in the Old Covenant, the means of salvation was faith in the promise of the Messiah and Savior, and not the law. They made it clear that to add anything to Christ as necessary for salvation, whether circumcision or any human work, was to deny that Christ alone is the complete Savior, and put something human on a par with Him. And that is fatal. The debate was ended. Not a voice was raised in contradiction to what Peter had said. Paul and Barnabas clinched Peter's words by telling the whole assembly about their success in taking the Gospel to the Gentiles, and how God had bestowed on the Gentile believers the same miraculous manifestations as He had bestowed on the Jewish believers at Pentecost. The only requirements the Apostles laid on the Gentiles was that they abstain from certain idolatrous practices concerning the meat of animals and blood, and abstain from sexual immorality, adultery and fornication, which were all common in the Gentile world.

In their action and decision, that Church Council guarded the faith against heresy and false teaching. But false teaching has a way of raising its ugly head again and again. In the church in Galatia, which Paul had planted, Judaizers again insisted that Gentiles be circumcised and observe the law of Moses. Just as Paul had not yielded an inch at Jerusalem, so he did not yield an inch of Gospel truth to those troublemakers in Galatia. He reminded them of that Jerusalem council and its decision, and then he comes down hard on them. In Galatians 3: 1-3, he tells them: "You foolish Galatians! Who has bewitched you?.....I would like to learn just one thing from you: Did you receive the Holy Spirit by observing the law or by believing what you heard (the Gospel)? Are you so foolish? After beginning with the Spirit, are you now trying to attain your goal by human effort?"

Paul's rebuke of those Galatians for allowing themselves to be deceived is a rebuke that can be applied to many Christians today who have allowed society, culture, false teachers, to lead them astray and compromise God's Word. The notion that our modern times need a

116

different gospel, the gospel of humanism, is false. It is rank heresy and a direct insult to Christ, Who is the Gospel of salvation and truth, Who is the living Word of God. But many short-sighted and weak-kneed Christians, including some pastors, church officials, and even denominations, have yielded to society, culture, and false teachers, and accept, condone, and even approve of things that are in clear and flagrant violation of God's Word, and they justify their action on the mistaken notion of love.

Two of those things immediately come to mind - the two hot-button issues facing the Church and the nation today - abortion and homosexuality, including same-sex marriage - both clearly in opposition to God's Word. But many church officials hesitate to address those issues for fear of the criticism that will follow. They fail to understand that to compromise with the world and the world's secular-humanism, is to compromise God's Word and the Gospel of Christ, and to compromise Christ and God's Word is to compromise with the devil, and that is never an act of love. It is an act of pure hatred toward God and our fellowman. Such compromise disrupts the unity of the Body of Christ - the Church - and causes fissures and conflicts that only hurt the Gospel and its work here and around the world.

There are those who say that the church should stay out of these controversies, that they are political issues. No! They are first and foremost moral issues that bear directly on the Christian faith. Both the former president, and the current president of the Lutheran Church - Missouri Synod understood this. Our former Synod president, Dr. Jerry Kieschnick, actively defended God's institution of marriage as the lifelong union of one man and one woman during his nine years of presidency. He was actively involved in supporting the 2008 ballot initiatives in California, Florida, and Arizona defining traditional marriage, and he supported a constitutional amendment clearly defining marriage as such. Our current Synod president, Dr. Matthew Harrison, has been called a "cultural warrior" in the struggle for the soul of this nation founded on solid Judeo-Christian principles. He testified before a House of Representatives Oversight committee against the mandate requiring religious organizations to pay for and facilitate drugs and procedures that take the lives of unborn children which violates the Biblical teaching of the sanctity of life. He insisted that freedom of religion included the right to exercise ones faith in the public square and in response to Christ's call. He also said: "I and the Lutheran Church - Missouri Synod will not be missing in action from the public square.

What is our responsibility, yours and mine as believing Christians in this matter? It is the same as the Apostles', as Paul's, as the church leaders and lay persons throughout the centuries since Christ established the Church. And that responsibility is to "guard the faith." Every Christian is called to be a guardian of the faith. Wise and good Christians desire to avoid conflicts and disputes as much as they can. However, when false teachings oppose the clear truths of Holy Scripture, and lead people astray, we must oppose them, we are commanded to oppose them. We oppose them with Christian love and God's grace, but nevertheless, we oppose them. God commands us to "guard the faith."

How do we guard the faith? First. by being steadfast, immovable, in that faith ourselves, in our confession of faith. And what is our confession of faith? The same as Peter's in our Gospel reading. "When Jesus asked His disciples, "Who do you say I am?" Peter, as spokesman, answered for all of them: "You are the Christ, the Son of the living God." There are many who confess Jesus with their lips, but not their hearts. Jesus, Who knows the heart, in Matthew 15:8, said of some who followed Him: "These people honor Me with their lips, but their hearts are far from Me." A confession of the lips must be a true expression of the heart's conviction. Any other confession is a lie. And a confession of the heart involves obedience to God's Word, and not the word of man. It involves opposition to all policies and decisions that violate God's Word, whether those policies and decisions come from other churches, the government, the courts, or wherever. And that opposition can take many peaceful forms including one that we can all do - writing to our representatives in Congress.

We know that Peter did not always live up to his confession, just as we do not always live up to our confession. We sin daily, but this changes nothing of the substance and truth of our confession if it is a confession of the heart. We confess and repent of our sins and failures, and based on our confession of Christ as Messiah and Son of the living God, as Savior and Lord, we are forgiven, cleansed, and reconciled to our living God. We guard the faith by insuring, through the power of the Holy Spirit, that our confession of Christ is both a confession of the lips and a confession of the heart.

Second, we guard the faith by obeying Jesus' command to be "wise as serpents and innocent as doves." Being innocent as doves means that we reach out to others, even enemies of the Church, with Christian love and the grace of God, doing nothing that brings scandal and division to the Body of Christ. Being wise as serpents means using the wisdom, discernment, knowledge that God gives us in His Word and through the Holy Spirit dwelling within us to guard against being deceived by the smooth words of false teachers who may confess Christ with their lips, but their deeds and acts are in opposition to God's Word. The Apostle John tells us to test the spirits to see whether they be of God. We do that by evaluating both the words and the deeds of individuals and organizations. When the confession of words and the confession of deeds clash, it is the confession of deeds that is the real confession.

There are some who naively believe that decisions by church officials, church councils, or denominations carry the weight of Scripture. No! No! Church history proves that wrong. It is Scripture alone that is the final authority for doctrine, faith and life. Dr. M. Loy, a theologian and pastor, once told a church convention that had passed a foolish resolution by a great majority, that in the inscrutable wisdom of God, they had been allowed to make jackasses of themselves. Many today are making jackasses of themselves by trying to combine the Gospel of Christ with the world's gospel of secular humanism. They fail or refuse to understand that if their bridge to heaven is 99% Christ and 1% humanism, that 1% humanism still leaves them hanging over the abyss with heaven far away. Only if our confession is 100% Christ can we avoid being deceived, can we be wise as serpents and innocent as doves, and have the gates of heaven open to us.

Finally, we "guard the faith" by obeying Jesus' command to take up our cross daily and follow Him. If you are 100% Christ's, adhere to His Word and reject all efforts to dilute that Word with the straw and mush of humanism, you will be ridiculed, mocked, cursed, as a radical fundamentalist, bigot, homophobe, etc. Jesus said: "If they mock and persecute Me, they will do the same to you who follow Me." It is the highest honor to be ridiculed, mocked, cursed, and persecuted for Christ. A pastor and theologian who many of you knew spoke of this - Pastor Arthur T.J. Irmer - who planted this church and pastored it for many years. After the Lord took him to heaven, Mom Irmer gave me many of his books and commentaries which are filled with his notes which I enjoy and benefit from. I found this note of his while preparing this message. Pastor Irmer said: "People who ridicule and mock Christ and His teaching ridicule and mock you who believe, and it is always their tendency to draw us away from Him." In his preaching, teaching, and pastoral ministry, Pastor Irmer guarded the faith.

God grant each of us the strength and power of the Holy Spirit to be steadfast and immovable in our confession of Christ. God grant each of us the wisdom and discernment to be wise as serpents and innocent as doves in our dealings with this world and the enemies of Christ. God grant each of us to take the Words God spoke to Joshua before he was to lead the Israelites in the conquest of the land of Canaan, as given to us in our mission of guarding the faith: "Have I not commanded you? Be strong and courageous. Do not be terrified; do not be discouraged, for the Lord your God will be with you wherever you go." And God grant each of us the courage to take up our crosses daily and follow our Lord. If we do this, then we too will truly be guardians of the faith. Grant this Lord, for Your Name's sake. Amen.

FAITH NOT TO FAIL

Text: Numbers 21: 4-7; James 5: 13-18; Luke 22: 31-34.

Theme: Falling, but not Failing.

Theme Statement: If faith is maintained in an hour of testing and temptation, though we may fall, yet we shall not be utterly cast down in failure. Faith will quench the fiery darts of satan. Though there may be many failings in the faith walk of true believers, yet there shall not be a total and final failure of their faith. Why not? Because of the mediation and intercession of our Lord and Savior Jesus Christ, Who prays for all His disciples, and for each of us by name, just as He prayed for Peter that his faith would not fail. Jesus and the Holy Spirit will see to it that our faith, though sometimes sadly shaken, will not fail. Though God's people may sometimes be brought low, yet our Lord is always there to bear us up, to help us in our afflictions. Though He may allow our faith to be tested, and yes, at times even severely, yet He will not leave us because He paid for us with His Body and His Blood on the cross. We are His! He will strengthen us in the faith that does not fail.

Key Passage: Luke 22: 31-32. "Simon, Simon, satan has asked to sift you as wheat. But I have prayed for you, Simon, that your faith may not fail. And when you have turned back, strengthen your brothers."

†

Every Christian is a target of Satan. He attacks us in the spiritual, physical, emotional, and material realms of our lives. And he has one objective - to undermine, weaken, and destroy our faith. Here, I want us to consider two examples of faith - a faith that fails under his attacks, and a faith that does not fail, and what we can learn from these two examples. First, a faith that fails.

In our Old Testament reading, the people again became impatient, discouraged, and complained against God and Moses. "There is no bread; there is no water!" they complained. God, on numerous occasions, had saved them from their enemies, provided all their needs in the wilderness, gave them bread to spare - manna from heaven - provided water out of rock; yet, whenever things got tough, they forgot all that, and their faith that God would keep His Word to provide all their needs failed. Not only that, but they insulted God's provision of bread from heaven. "We detest this miserable food," they said. There are many today who, like those Israelites, detest and reject the true Bread from Heaven, the Bread of Life, Jesus Christ. And they will come under judgment, just as those Israelites came under judgment.

God sent venomous snakes among them and many of them died. Now they confess their sin and ask Moses to pray for them that the Lord take the snakes away. Consider the irony here. They who complained against Moses and scorned his prayers for them now ask him to pray for them and be their advocate with God. Moses here was a type of Christ, symbolizing Him Who would pray and intercede for His persecutors, and Who commanded us to do the same.

God did not take the snakes away as the people wanted. He had a prophetic lesson to teach them. God instructs Moses to make a snake and put it on a pole. Everyone bitten by a snake and who looked at that snake on the pole was saved. They could only receive their cure from God by looking at that bronze snake on the pole. That snake represented another Who centuries later would hang from a pole - a cross - the Christ, Son of God and Son of Man. Only by looking to that bronze snake could the people be cured of the venomous poison within them. Only by looking to Christ on the cross can we be saved from the venomous poison of sin that leads to death and damnation. Jesus tells us in John 3: 14-15, "Just as Moses lifted up the snake in the desert, so the Son of Man must be lifted up, that everyone who believes in Him may have eternal life."

Why a snake, a serpent? A serpent tempted Adam and Eve, who fell and brought sin into the world. How can a serpent that represents sin represent Christ on the cross? Because Christ, Who was without sin, perfect and pure in holiness, was made to be sin for us - that is, to have all the sins of humanity poured out on Him. As Scripture tells us: "He Who was without sin was made to be sin for us, that we might be cleansed and forgiven and be made children of God.

This passage is only one of many times the faith of those Israelites failed during their time in the wilderness. Finally, the culmination of all their failures in faith came when they refused to go into the Promised Land because of fear, because of their distrust in God to keep His promise to give them victory over all their enemies. This final failure of faith resulted in God's judgment that that generation of Israelites would never enter the Promised Land. They lost the great blessings God had in store for them. It would be their children who would receive these blessings and inherit the Promised Land. A faith that fails forfeits God's blessings.

Now fast forward to our Gospel passage and an example of a faith that fell, but did not fail. Satan desired to bring Jesus' disciples to spiritual ruin, especially Peter. It was Simon Peter, impetuous, headstrong, Simon Peter who would get into the greatest danger because of his self-pride and confidence in his own strength. And Jesus knew this. So Jesus tells Peter: "Simon, Simon, satan has asked to sift you as wheat. But I have prayed for you, Simon, that your faith may not fail." Jesus here is speaking of a total and final failure of faith, such as Judas' failure of faith. Did Jesus pray for the rest of His disciples? Yes, we see that in John 17. But Jesus' prayer for Peter is specifically mentioned because satan's testing and temptation of Peter would be more severe. Why? Because Peter was the spokesman for the disciples, you might say their leader under Christ. It was Peter who, in front of all of them, had given that great confession to Jesus: " You are the Christ, the Son of the Living God." Satan knew that if he could destroy Peter's faith, bring Peter's faith to final and total failure, it would have a devastating effect on the others, and perhaps cause their faith to fail completely also.

"Satan has asked to sift you as wheat," Jesus tells Peter. We are reminded of satan's request to test Job. Now he is asking to test Peter.

There is a lesson here that is of mighty comfort to all of us. Satan is not free to assail us at will and with what power he pleases. He may test us only by God's permission and only to the extent of that permission. Jesus could have kept Peter and the rest from being tested. He could have forbidden satan from testing them, and from testing Peter most severely. But He didn't! Why? Because of His grand plan for them, the Great Commission He would give them to take the Gospel to all the world. Jesus knew each of their weaknesses; He knew Peter's weaknesses, and He knew that they could only carry out His Great Commission if their weaknesses were removed and their faith strengthened into a faith not to fail. And that could only be accomplished through testing, even severe testing.

It is the same with us. Just as Jesus knew the weaknesses of Peter and the others, so He knows our weaknesses. He knows each of us better than we know ourselves. He knows the evil we are capable of due to our sinful nature, which we ourselves do not know, or even suspect, just as Peter did not suspect the evil he would soon commit. But there is immense comfort for us in knowing that Christ knows our weaknesses better than we do, and that though He may allow us to be tested and tempted, He does so to strengthen us in a faith that does not fail, a faith that enables us to fulfill His perfect will and purpose for us and reach our highest good that He ordained for each of us before we were created. And He sets the limits to that testing and temptation - not satan. In His all-knowing wisdom, He tells satan, "This far, and no farther." Our Lord Himself had to undergo testing and temptation, in every way we are tested and tempted, in fact more severe than any we are called on to bear.

The Holy Spirit knows exactly how much and what kind of testing is necessary for each of us in order to form and shape us into who and what He created us to be. Scripture refers to it as the Potter forming the clay. We can think of it too as preparing a meal. When I cook a meal, I use a recipe, and.....On second thought, I better not go there. When my wife cooks a meal, she uses a recipe - a little of this, a little of that, not too much or too little. And it invariably comes out a masterpiece. It's the same with the Holy Spirit sanctifying us, shaping us. The Spirit knows exactly the ingredients necessary to make us into the masterpieces God intended - how much testing, how much joy, sorrow, loss, success, failure, and although we might at times say, "Lord, it is too much; I cannot take this," yet, the Spirit makes no mistakes and God's grace is all sufficient for all things and in all circumstances for us just as it was for Peter and the others.

Jesus tells Peter, "But I have prayed for you, Simon, that your faith may not fail." Peter probably did not realize the full import of these words at the time, but they must have certainly comforted and assured him after his great fall. Knowing that the Son of God Himself was praying for him would have assured him that, despite how far he had fallen, God's grace was still available to him and all-sufficient for his forgiveness, reconciliation, and restoration. That assurance is ours also. In our testings, temptations, battles against our sinful nature and the evil spiritual powers of this world, God's Word assures us that the Son of God and the Holy Spirit are both interceding and praying for us personally, for you and for me by name. Jesus' prayers for Simon were not in vain. Jesus' prayers for you and me are not in vain. Some have asked, "Would Judas have repented as Simon did if Jesus had interceded for him?" The answer is, Jesus did intercede for Judas. He gave Judas strong warnings about his plans to betray Jesus. But Judas would have none of it. It was Judas' free will, his wicked will, unbelief, rebellion, and rejection of God's grace that damned him, not any lack of warning or intercession on Jesus' part. And so it is with many people today.

Jesus tells Peter, "And when you have turned back, strengthen your brothers." "Turned back" refers to his being brought to repentance by the grace of God. Jesus, in His foreknowledge, knew that Peter would repent in tears and grief and great sorrow. Jesus, in effect, was telling Peter, "your faith will not fail. Although you and the others will be struck down by satan's assault, your escape and recovery are already planned." Why did Jesus tell Peter, "strengthen your brothers?" Because Peter fell so far, fell as none of the rest fell. Therefore, when he turned back, he was the one who could help the others by means of his own experience, make the wavering faith of the others strong and firm again into a faith not to fail. There's a lesson here for us. Often, God will allow a child of His to go through severe testing so that they, through experience, can comfort, strengthen, and encourage others who are experiencing such testing.

Peter tells Jesus: "Lord, I am ready to go with You to prison and to death." Notice that he did not say, "with your help," or "with God's help." It's as if Peter is saying, "Jesus, You can count on me. As brave as I am, You don't have to worry about me, even if it means prison or death." Did Peter mean it? Of course he did! Just as Judas' heart was set on betraying Christ, so Peter's heart was set on going to prison, or even death, with Christ.

And then, Jesus gives Peter His prediction: "I tell you, Peter, before the rooster crows today, you will deny three times that you know Me." Notice that where before Jesus calls him Simon, here He calls him Peter, which means stone or rock. It's as if Jesus is telling him, "Your name may identify you as stone, but you will be like straw in the hurricane of testing that is about to descend on you." In telling Peter of the rooster crowing and his three denials, Jesus prepared the way to help raise Peter from his great fall. Peter will hear the crowing of the rooster and that will bring Jesus' words to his mind, and this, together with a look from Jesus' eyes, will cause the tears of repentance to flow, the repentance that led to forgiveness, reconciliation, and restoration as Jesus' apostle.

Satan's assaults against God's people, you and me, are always directed against faith, and his objective is to produce unbelief and a faith that fails. Our enemies are so mighty and our strength is so small; the world is so full of traps and our hearts are so weak, that it seems at times impossible not to fail. But with God, nothing is impossible. Though He may allow satan to test us, and yes, at times even severely, yet He will never leave us or forsake us. We have His Word on that!

Though there may be many fallings in the faith of true believers, including you and me, yet there shall not be a total and final failure of our faith. Why not? Because our Lord won't let His true disciples fail.

He paid too high a price for us, He has too much invested in us - His very Body and Blood. He is always there to help us, to bear us up, to lift us up. We have a mighty Friend at the right hand of God, Who with the Holy Spirit, always intercedes for us and prays for us just as He prayed for Peter and the others. We have an Advocate Who daily pleads for you and me, Who sees all our testings, our temptations, our troubles, our sorrows, Who, as His Word tells us, sympathizes with us because He suffered all the testings and temptations we experience, yet was without sin. He daily and richly supplies mercy and grace and the forgiveness which He purchased for us with His Body and His Blood.

If we keep our eyes on Jesus and the cross and open tomb, the Holy Spirit will sanctify us in the one true saving faith that does not fail, a faith that all the powers of hell and this world cannot cause to fail. Lord Jesus, pray for us and keep us in that faith. Amen.

CHAPTER 5 - FOUNDATIONS

In suffering, be your love my peace. In weakness, be your love my power. And when the storms of life shall cease, O Jesus, in that final hour, Be your love my strength and guide, And draw me safely to your side.

Amen

GOOD TREE; GOOD FRUIT

Text: Deuteronomy 11:18-21;   Romans 3:21-25;   Matthew 7:15-18.

Theme: Only two types of trees, spiritually speaking - good or bad. Only two types of fruit - good or bad.

Theme Statement: Only a good tree, a tree solidly rooted in God's Living Word - Jesus Christ - can bear the fruit of abundant life here and everlasting life in heaven.

Key Passage: Matthew 7:15-17. "Watch out for false prophets. They come to you in sheep's clothing, but inwardly they are ferocious wolves. By their fruit you will recognize them. Do people pick grapes from thorn bushes, or figs from thistles? Likewise every good tree bears good fruit, but a bad tree bears bad fruit. A good tree cannot bear bad fruit, and a bad tree cannot bear good fruit."

If I were asked to select one word which best describes the state of society at large today, I would choose the word confusion. The majority of people, I believe, sense that something is dreadfully wrong, that society has, to a large extent, lost its moorings and is dangerously adrift. And they are confused as to why. Today, it is common for that which is good according to God's standard, and society's standard some years ago, to be called bad, and for that which is, and was, some years ago, bad to be called good; for the wise according to God's standard to be called foolish, and for the foolish according to God's standard, to be called wise. Things in the media, the arts, in politics, in our schools and universities, and even in some churches, which would have been considered intolerable some years ago, are not only tolerated by many today but approved of, promoted, and supported. God's established order of creation regarding life, human relations, and family has been dangerously weakened by attempts to replace it with man's idea of what the order of creation should be. Even the Christian faith is being attacked today as never before, and more Christians are being persecuted for their faith today than in any previous period of history. People are confused and ask "Why?" What happened to the old reliable Biblical standards of right and wrong, good and evil, wise and foolish? And what can we do to reverse the decline of those standards?

There are many out there who claim to have answers, so called experts in the social sciences and other fields. And their solutions usually entail more laws, more government programs, more money for this or that policy. But all their solutions ignore the basic, fundamental, underlying problem - and that is sin. Sin is not a subject many people want to consider. Either they deny it or they have their own definition of what sin is. God's Word, however, which I think most citizens still acknowledge as the highest authority, is very clear on what sin is: rebellion against God. Sin is violating God's standards for the order of creation, violating the rules for human relationships summarized in the Ten Commandments. Our major problems in our institutions and society today stem from a single cause, and that is that too many of those in authority and a multitude of citizens do not take sin seriously. And if a people don't take sin seriously, they don't take God seriously. And not taking God seriously leads a nation and a people to a precipice of disaster of such monumental proportions that the human mind cannot even comprehend it.

Moses understood this perfectly. He understood the dangers of not taking sin seriously, and that forgetting that everything is a gift from God, and being ungrateful and rebellious towards God is inviting disaster. In our Old Testament passage, we hear his charge, his command to the Israelites before they were to cross the Jordan River and take the land God had promised to them. Moses foresaw the dangers they would face, the temptations to turn away from God, worship the false Gods of heathen peoples, and take up their sinful lifestyles. And he knew that the only thing that would save them, sustain them was the Word of God. The intensity that Moses felt stands out clearly in his words. He tells the people to <u>fix</u> God's Word in their hearts and minds; to tie God's Word as symbols on their hands; to bind God's Word on their foreheads; to teach God's Word to their children; to talk about God's Word when they sit at home and when they walk along the road, when they lie down and when they get up; to write God's Word on the doorframes of their houses and on their gates. In other words, Moses was telling them that God's Word was to be the guiding principle and standard for every aspect of their lives.

Why for every aspect of their lives - religious, moral, political, educational, and social - in other words, for all their relations with Him and with their fellowmen? And they were to teach this to their children. Why? So that in whatever circumstances of life they might find themselves, whatever questions they might be faced with in life, they would know what was the will of God, and therefore know and do that which would please Him. Many of you, I'm sure have heard of the book, "Everything I needed to know about life I learned in kindergarten." It's a humorous book of homespun wisdom. Well, a child of God raised according to Moses' instructions could write a book entitled "Everything I needed to know about life I learned from those Bible stories Mom and Dad read to me during family devotions."

The Israelites failed to follow Moses' instructions, just as to a great extent, our society has failed to teach the younger generations their Judeo-Christian heritage. The theologian David Allan Hubbard made the following comment some years ago, which I will paraphrase: "Ours may be the first generation in civilized times that has not raised its young on the Biblical Proverbs. From the beginning of recorded history, these concise sayings which describe the benefit of good conduct and the harm of bad conduct have been used to teach children right from wrong. The Biblical Proverbs have helped past generations of parents to coach their children in the art of successful living. But Proverbs seemed too preachy to many people, and nearly entire generations sought to discover their own values rather than conserve the values of the past. The result is a world burned and scarred by new values that proved false, new values that had no solid foundation, new values built upon the straw and mush of feelings and emotions, and relative truth and morality, instead of absolute Truth. Perhaps societies confused and bitter at the absence of solid values much needed may turn back to Proverbs again to regain its sense of direction and bring some order to the chaos of living.

Israel's defeat arose from their failure to follow Moses' direction and apply God's Word of Truth to all aspects of their daily lives. The prophets of the 8th century B.C. spoke out strongly on that. Our failure as a society today also arises from a failure to apply God's Word of Truth to all aspects of our daily lives. Our Founding Fathers and many of their successors gave strong warning of this. Washington, Adams, Jefferson, Madison, John Quincy Adams, Samuel Adams, and on and on, all warned that if we ever turned away from our Judeo-Christian foundation, from our Christian heritage and moral standards of the Ten Commandments, our Democratic Republic which they established could not survive. Washington said that "Without God and the Bible, it is impossible to govern." John Adams said: "Our Constitution was made for a religious and moral people; it is totally unsuitable for any other." James Madison said: "Our entire system of government and society is dependent on our leaders and citizens conducting themselves, sustaining themselves, according to the Ten Commandments of God."

Israel had no excuse for failure, for they had everything they needed to fulfill God's purpose for them - to be a light to all the nations. They had the Law and they had God's promise of salvation through a Messiah, a Savior, Who would come. And we certainly have no excuse for failure, since we have even more. We have the Law, but we also have the promise of salvation fulfilled, the Gospel. We have Jesus Christ, Son of God and Son of Man, Who came, Who died for us, and Who rose again. We have Christ, through Whom God the Father completed His plan for our redemption.

We have Christ, through Whom God the Father gives us the perfect model for all of life.

We have Christ, through Whom God the Father pours out His mercy and forgiveness for all our failures caused by sin because He suffered the full and terrible punishment for our sins for us.

Through faith in Christ, we are declared righteous by God the Father Himself, as the Apostle Paul tells us in our Epistle reading. This declaration of righteousness is only for believers, for there is no righteousness apart from Christ.

Israel fell victim to the false teachers and false prophets who appealed to the people's sinful nature, telling them what they wanted to hear, approving their sinful acts. And over time, the solid foundation of Truth given them by God through Moses was essentially forgotten, and the result was disaster and destruction, as Moses prophesied. In our Gospel passage, which is taken from our Lord's Sermon on the Mount, Jesus speaks of the dangers of false teaching and He gives us the key, the practical test, for discerning truth from falsehood, good from evil, wisdom from foolishness, right from wrong. It is a test that every Christian must be proficient in using to prevent being deceived and misled.

The passage starts with a warning to watch out for false prophets. Another translation is even stronger - "Beware of false prophets." False prophets have been around since the earliest days of Biblical history. They were there in Abraham's day. They were there when Jesus walked this earth, else He would not have warned against them. They were there when the Church was first established. And they are with us today. The number of false prophets today is legion. And unfortunately, some of them are in the Church.

We Christians must have a clear understanding of what a false prophet is if we are going to be able to effectively defend ourselves and our loved ones against them. A false prophet is one who perverts or denies the fundamental doctrines of the faith, the Gospel, and yet claims to be a true prophet, minister, or pastor. To the extent that any person preaches or teaches what is false, contrary to God's Word, as if it were God's Word, that person is a false prophet. And Jesus tells us,

134

"Watch out, beware!" False prophets are extremely dangerous for they can lead many astray. They can pretend to be harmless; they can appear as gentle sheep, one of the flock, and what they say can even sound reasonable and true. But Jesus tells us that inwardly they are ferocious wolves. False prophets and their teaching are like the leaven Jesus mentioned when He said that a little leaven leavens the whole loaf. A lie here, a falsehood there, a compromise here and there, and pretty soon corruption is widespread. False prophets can appear to be sincere Christians, and they are sincerely wrong.

Jesus tells us how to judge rightly between that which is true and that which is false, between true prophets and false prophets, so we can protect ourselves and safeguard the faith. He tells us to check the fruit. What did He mean by fruit? Personal works are fruit which stem from what a person believes. Yet personal works cannot be considered as the main or sole criteria for recognizing false prophets because they can be misleading. Even the most committed and true believers sin, for we are all sinners and fall short of the grace of God. Therefore, a true prophet could be mistaken for a false prophet. Then too, false prophets may appear holy in their personal works. The Scribes and Pharisees appeared holy; yet, many of them were false prophets.

No, we need something more certain than personal works. We need to judge the fruit, the results, the effects, the outworking of their teachings and doctrines, as Jesus tells us to do. Every teaching, every doctrine, every law, can be judged by the means of God's revealed Word of Truth, in the light of God's Word. All teaching, all doctrine, all law, produces results which can be discerned and known - in other words, fruit - and whether or not that fruit corresponds to God's will as revealed in His Word and the Gospel of Christ is the ultimate test of truth or falsehood. Every Christian, armed with the Word of God and the leading of the Holy Spirit, is equipped to apply such a test and judge the fruit, and we should not hesitate to do so.

Perhaps a couple of examples may help clarify how such testing can occur. It is a popular belief among many people that there are many ways to God, and if one lives a good life, abstains from evil, is generous and helpful to his fellowman, God will certainly allow him into heaven. If we test the truth or falsehood of this using God's Word, we find that it is demonstrably false. We find in John 14:6 Jesus' statement: "I am the Way and the Truth, and the Life. No one comes to the Father except through Me." Jesus makes it totally clear that there is no other way to God except through faith in Him. Period. Two other examples which are hot button issues today: abortion and homosexuality. There are many who say that God would approve of abortion in certain cases. There is no passage in Scripture that supports such a view. In fact, Psalm 139 is a very beautiful and intimate description of God's relations with babies in the womb which thoroughly refutes abortion as the evil that it is. As far as homosexuality is concerned, many believe that God approves of homosexuality on the basis of love. 1Corinthians 6:9-10 and Romans 1:26-27 and many other passages both Old Testament and New Testament, refute this. Does God accept the homosexual who comes to Him? Yes! Does God love the homosexual as His creation? Yes! Are we to accept the homosexual in friendship? Yes! Are we to love the homosexual as God's creation? Yes! Does God approve of the homosexual lifestyle? No! Are we to approve of the homosexual lifestyle? No! Again, the ultimate test is God's Word. We either accept it or we don't. There is no middle ground.

Jesus tells us that grapes are not gathered from thorn bushes or figs from thistles. Grapes and figs symbolize true spiritual food which grows from the Word of God alone. He tells us that the kind of tree determines the nature of the fruit. It is impossible for a tree to bear fruit contrary to its nature. And there are only two types of trees - good or bad; only two types of fruit - good or bad. Good fruit is that which conforms to God's Word, the Truth, not in a mere intellectual sense, but in practical results. Bad fruit is that which is in conflict with God's Word. And notice that there is no in-between, no compromise. For Truth is Truth! Truth is not relative.

The world would like for truth to be relative, for truth to be what each person wants it to be. There are many who would like to see God's

Word compromised, watered down, tailored more to their liking. False prophets would like God to conform to their image of Him. They would like to fit God into their purpose, into their agenda, whether it be religious, political, educational, or cultural. The true prophet and teacher, the true Christian, allows God to fit them into His purpose, into His plan. In the passage just preceding our Gospel lesson, Jesus talks about the narrow gate that leads to life, and the broad gate that leads to destruction. There are many who prefer the broad gate because it entails permissiveness, whereas they consider the narrow gate too restrictive. They are like those who the Apostle Paul describes in 2Timothy 4:3-4 where he writes: "The time will come when men will not put up with sound doctrine. They will gather around them a great number of teachers who will say what their itching ears want to hear. They will turn their ears away from the Truth and turn aside to myths."

We are living in such a time today. But you and I, as followers of Christ, have nothing to fear if we obey the commands of our Lord to "beware" and "be watchful," if we hold fast God's Word of Truth, and if we evaluate and judge all things according to that Word of Truth. We are not to condemn; only God condemns. And we are not to judge in a biased, unfair manner. Jesus made this clear in His Sermon on the Mount. But we are to judge fairly and wisely, judge between the good tree and the bad tree; between the good fruit and the bad fruit. God has given us the means to identify falsehood and false teachers through His Word of Truth and the Holy Spirit, and He expects us, commands us, to apply this test of His Word to all things, because it is a reasonable test, a sensible test, a simple test, a just test, a sure test. The only sure test.

By their fruits you shall know them. Only a good tree can bear good fruit, the fruit of everlasting life. As followers of Christ, we are called to be good trees bearing good fruit as witnesses for Christ to a fallen world. How does one become a good tree? By being solidly rooted in God's Word, by going to the foot of the cross and honestly confessing our sins each day and receiving God the Father's forgiveness for the sake of His Son Jesus, our Savior, and by committing our lives to that

Savior. And we become good trees by following the Apostle Paul's instructions in 1Corinthians 3:18-20 where he says: "If anyone of you thinks he is wise by the standards of this age, he should become a fool so that he may become wise. For the wisdom of this world is foolishness in God's sight." We become good trees by becoming fools for God.

A true Christian is a tree that is grafted into Christ, and if that is the case, good fruit will assuredly follow, fruit that will be seen in time and eternity. And we should never be tricked into thinking of our good fruit as small or insignificant, for God can and does do great things with the small or seemingly insignificant. Dr. Lyman Beecher, one of the great American preachers, was once asked to preach for a minister whose church was in a remote district. It was winter, the day was stormy and cold, and snow lay so deep that he could scarcely find his way. On his arrival, he found the church empty. Nevertheless, he took his seat in the pulpit, for it was time to begin the service. After a time, just one man came in and sat down. Dr. Beecher arose and conducted the service, after which the solitary attendant departed. Twenty years later, Dr. Beecher was traveling in Ohio when a stranger approached him and asked: "Do you remember preaching once to one man?" "Yes," said Dr. Beecher, "and if you are that man, I have often wished to see you." The man said: "Your sermon that day changed my life; it made a minister out of me." And pointing, he said, "And over there is my church. The converts, due to your sermon, sir, are all over this state." Little had Dr. Beecher known that his sermon that day long ago had been greatly used by God. Little do you and I know how greatly God has used the fruit of our faith in our walk with Christ.

Jesus tells us: "I am the vine, you are the branches. He that abides in Me and I in him, the same bears much fruit. Without Me, you can do nothing." The only successful life is a fruitful life. And a fruitful life is a life centered in Christ. Be a good tree, a fruitful tree for your Lord. Don't let this world and its false prophets mislead you. Use the rock solid, unchanging standard for judging between truth and falsehood, between good and evil, between wisdom and foolishness, that God has given us, the standard of His Word, and the Living Word Jesus Christ, the same yesterday, today, and forever. Christ is our Standard. Christ is our Righteousness. Christ is our Truth. Christ is our Hope. And Christ is our Life.

God grant, in the Name of Jesus and in the power of the Holy Spirit, that each of us become the very best trees we can be, bearing abundant fruit to the honor and glory of His Holy Name. Amen.

THE NOBLEST PRAYER

Text: Psalm 116; Matthew 6:5-15.

Theme: The Lord's Prayer

Theme Statement: We pray the Lord's Prayer as individual children of God and as the family of God. We are able to do so only because of Jesus, Who not only gave us the prayer, but made it possible for us to pray it individually and corporately through His suffering, death, and resurrection. Thus, the Lord's Prayer can also rightfully be considered as the Noblest Prayer, and an important part of every worship service..

Key Passage: Matthew 6:9. "Our Father Who art in heaven."

P rayer is the Christian's greatest weapon against the constant temptations we experience from the devil, the world, and our sinful flesh. Scripture tells us to "pray without ceasing," that is, be in a constant attitude of prayer, open to the Holy Spirit's leading and ready anytime to send a prayer to heaven for help, strength, and guidance.

In Psalm 116, the Psalmist emphasizes God's readiness, and even eagerness, to hear our prayers. Overcome by trouble and sorrow, near death, he cried out to God. "O Lord, save me!" And he says, "I love the Lord, for He heard my voice, my cry for mercy; because He turned His ear to me, I will call on Him as long as I live." The Psalmist has a great lesson for us. As long as we continue living, we must continue praying, right up to the last day when we breathe our last. We have the great example of Jesus our Lord, Who throughout His ministry on earth, was constant in prayer right up to His last breath on the cross which was a prayer in itself: "Father, into your hands, I commit my Spirit." Our prayers are as precious, holy, and pleasing to God as those of St. Paul and the other apostles and saints, because our prayers rest on the same commandment of Jesus to pray that theirs rested on.

There is no nobler prayer under the heavens than the Lord's Prayer. Why? Because it was spoken and taught to the disciples by God Himself, the Son of God as Son of Man. The Lord's Prayer is also a perfect prayer, not only because it was spoken by the Christ, but because, in its petitions, is included every need of mankind. There are two reasons for praying the Lord's Prayer frequently. One is that God the Father loves to hear the prayer of His Son as Son of Man, and the other is that it addresses all our needs in this life. Jesus gave us the Lord's Prayer so that we can know how to pray and what to pray for.. Luther advised setting times throughout the day to pray the Lord's prayer. The Lord's Prayer can also rightfully be considered as an essential part of every worship service, every Bible study, and every personal meditation. You ask, "what is it about the Lord's Prayer that is so noble and makes it so essential?" Well, let's consider this unique and special prayer.

First, we pray, "Our Father Who art in heaven." Right from the beginning of the Lord's Prayer to the last petition, Jesus, the composer, uses the plural instead of the singular. We pray "Our Father," "Give us," "forgive us," "lead us," "deliver us," emphasizing our status as members of God's family, members of the Communion of Saints. How can we be so bold as to call God our Father? Because of Jesus, and Jesus alone, whose suffering, death, and resurrection made it possible for us to be adopted into the family of God and given the highest privilege of calling Almighty God "Father." And the Father sent His Son to pay the terrible price for our redemption and salvation because He wanted us to be able to call Him Father because of HIs great love for us.

At the University of California at Berkley, there is a monument which is engraved with the words: "You are all sons of God...." It is taken from Galatians 3:26 which reads: "You are all sons of God through faith in Christ Jesus." Notice that they left the part about faith in Christ Jesus out, giving the impression that everyone is a member of God's family. This is deliberate falsehood, deception, and blasphemy. Only faith in Christ and His suffering, death, and resurrection makes a true child of God, and only a true child of God can address God as Father, and not only Father, but ABBA Father, an expression of family love and intimacy. To all others, God says, "I never knew you." Jesus and His atonement is the reason we can call God "Our Father." Therefore, whenever we pray, "Our Father in heaven," we are expressing our faith in Christ, and praying the prayer given us by Christ.

Next we pray, "Hallowed be Thy Name." God's Name was given to us when we became Christian, and when in our baptism, we became members of God's family. To hallow God's Name is to set it apart, to esteem, prize, honor, reverence it, and adore the Living Word Christ, above all else. We pray that God's Name be hallowed by making His Word and Revelation in Christ Jesus supreme in the hearts of men, with the centerpiece of that revelation the suffering, death, and resurrection of the Christ to atone for the sins of us all. If that centerpiece of Christ's atonement is missing, God's Name is not hallowed, but profaned. Thus, all of man's religions, in effect, profane the Name of God, and only the Christian Faith hallows the Name of God. Thus, when we pray "Hallowed be Thy Name," we express our Christian faith and pray our Christian prayer.

Next, we pray "Thy Kingdom Come." God's Kingdom comes to us in two ways. It comes to us here in time through the Word and Sacraments and faith. It comes to us in eternity when Christ returns, the devil, sin, and death are destroyed once for all, and the new heaven and the new earth of God's Kingdom are consummated in which God dwells personally with His people in perfect righteousness, holiness, and blessedness. Only we Christians can pray "Thy Kingdom Come" with overwhelming joy and eager anticipation because it is for us that the new heaven and the new earth are created. God wants us to do great things for Him in this life to build that Kingdom, but too often we hesitate or hold back out of fear, doubt, and uncertainty. In Ephesians 3:20, He tells us He is able to do exceedingly above all we can possibly imagine or comprehend. Too often, we ask for a piece of bread, and often that with doubt, when God wants to give us the whole loaf.

When we pray "Thy Kingdom Come," we are praying for the whole loaf, the greatest gift of all, the eternal, inestimable, incomprehensible treasure of God the Father, Son, and Holy Spirit. And we can do so with boldness and confidence, because of the salvation we have, the salvation God's Son, our Lord and Savior Jesus Christ, purchased for us with His Body and Blood, with His suffering, death, and resurrection that opened the gates of heaven, the Kingdom of Glory, to us. Yes, when we pray, "Thy Kingdom Come," we express our Christian faith, and pray our Christian prayer.

Next we pray, "Thy will be done on earth as it is in heaven." In this petition, we pray that God empower us through the Holy Spirit to submit our wills, weak as they are, to His will, just as Jesus did when He took on our humanity and took up the cross. Sometimes this may involve our having to endure crosses, trials, and sufferings when we don't understand God's will. But God promises us in Romans 8:28 that, in all things, He will work out the highest good for His children. God's will is symbolized for us in the cross, that through His Son's perfect sacrifice of Body and Blood on that cross, all men may come to the knowledge of the Truth, submit their wills to God, and be saved through Christ. The cross drives the devil into a rage because it is the proof of his defeat and the fulfillment of the Father's will through His Son's sacrifice on the cross. In his rage, the devil exerts all his power, the allurements of a sinful, wicked world, and the weakness of our sinful flesh in his attacks against the children of God to keep us from submitting our wills to God's will. We pray this petition for our own, and our brother's and sister's, protection and defense. And every time we fail to submit our will to God's will, which invariably leads to sin, we flee to the cross, and there with confession and repentance, seek and receive God's forgiveness, cleansing, and renewal for the sake of His Son, Who was mocked, beaten, spit upon, scourged, and nailed to the cross to pay for our sin. Yes, every time we pray, "Thy will be done on earth as it is in heaven," we express our Christian faith and pray our Christian prayer.

Next we pray, "Give us this day our daily bread." Daily bread symbolizes and encompasses all that we need for our daily life. Notice that the petition says "this day," and "daily," which should remind us of the Israelites' sin in the wilderness with the "manna" God provided from heaven, when in their greed, they took more than a daily amount and tried to hoard it. Their sin is a warning to us against greed, covetousness, seeking our treasure on earth instead of heaven. The Bread of this petition also reminds us of the Supreme Bread, the Bread of Life. Jesus says, "I am the Bread of Life. Whoever eats of this Bread will never die." Jesus also says, "I am the Living Water. Whoever drinks of this water will never thirst." The Bread of Life is His Body nailed to the cross for us. The Living Water is His Blood poured out for us. The bread of the oven and the water of the well strengthen us for this life on earth; the Bread of Life, Christ's Body, and the Living Water, Christ's Blood, strengthens us for both this life on earth and the new life, the life eternal. And so, when we pray "Give us this day our daily bread," we express our Christian faith and pray our Christian prayer.

Next we pray, "And forgive us our trespasses as we forgive those who trespass against us." We are God's children, new creations, through faith in His Son. Yet, our sinful nature still resides within us, and always will as long as we live on this earth. The devil tempts and attacks us through our sinful nature, and in our weakness, we daily sin in thought, word, and deed. In this petition, we pray that God would forgive us, as He has promised, for the sake of His Son. There is a qualification - "as we forgive those who trespass against us." If we do not forgive others, we dare not think that God will forgive us. But if we do forgive others, as the Father forgives us for the sake of His Son, then we have the comfort and assurance that we are forgiven by God. But we cannot take credit for forgiving others. Jesus made it possible for us both to be forgiven and to forgive others through His suffering, death, and resurrection. Apart from Christ and His sacrifice of atonement, and the Holy Spirit working through that redemptive power of Christ, it would be impossible for us to forgive others because of our sinful nature. Thus, our forgiving others in the Name of Christ, is not only a sign that the Holy Spirit dwells in us, but also that we are forgiven, all as a result of Christ's sacrifice. Here too then, when we pray "And forgive us our trespasses as we forgive those who trespass against us," we are expressing our Christian faith and praying our Christian prayer.

Next we pray, "And lead us not into temptation." We have referred to the three-fold source of all temptation - our sinful human flesh, the world with its wickedness, hatred, and hostility, and the devil, lying, deceiving, accusing, and using the world and our sinful nature in attempts to tear us away from faith, hope, love, trust in God, and lead us into despair, blasphemy, and unbelief. When we pray, "And lead us not into temptation, we are not asking God to take away the temptation. We are asking God to strengthen us through the Holy Spirit to overcome it. We are reminding God of His promise given to us in 1Corinthians which says: "God is faithful; He will not let you be tempted beyond what you can bear. But when you are tempted, He will also provide a way out so that you can stand up under it." Experiencing temptation is not a sin; submitting to it is. Jesus, in order to be the perfect sacrifice for our sin, had to experience every type of temptation we experience, without sinning.

If the devil tempts us so strongly, think of how he tempted Jesus during His ministry here on earth, for the devil understood fully the mission of this Messiah, the redemption of mankind. He understood the monumental, universal, and eternal stakes involved in this gigantic battle with the Incarnate Son of God Who had come in the flesh. The supreme agonies of Jesus' temptations in the wilderness, in Gethsemane, and on the cross, when all the powers of the devil, his demons, and hell itself were thrown at Jesus in the devil's desperate attempts to get Him to sin, were only the worst of the constant temptations Jesus had to endure and overcome for our salvation. Yes, when we pray, "And lead us not into temptation," we confess our Christian faith and pray our Christian prayer.

Next we pray, "But deliver us from evil." Evil here is all-inclusive, spiritual, material, and physical. In this petition, God commands us to seek and expect help and deliverance from evil only from Him, for unless He preserves us, we would not be safe from our enemy for even a moment. Finally, in this petition, we pray for deliverance from this sinful, wicked world and its evil, through a blessed death in Christ. And since a blessed death in Christ is ours only through faith in Christ as our Lord and Savior and through His suffering, death, and resurrection, in this last petition also we confess our Christian faith and pray our Christian prayer.

The doxology, "For Thine is the Kingdom and the Power and and the Glory forever and ever," was apparently inserted when the prayer was given continued usage in the Church. And with its praise eminently fitting the prayer, it remains as part of the Lord's Prayer. We pray: "For Thine is the Kingdom…" The Kingdom is the new heaven and the new earth of Revelation 21:1 in all its unimaginable glory, created for us, the family of God, through Jesus Christ Who made it possible through His suffering, death, and resurrection. We pray, "And the power…" The power we read of in Revelation 20:10: "And the devil…was thrown into the lake of burning sulphur, where the beast and the false prophet (the devil's minions) had been thrown. They will be tormented day and night forever and ever." This is the power of Christ's atonement, of Christ's victory over the devil and all the powers of hell. We pray, "And the glory…" The glory we are told of in Revelation 21:2: "I saw the Holy City, the New Jerusalem, coming down out of heaven from God, prepared as a bride beautifully dressed for her husband." What husband? Christ, whose victorious atonement for my sins, your sins, the sins of mankind, made possible the new heaven and new earth, made possible the destruction of the devil and his kingdom, made possible the New Jerusalem, where one day you and I and all our brothers and sisters in Christ will live. Yes, even as we pray this doxology, we express our Christian faith and pray our Christian prayer.

We have shown that the Lord's Prayer is inseparably linked to our worship, study, and meditation. Every time we pray it, whether alone

146

or in union as the family of God, our hearts and minds should go to the cross in praise and thanksgiving to our Lord and Savior Who made it all possible. We mentioned that the Father loves to hear the Lord's Prayer, composed by His Son and taught to His disciples, and us, to the glory of His Father. With that in mind, let us close this message by giving our Heavenly Father the pleasure and enjoyment of hearing His Son's prayer again. We pray: "Our Father Who art in heaven, Hallowed be Thy Name, Thy Kingdom come, Thy will be done on earth as it is in heaven, Give us this day our daily bread, And forgive us our trespasses, as we forgive those who trespass against us, And lead us not into temptation, But deliver us from evil, For Thine is the Kingdom, and the Power, and the Glory, forever and ever. Amen.

THE THREE SANCTITIES

Text: Psalm 139:1-18; Romans 12:6-16; John 2:1-11.

Theme: Life, Marriage, Family.

Theme Statement: God is Sovereign over every aspect of our life. Thus, every decision, every act, has a spiritual, ethical dimension. In view of this, how then does this, or should this, affect consideration of such current hot-button issues as abortion, homosexual marriage, and family disintegration which are clearly in contradiction to God's Word and Will?

Key Passage: Psalm 139:13-14. "For You created my inmost being; You knit me together in my mother's womb. I praise You because I am fearfully and wonderfully made; Your works are wonderful, I know that full well."

We are all familiar with the statement: "Don't mix religion and politics." The statement is foolish and unrealistic because God's sovereignty is total and encompasses every aspect of our lives. Thus, every decision, every act, has a spiritual, ethical dimension to it. George Washington said: "Without religion, morality has no roots." The moral, ethical nature of something cannot be properly evaluated apart from its theological aspects, for the two are inseparable. This perhaps is why the seers, the wise men of the past, considered theology to be the queen of the sciences. As both Creator and Redeemer, God is Lord, Sovereign over both the spiritual and the secular. What does this mean insofar as our consideration of such controversial issues as abortion, homosexual marriage, and family disintegration is concerned?

Separation of science and the secular from the theological and the moral / ethical, in other words humanism, is at the heart of the great social controversies mentioned above, as well as some others like

148

euthanasia and cloning. It has also tended to move us away from the foundation of Judeo-Christian morals and ethics our Founders insisted they had built this nation on. The Founding Fathers charged the citizens of this country with the solemn duty and responsibility to hold our elected officials accountable for any laws, policies that contradicted that Judeo-Christian foundation. To deny God's sovereignty over the nation, in their opinion, justified revolt. The Founders would have fully agreed with the Apostles John and Peter, who when they were told by the governing authorities to stop preaching in the Name of Jesus, answered, "We must obey God rather than man." Let us consider the results of this chipping away of our Judeo-Christian foundation on the Three Sanctities which are the cornerstones of all societies and civilization itself - the Sanctity of Life, the Sanctity of Marriage, and the Sanctity of Family. Let us consider first the Sanctity of Marriage and the Sanctity of Family.

Our Gospel lesson tells us of the wedding at Cana at which Jesus performed His first miracle of changing water into wine at the outset of His ministry. From the description of events, it seems that Jesus' mother was helping the wedding party with the serving of guests. Jesus and His disciples were invited, perhaps as a result of Mary's relationship with the wedding family. In her service, Mary became aware that the wedding party was running out of wine. She came and told Jesus. Why? What did she expect Him to do? She had never seen Him perform a miracle, and it is doubtful she expected that. Nevertheless, given what she had heard and seen all those years ago from the shepherds, the wise men, Simeon and Anna at the temple, and which we are told she pondered in her heart and undoubtedly still pondered, it is understandable she would turn to Him and also tell the servants to do whatever He said.

Weddings at the time could go on for days and the wedding feast was very important. From the situation with the wine, this wedding was probably much shorter and the groom's family poor. To run out of wine was more than just a minor social embarrassment; it would have been considered an act of discourtesy to the guests and a source of acute embarrassment to the groom to fail to provide wine for his guests.

When the master of the banquet tasted the water made wine by Jesus, he chided the groom for serving the poorer wine first and saving this best wine until later. He didn't know where the wine came from and neither did the groom, but they surely found out from the servants who had filled the water jugs, who, when in their amazement they realized what Jesus had done, certainly shared their amazement with the others. And Mary certainly knew. And we know the disciples were astounded because we're told that it led them to believe on Him. And I'm sure the groom was very grateful to Jesus for saving his reputation, along with being grateful to Jesus for His wedding gift to him and his bride of 120 gallons of the most excellent wine.

At this village marriage, with His first public appearance in any company, with His first miracle of His earthly ministry, with the first sign of His Messiahship, and with His first manifestation of His glory, Jesus honors the sanctity of marriage and the sanctity of family. And He honors marriage as it was instituted by God Himself in the Garden of Eden - one man, one woman, becoming one in the flesh, commanded by God to reproduce and become the core of the sanctity of family, which God also instituted in the Garden as one man (father), one woman (mother) and children. And Jesus would later honor marriage even more by using it to describe the oneness between Himself and His followers - the Church - Christ the Bridegroom and the Church His Bride.

Today the holy estate of marriage has been radically corrupted by judges, a segment of citizens, and even some religious authorities who apparently consider themselves wiser than the sages of past millennia, wiser than God Himself Who instituted Holy Marriage, and who magically found within the scope of the Constitution a right to same sex marriage that was completely unknown or even undreamt of by those who drafted the Constitution, as well as all the justices, some of

150

them renowned, who followed them during the intervening more than one hundred fifty years.

Perhaps it was undreamt of because same sex marriage is irrational and doesn't make sense. The primary purpose of marriage, as stated by God Himself, is to reproduce, have children and replenish the human race. Same sex marriage cannot do that in and of itself; therefore, it is not true marriage as instituted by God. Thus, our legal and political and some religious authorities have approved a type of marriage in which it is impossible to accomplish the primary objective of marriage. How foolish is that? They demand the so-called right of marriage in order to try and legitimize a relationship that is blatantly against God's Word and will. Furthermore, the corruption of marriage is interrelated to the corruption of family. The two are inseparable. This is appalling ignorance and also blatant blasphemy against Christ and His depiction of the husband / wife relationship as a picture of the relationship between Himself and the Church, His family, the Church Christ loves and sacrificed Himself for, the Church Christ cherishes and nourishes with Word and Sacrament.

Let us now consider the Sanctity of Life. It has been 49 years since Roe vs. Wade was passed by the Supreme Court which legalized abortion. By the grace of God, it has been repealed by the Supreme Court this year 2022, on the grounds that it is unconstitutional and a matter for the States to decide. Back in 1973 when it passed, Chief Justice Rehnquist, one of the two dissenting justices, stated in his dissenting opinion that the seven liberal judges, in order to pass it, had to find within the scope of the Constitution a right that was apparently completely unknown or even undreamt of by the drafters of the Constitution or subsequent justices over the intervening more than 150 years. The so-called "right to privacy," used to justify abortion, is not mentioned in any of our founding documents - not in the Declaration of Independence, not in the Constitution, not in the first ten amendments to the Constitution called the Bill of Rights. It was a figment of the imaginations of the radical liberal judges, who being in the majority, overrode the conservative judges' constitutional agenda with their secular progressive agenda and passed it into law. Can anyone seriously believe that the Founding Fathers, who insisted in the Declaration of Independence that the right to life given by God superseded all other rights, would agree with a right to abortion, especially since at the time, abortion was a crime?

Over the years, abortion came to be considered as a civil right and many still consider it so. This belittles the historical civil rights movement which was a courageous and noble chapter of our history. Consider the utter ignorance and stupidity of calling abortion a civil right. In order to exercise abortion as a civil right, you have to deny and cancel the most basic, fundamental, and foundational civil right of all - Life, and in cancelling that, you effectively cancel all civil rights of the person. Let us consider the appalling judicial, physical, and spiritual abominations of this law and its devastating effects individually and nationally over the past 49 years before it was finally consigned to the dustbin of judicial history.

First, the spiritual. The greatest argument against abortion, the open and shut case which clearly condemns abortion, is our Old Testament lesson from Psalm 139. We're told by David the Psalmist, through the Holy Spirit, that God knew us before we were born, before the creation of this world. He knew us not remotely, but intimately and totally. And then, David prays, "You created my inmost being; You knit me together in my mother's womb. My frame was not hidden from You when I was made in the secret place. When I was woven together in the depths of the earth, Your eyes saw my unformed body. All the days ordained for me were written in Your book before one of them came to be."

The Psalmist sees himself, as each of us should see ourselves, not as an accident, but as one known, brought into being, given an allotted time, and encompassed by the everlasting God. As our Creator, God shapes our complex individuality, gives it life, and directs it toward our future with the works He has ordained for us. It is like the Lord's words to Jeremiah at the time of his call: "Before I formed you in the womb,

152

I knew you, and before you were born, I set you apart; I appointed you as a prophet to the nations." As God's creation, we are brought into existence for a purpose, a mission, which fits into God's grand design. Ephesians 2:10 tells us: For we are God's workmanship, created in Christ Jesus to do good works, which God prepared in advance for us to do." In advance of what? In advance of our creation; in advance of the world's creation.

The Psalmist lifts his voice in praise: "I praise You because I am fearfully and wonderfully made; Your works are wonderful, I know that full well." We can also cry that out to God for each of us is fearfully and wonderfully made. God made it clear that He created man in His own image, "in the image of God He created him, male and female He created them." Every human being bears the image of God. That is what makes us human and separates us from the animal world. That being the case, consider this: With every baby that is aborted, the image of God is aborted. God's plans for that baby are aborted. God's works that He ordained for that baby are aborted. Every abortion is a direct attack, a heinous act against God Himself, against His image, against God's sovereignty over life, against God's ownership of that precious life He created, formed, and knit together in the womb.

How is it that man can acknowledge God as Creator, the One Who formed him in the womb, and yet commit the most horrible genocide against the most innocent and helpless among us, those babies in the womb, and even outside the womb, through the satanic evil of abortion? Babies are chopped to pieces in the womb, the pieces extracted from the woman's body and pieced together on the table to make sure all the parts are there, like putting a jigsaw puzzle together, only these parts are the bloody pieces of a baby's remains. And consider the fact that the baby, early in his/her development, can feel pain. How horrible is that?

Statistics tell us that every month 133 thousand babies are aborted. Since 1973 when abortion was legalized, over 63 million babies have been aborted. That's nearly twice the entire population of California.

Through abortion alone, we have committed more murders than three of the greatest mass murderers in modern history - Hitler of Germany, Stalin of Russia, and Mao Tse Tung of China. A few years ago in Los Angeles, over 17 thousand aborted babies were found in a dumpster. The largest abortion provider in the country is Planned Parenthood. It was founded around 100 years ago by Margaret Sanger, whose primary purpose was eugenics, controlling the black population by aborting black babies. Did you know that, to this day, Congress allocates in the yearly budget over half a billion dollars to Planned Parenthood - that's your tax money and mine - which enables them to butcher more babies? Did you know that, at a Planned Parenthood event, our former President Obama, in a speech, asked God to bless Planned Parenthood? Imagine that - a black President asking God to bless an organization drenched in the blood of black babies as well as others. Did you know that in the 2020 presidential election campaign, all eighteen, or whatever the number was, of the Democratic presidential candidates strongly supported abortion throughout the nine month period, right up to the moment of birth? Did you know that many strong pro-abortionists claim to be devout Christians? How ignorant is that?

The pro-abortion faction goes to great efforts to convince people that that baby in the womb is just a mass of tissue and not life. Really? Is that what God formed in the womb, just a mass of tissue? Do they want to tell God that? Many people don't want to know the details about abortion, thinking that if they don't know about it, they don't have to feel guilty about ignoring it. But it is vitally important that people understand clearly what abortion is, and the devastation - spiritual, physical, and emotional it causes. Since Roe vs. Wade has been reversed, the battle now reverts back to the States, snd the sooner the majority of citizens become knowledgeable of the horror and pure evil of abortion, the sooner irresistible pressure can be put on our elected State officials to remove from each State's national social fabric the disgusting, abominable, and filthy stain of abortion. Evil can only be defeated by shining the light of truth on it. Let me briefly summarize what abortion is and the devastation it brings:

Abortion is the ultimate civil rights discrimination against the most innocent and helpless among us - our babies in the womb.

Abortion brutally murders someone created by the hands of a loving God. Abortion brutally murders someone redeemed by their loving Savior Who was brutally murdered on the cross for them.

Abortion brutally murders someone who will never be the person - black, white, red, brown, yellow - that God intended for them to be.

Abortion brutally murders someone who will never accomplish the works, deeds, goals, that God ordained for them to accomplish in His good and perfect plan for them.

Abortion not only brutally murders someone, but often brutally wounds that someone's mother with sorrow, guilt, depression, and regret, as well as that someone's father and that someone's family.

The good news is that there is hope and help for those experiencing an unplanned pregnancy. Organizations like Crisis Pregnancy Centers are there to help and support the person to carry the child to birth, and then if the mother wishes, help place the child up for adoption. The good news for those suffering from depression and guilt over having had an abortion is that, although abortion is sin, like all sin it can be confessed, repented of, the sinner forgiven, washed clean of it with the Blood of Christ, and freed of the sin and guilt once and for all.

We Christians must love our sisters suffering so with the love the Apostle Paul speaks of in our Epistle lesson, *agape* love, the love of intelligence and purpose, the love of action and not just words, the sacrificial, encompassing love, the love with which Christ loved us. Also, and this is extremely difficult and can only be done in the strength of the Holy Spirit, our Christian love must extend to the abortionist and those who support abortion, that their eyes be opened to the horror and evil of it, that they go to the cross of Christ in confession and repentance, and receive God's mercy and pardon.

The Psalmist says: "When I awake, I am still with You." The Psalmist not only assures us that God knew us before we even came into being, he assures us that God knows us after we go out of being. "When I awake," (awake from what? From death!), "I am still with YOU!" The Omnipresence of God gives us the certainty that God is present everywhere we are. The Psalmist emphasizes this inescapability of God. Death cannot cut us off from the presence of God. That includes every one of those 63 million aborted babies. We don't know their form, shape, or current state, but their Creator has taken care of that. We do know that they are in His Presence now and will be with Him at the Resurrection. Our Creator does not waste His precious creations. Only sinful man does that.

God is loving, patient, merciful, compassionate, forgiving, but God is also just. If men and nations do not repent of their sin and evil, God will eventually use judgment to restore justice. Both Biblical and secular history clearly show this. If we continue as a nation promoting actions and lifestyles that are in direct, flagrant, arrogant, opposition to God's Word, the time will come when God says: "Enough! It is time for judgment to cleanse my people." Thomas Jefferson understood this clearly when he said: "When I consider that God is just, and that HIs justice cannot be delayed indefinitely, I tremble for my country." God grant us the wisdom to tremble for our country, and the steadfastness to stand fast against those corrupting God's Word, and against those corrupting the Constitution that God, in His wisdom, gave us through our Founding Fathers. God grant this for Jesus' sake. Amen.

CHAPTER 6 - EXAMPLES

"To be thought of as a fool for Christ is the greatest compliment. To know nothing but Christ crucified and risen, is the purest form of wisdom. To be consumed with love for Christ so intense that it becomes a holy madness, is the highest form of sanity. To be counted worthy to suffer for Christ, is the highest honor."

The Apostle Paul

A PROFILE OF BOLDNESS AND HUMILITY

Text: Malachi 3:1-5, 4:5-6; Matthew 11: 11-15.

Theme: The character and ministry of John the Baptist.

Theme Statement: John the Baptist was God's messenger and forerunner for His Son, the Messiah Jesus Christ. He ministered in the spirit and power of Elijah, as prophesied by Malachi, to prepare God's people for the Lord's coming. He was fearsome in appearance, bold in preaching "Repent, for the Kingdom of Heaven is near," and humble in character. He referred to himself as simply "a voice in the wilderness," and told his disciples that he must decrease and the Christ must increase, that he must become less, and the Christ become greater. The humility of John the Baptist, and the boldness of his witness to Christ, serve as strong examples to us, for only in such humility and boldness, can we properly prepare to celebrate Christ's First Advent of Christmas and to eagerly and faithfully await His Second Advent.

Key Passage: Matthew 11:11. "I tell you the truth: Among those born of women there has not risen anyone greater than John the Baptist."

✝

He must have been quite a sight, this John the Baptist. He was strange, wild looking, and a bit fearsome. His clothes were camel's hair with a leather belt, and his diet was locusts and wild honey. And he could be a bit testy. He called the Pharisees and Sadducees a brood of vipers. I imagine if John the Baptist came to church on Sunday morning, many churches would be very uncomfortable with his presence. The ushers would probably seat him in the far rear out of sight, and then quickly usher him out as the service was ending. In short, John the Baptist would probably not be welcome in polite society.

And yet, he received the highest praise possible, and that praise came from God Himself, Jesus Christ. Jesus told the people, "I tell you the truth: Among those born of women there has not risen anyone greater than John the Baptist..." Can you imagine receiving such praise from the Son of God Himself? Let's consider this man to whom Jesus gave such high praise.

In our reading from the prophet Malachi, the Lord tells us, "See, I will send my messenger, who will prepare the way before Me." John the Baptist, foretold here, was also foretold long before by the prophet Isaiah who referred to John as "A voice of one calling: 'In the desert prepare the way for the Lord; make straight in the wilderness a highway for our God.'" John the Baptist was more than a prophet; he was God's messenger and forerunner of Jesus Christ to prepare the people for receiving their Messiah, raising their expectation of Him, giving notice of the approach of Him who Malachi describes as the Lord Who would come to His temple, Who would be like a refiner's fire or a launderer's soap, purifying His servants of their sins and unfaithfulness, Who would judge the sorcerers who dealt in spiritual wickedness and idolatry, the adulterers and perjurers, those who defraud, oppress, and deprive the people of justice, those who do not fear the Lord. All those John the Baptist was to call to repentance to prepare them for the arrival of that Lord, the Messiah, and His Kingdom. And his basic message was: "Repent, for the Kingdom of Heaven is near."

Other prophets had spoken of the Messiah's coming, but John the Baptist could point to Him and say, "Look, the Lamb of God Who takes away the sin of the world." John the Baptist testified, " I saw the Spirit come down from heaven as a dove and remain on Him. I have seen and I testify that this is the Son of God." John the Baptist is proof that Jesus Christ is the Messiah.

John the Baptist performed the great ministry God gave him with boldness and humility. In fact, John the Baptist is a profile of boldness and humility. Let's consider these characteristics of his. First, boldness. It has been rightly said that "shallow preaching disgusts; timid preaching leaves poor souls fast asleep; whereas bold preaching is the only preaching that is owned of God." In other words, preachers are not like weather vanes, letting the winds of popular opinion or the culture of the times turn them about, but which always point in the same direction - Christ crucified and risen! Well, there was nothing timid about John the Baptist, whether in his person or in his preaching.

When Malachi prophesied the coming of God's messenger to prepare the hearts of the people for the Messiah, he referred to that messenger as Elijah. When the angel announced to Zechariah that he and Elizabeth would have a son they were to name John, the angel said of that son: "He will go on before the Lord, in the spirit and power of Elijah, to turn the hearts of the fathers to their children and the disobedient to the wisdom of the righteous - to make ready a people prepared for the Lord." John the Baptist ministered in the spirit and power of Elijah.

The Jews interpreted Malachi's prophecy to mean that the actual Elijah would return as God's messenger. Remember that Elijah did not die, but was taken to heaven in a fiery chariot. But the words of the angel, and Jesus' own words concerning John the Baptist disprove this and show that it was John the Baptist who would come in the spirit and power of Elijah. Why this comparison of John the Baptist with Elijah?

Elijah prophesied at a time of great idolatry, wickedness, and unfaithfulness in the land of Israel. Their king was Ahab, one of the wickedest of Israel's kings, and his wife Jezebel, considered to be the wickedest woman in Scripture. Elijah was persecuted, criticized, and suffered much. He was a man of great austerity, zealous for God, bold in his preaching, condemning idolatry and false prophets, and calling people to repentance. Remember his great victory over the prophets of Baal on Mt. Carmel.

John the Baptist was of the same spirit and power of Elijah. He preached repentance and reformation as Elijah had done. John, like Elijah, made a bold stand against the sin and impiety and unfaithfulness that was in full force in the land. He rebuked the people for their slothfulness and complacency toward God. He rebuked the religious leaders for their hypocrisy and self-righteousness in the strongest language, just as the One he was preparing the way for would Himself later do. He pulled no punches in preaching to the people God's demand for repentance. The people, the religious leaders, and even King Herod had a healthy fear of John, and that healthy fear led multitudes of the people, if not the religious leaders and government officials, to receive his baptism of repentance. In Malachi, God threatened to come and strike the land with a curse. Israel had, by its impiety and impenitence, laid itself open to the curse of God. There's a lesson there for nations and peoples today, including our nation and people. Only God's mercy, unfathomable love, and incredible patience is delaying that curse, and His servants today, like John the Baptist, are crying out for repentance and turning to God.

As an instrument in God's hand, John, through his stern and bold preaching, his call to repentance and baptism of repentance, his total commitment to his call as God's messenger, turned many to righteousness, to the Lord their God. Many had their consciences awakened and came to repentance. Luke tells us of the great fruitfulness of John's ministry. In Luke 7:29-30, Luke says: "All the people, even the tax collectors, when they heard Jesus' words, acknowledged that God's way was right, because they had been baptized by John." All the people recognized John as a great prophet and that his baptism for the forgiveness of sins was from heaven and not men. They rejoiced that a prophet from God was again in their midst, for with the conclusion of Malachi's ministry, prophecy ceased until John the Baptist. Truly John did minister in the spirit, power, and boldness of Elijah and prepare the way for the coming Messiah.

Jesus referred to John as more than prophet, and confirmed to the people that John was the one prophesied by Isaiah and Malachi. When Jesus gave His high praise of John by saying, "I tell you the truth: Among those born of woman there has not risen anyone greater than John the Baptist," He continued on to say, "Yet he, who is least in the Kingdom of Heaven, is greater than he." Greater how? Greater accomplishments than John? No! Greater in faith than John? No! What did Jesus mean? Two schools of thought are as follows: First, the greatness of those least in the Kingdom of Heaven - that's you and me and all our brothers and sisters in Christ - consists of the great treasures of revelation given us by God. In Matthew 13:16-17, Jesus tells His disciples and us: "Blessed are your eyes because they see, and your ears because they hear. For I tell you the truth, many prophets and righteous men longed to see what you see but did not see it, and to hear what you hear, but did not hear it."

Thrown in prison and soon to be killed by Herod, John, for all his greatness, could not see the great miracles Jesus was working. He would not see the consummation of Jesus' work - His death and resurrection, the completion of His redemption of mankind. All the believers who witnessed these things at the time, and all believers who witnessed these things afterward through faith and the means of grace - that's us - are greater than John, not in stature or deeds, but in revelation.

Another possibility of Jesus' meaning concerning the least being greater than John comes from His response when His disciples asked Him, "Who is greatest in the Kingdom of Heaven?" Jesus called a little child to them and said: "I tell you the truth, whoever humbles himself like this little child is the greatest in the Kingdom of Heaven." In other words, those who become childlike in faith, humility, and trust are to be regarded by God as greatest in the Kingdom of Heaven. Then too, perhaps Jesus was making the point that in heaven there is no hierarchy of personal stature.

Jesus said that "From the days of John the Baptist until now the Kingdom of Heaven has been forcefully advancing, and forceful men lay hold of it." Forcefully advancing by whom? By John and Jesus. From the day when John began to baptize until when Jesus was in the fullness of His ministry, the Kingdom of Heaven was forcefully advancing. And that "until now" goes on and on right up to the present day and beyond with the Kingdom of Heaven forcefully advancing until the Day of the Lord when Christ returns. And the forceful advance of the Kingdom of Heaven with its gift of salvation, its treasures and blessings of oneness with our Lord and Savior, and the promise of eternal life, leads people, through the Holy Spirit, to forcefully lay hold of it in faith and obedience to Him Who opened the door to that Kingdom of Heaven to us through His suffering, death, and resurrection.

Jesus went on to say, "For all the Prophets and the Law prophesied until John." What did He mean? John the Baptist marked the grand new era of the New Covenant. For 430 years, since the last prophet Malachi spoke and wrote, the Old Testament Scriptures, the Old Covenant, was complete. Their fulfillment began when John the Baptist appeared announcing the arrival of the Messiah. It was then that the Kingdom pressed forward as never before. The ministry of John the Baptist was the dividing line between the Old Covenant and the New Covenant.

I said that John the Baptist was a profile of boldness and humility. We've spoken of his boldness. Now let us consider his humility. When the Jews were wondering if John was the Christ, he emphatically declared: "I am not the Christ!" When they asked if he was Elijah, he said "No!" In his humility, he did not claim to be the Elijah who was to come, even though he was. When they asked if he was the Prophet who was to come, he said "No!" In his humility, he did not claim to be even a prophet. When asked who he was, he simply referred to himself as "a voice crying in the wilderness."

In his humility, John regarded the baptism he was giving as merely preparatory. He told the people, "I baptize with water, but there is one coming Who will baptize with the Holy Spirit and fire." When Jesus came to him to be baptized by him, he initially refused, saying, "I need to be baptized by you, and do you come to me?" Only when Jesus said, "It is proper for us to do this to fulfill all righteousness," did John consent. And then, there is the statement John made to his disciples when they told him that everyone was going to Jesus: He said, "He must increase and I must decrease. He must become greater; I must become less." And with that statement, John gives us the essential key, the first step, to true greatness, to achieving our highest good that God wants for each of us. And that first step is humility.

People strive for success in this life, strive to be all they can be, their very best. Bookstore shelves are filled with self-help books telling them how to do this. But they are all worthless, meaningless, without that first step - humbling oneself before God by becoming less so He, the Christ, can become greater in our lives. There is no true success without that. Without humility, it is impossible to please God. Politicians and other celebrities strive to have a lasting legacy, and their efforts are futile without that first step John gives us, because only that first step of becoming less so He, the Christ, can become greater, leads to the only lasting legacy, the only legacy that lasts for eternity, the legacy of when we see Jesus face-to-face and hearing Him say, "Well done, good and faithful servant."

That first step, "I must become less; He must become greater;" "I must decrease and He must increase," prepares our Lord's way into our hearts and lives, for it is there that He would enter and rule. That first step is the key to the whole Christian life; it is the key to proper preparation for celebrating in remembrance of the First Advent of our Lord and Savior as the Babe of Bethlehem, of celebrating His coming in Word and Sacrament and preparing for His coming in power and glory with His Second Advent. Only if we become less and He become greater in our lives can we welcome Him with a holy awe and reverence appropriate for our God and King.

How do we become less? We become less and He becomes greater when we renounce this world's values, ambitions, gains, and vanities for His sake. We become less and He becomes greater when we hold nothing in this life as tight as we hold the Gospel of Christ, Who is the Way, the Truth, and the Life. We become less and He becomes greater when we are ready to drop all that is ours so that we may hold fast to all that is Christ's. We become less and He becomes greater when we bring to Him our offerings of faith, worship, prayer, praise, thanksgiving, obedience, tithes, and service. In Christ alone there is true greatness, and in Him alone can that greatness be ours which He ascribed to John the Baptist.

"Christ stands among you!" That was John the Baptist's message to the people. And it is his message to us today. God grant us ears to hear it, minds to understand it, and hearts to receive it, for Jesus' sake. Amen.

THE HEALING TOUCH

Text: Mark 5:25-34

Theme: Healing only in Christ.

Theme Statement: The need for healing involves every aspect of our lives. The trials and tribulations of life, personal failures, broken relationships, job problems, physical problems, financial problems - all can rob us of our joy and fill us with disappointment, discouragement, and depression. We need spiritual, emotional, and physical healing. The woman in our text desperately needed healing, for she suffered from a disease that rendered her ceremonially and physically unclean, thereby isolating her spiritually, physically, and socially. She was at the end of her rope, and had only one hope remaining - Jesus.

Key Passage: Mark 5:28,29. "She thought, 'If I just touch His clothes, I will be healed.' Immediately her bleeding stopped and she felt in her body that she was freed from her suffering."

†

It was turning out to be another busy and exhausting day for Jesus. Earlier, on the far shore of the Sea of Galilee, Jesus had healed a man who was possessed by a legion of demons. And for this, the people of the region, struck with fear, begged Jesus to leave their area. So, Jesus and His disciples got into a boat and crossed over to the other side. A large crowd surrounded Jesus, and in that crowd, was another person with a desperate need, a woman who had reached the end of her rope. Life had been exceptionally cruel to this woman. A wall, an obstacle, had been placed in her life that neither she or anyone else could remove. And that wall, that obstacle, blocked her from the joys of life that others, including us, take for granted. Consider for a moment her situation.

She had an issue of blood. We're not told exactly what it was - perhaps a menstrual disorder. Whatever it was, she had been bleeding for twelve years, and this had a devastating effect on all areas of her life. Her condition made her Levitically, or ceremonially, unclean. That meant that anyone or anything she touched, or that touched her, became unclean and had to go through a ritualistic cleansing. We're not told if she had a husband or children, but if she did, think of the devastating effect her condition had on her marriage and family life. Even household utensils she touched were considered unclean. Think of the terrible impact her condition had on her friendships and social life. She was not allowed to enter the temple in her condition. Spiritually, physically, and socially she was isolated, an outcast, ostracized by society. And she had suffered this bleeding and her isolation for twelve years.

All attempts at healing had failed. She had suffered much from many doctors over the years, and she had spent all she had. And her condition had only gotten worse. She was physically exhausted and drained of energy by the constant bleeding. She lived each day in a body she didn't want and no one else wanted either. She had reached the end of the line and was down to her last prayer and final ray of hope. And what was that final ray of hope, that last prayer? She had heard of the things about Jesus, the man who taught with authority and healed miraculously. And she thought to herself: "If I can just touch the bottom of his outer garment, I will be healed." She had no guarantee of healing. What she did have was the absolute conviction that Jesus could help, and the firm hope that He would help. And such conviction and hope is what makes up faith.

Faith is not the belief that God will do what we want Him to do; faith is the belief that God will do what is right for us. And only God knows what is right for us because only God knows us completely. Faith and hope go together like hand and glove. Hope without faith is futile, and faith without hope is an empty shell. The faith and hope of this woman is shown by her statement: "If I just touch his garment, I will be healed."

But faith requires action. To touch Jesus' garment, she must work her way through that crowd and reach out to touch Him. And this was a risky venture. To make her way through that crowd, she would surely touch others, and if anyone recognized her, she would be strongly rebuked and condemned since she was unclean. And then, what would be this man Jesus' response if He knew that she who was unclean had touched Him? Would He rebuke her and refuse to heal her? But she had no other alternative, only her hope and faith that she would receive healing if she touched his garment. Perhaps, in the excitement of the crowd, she could make her way to Jesus unnoticed, and if she approached Him from behind and just touched his cloak, He would not notice her.

Her motive was not to steal healing from Jesus, but to keep her disease hidden. If she came to Jesus openly, she would have to tell Him what her disease was and suffer the shame of it in front of Him and that crowd. And so, she dares to take the chance, dares to get close to Jesus and touch his cloak.

Like all true Jews, Jesus wore the Shimla, a large, square cloth that was used as an outer cloak or robe. It had tassels at the four corners. The tassels were attached to blue cords. Two of the corners of the cloak were thrown back over the shoulder so that two of the tassels hung down behind. The woman probably touched one of these tassels.

Immediately the bleeding stopped and the woman realized that she was healed of her scourge and freed from her suffering. But that is not the end of the miracle. There is more to come. The woman thought that after being healed, she could steal away in the crowd. But Jesus, knowing that power had gone out from Him, turned around and asked: "Who touched my clothes?" His disciples, surprised that He would ask this, said: "You see the people crowding against you, and yet you ask: "Who touched Me?" They didn't know that the woman's touch was different. It was the touch of faith, and that triggered a divine response from Jesus. God responds to the touch of faith.

Some say that this outgo of power from Jesus was without His knowledge or volition, but that is to misunderstand it. Nothing happens without God's knowledge, and being God as well as Man, Jesus divine power was always under the control of Jesus' conscious will. And being One with the Father and the Holy Spirit, Jesus' divine power and will are the same as the Father's and the Holy Spirit's divine power and will. God graciously healed the woman through his Son, but the instant the woman touched Jesus, in His all-knowing omniscience Jesus knew it, knew her ailment, willed her healing, and knew that power had gone out of Him to work a miracle.

Jesus insisted that the one who had touched Him come forward. Did He not know who it was? Of course He did! We're told that He looked around to see who had done it, and we can be sure His eyes looked into the eyes of the woman. The woman, who had touched Jesus secretly, was hoping she could leave the scene and no one would know what she had done. But this was not to be. Jesus made the woman reveal herself. Why? She came and fell at His feet, trembling with fear, knowing that she had to tell Him the truth, admit to Him amidst that crowd that she had violated the ritual law of uncleanness. Was this cruel of Jesus? No! He made her come forward for her own sake, and also for the sake of the people in that crowd thronging around Him. And there is an important lesson here for all of us, as follows.

The woman was healed of her physical disease, but Jesus had further healing in mind. For the healing process to be complete in the woman, it was necessary for her to speak the whole truth concerning her condition and her need to the One Who had healed her. Total honesty with Jesus was required for her to be completely healed - spiritually and emotionally, as well as physically. This was necessary to close for good that long chapter of suffering in her life.

Jesus knew that her needs went beyond just physical healing. He knew how she had suffered, and He knew that she needed to be assured that she had not done anything wrong or improper in touching Him in faith and receiving her healing that way. He assured her that there was nothing to be ashamed of or to hide in regard to the ailment and its miraculous removal. And He did that in front of that large crowd around Him, thus assuring that there would be no doubt of her healing on the part of the townspeople, and that her social isolation would end for good.

This is one of my favorite accounts of Jesus' healings. There is an awesome quality to this scene, a wondrous intimacy. Imagine if you will that dusty street and the milling crowd, the woman who was an outcast of society, prostrate before Jesus, pouring out her heart to Him. And imagine Jesus, the Son of God and Son of Man, in His full divinity and humanity, ignoring the crowd and giving His full attention to this poor woman. The woman abandons herself to her Creator and Redeemer, and her Creator and Redeemer personally ministers to her, speaking comfort and peace to her, assuring her of her healing and restoration. Jesus tells her: "Daughter, your faith has healed you. Go in peace and be freed from your suffering."

This is the only time that Jesus referred to an individual as "Daughter." And it was to an outcast of society and spoken in the midst of that crowd. His use of the term speaks of His loving concern for her. Imagine how this made the woman feel. Jesus not only removed the terrible burden of her physical disease; He removed the burden of her shame and He restored her dignity. And He gave her the gift of peace. The result - total healing.

In His ministry, death, and resurrection, Jesus made possible an intimacy between God and His human creation that had not existed since before the fall of man in the Garden of Eden. Jesus, the GodMan, became one of us, and experienced firsthand the obstacles, the hurts, the burdens in our lives. We all have our times of bleeding in this life. Sometimes we face obstacles and burdens that overwhelm us, that we can't remove or even budge, just like that woman. And no one else can remove it. Doctors, counselors, pastors, friends haven't been able to remove it. And so we bleed. Perhaps over the death of a loved one that ripped the fabric of life in two; perhaps over a marriage that has failed or is tottering on the brink; perhaps over a child who is struggling in life with an obstacle of their own that they can't budge, and that we can't remove for them; perhaps over a physical disability that drains all energy; perhaps over some dreaded news just received from the doctor; perhaps over a lost job or career, or financial crisis. Life has a way of making us bleed at times.

I know one obstacle, one burden we all have in common. And that is sin. Sin saps our energies, drains us just as physical bleeding does. Through sin, Satan tries to bleed us of our faith, our hope, our vitality. The woman in our passage was down to her last hope, her last prayer. There was nowhere else to turn but to Jesus. When you are down to your last hope, your last prayer, you are down to Jesus, and the only thing left is an act of faith. Reach out to Jesus. Reach out to touch Him and let Him touch you. To connect with the life-giving, life-sustaining, healing power of Jesus, you have got to reach out to Him. And you can be assured that Jesus never refuses a genuine act of faith. He has promised to response in His time, and in the way He knows will lead to our highest good.

For the woman in our passage, healing was immediate. For others, it may take longer. And for some, physical healing may not come until they see their Lord face-to-face. It is a fact that God may choose not to remove a person's physical disability because He wants to use that person and their disability to bring glory to Him and to that person, to serve as a strong witness of faith to others. This was the case with the Apostle Paul. Three times Paul begged the Lord to take away his disability, what he called his "thorn in the flesh," and three times the Lord told him "no." The Lord told him: "My grace is sufficient for all things, and my strength is made perfect in your weakness." What greater witness is there than a physically disabled person who, while struggling with their disability, lives a life of worship, faith, obedience, commitment, and service to their Lord. Such disciples are special to the Lord, and their reward will be great.

One thing we all can be absolutely sure of is that Jesus will do what is right and best for each of us. He will do what He knows is right for you because He created you, redeemed you, sustains you, loves you, and knows you and your needs completely. He has promised that whoever seeks Him, reaches out to Him, will most certainly find Him and be touched by Him.

Reaching out to Jesus can be a risky venture for us, just as it was for that woman. It requires an honesty with God that we might hesitate to give just as that woman didn't want Jesus or the crowd to know her condition. Reaching out to Jesus requires the courage to face the anger and ridicule of the crowd, or worse yet, the anger and ridicule of friends and those close to us. Reaching out to Jesus requires the faith and hope of that woman in the midst of the darkness and desperation surrounding us.

Reach out to Jesus. Scripture tells us that He sympathizes with our weaknesses. He understands better than we do the obstacles and burdens in our lives. He had a terrible burden in His life on this earth. His whole life was a journey towards that burden - the cross. And on that cross, He made it possible for our sins, our greatest burden, and the burden from which every other burden in life stems, to be healed and removed, washed clean in His Blood. His redeeming us from sin, death, and hell is the greatest healing of all time.

Reach out to Jesus Who hears and understands your cries of suffering and desperation, for He too cried out in desperation to His Father to remove His burden, the cross. But, in His case, the Father said "no!" It had to be "no" because if the Father had not said "no," the burden of our sin could not have been removed and we would be crushed into eternal death by its terrible weight. It was for our sakes the Father said "no" so the Rock of Salvation, Jesus Christ could remove the terrible burden of sin from us.

Reach out to Jesus with your bleeding condition, for He, more than anyone, knows what it is to bleed. On Calvary, in the dirt, grime, agony, and humiliation of the cross, Jesus, the GodMan Himself, poured out

His Blood to make it possible for our bleeding to be healed. And His Blood just keeps on cleansing and healing us day by day, every day, right up to the time we leave this life to go be with Him, or He returns to take us to glory with Him, whichever occurs first, when all bleeding will stop once and for all.

Don't let the times of bleeding in this life crush you. When your world is dark, remember that there is still light. Jesus said: "I am the Light of the world." All the powers of Satan, hell, and this world cannot extinguish that Light. And that Light is yours and mine through faith and hope.

God grant to each of us the courage, the faith and the hope of the woman with the bleeding condition to reach out to touch Jesus. God grant to each of us the honesty of that woman to be truthful with our Lord concerning our bleeding, our burdens, our sin and shame. And God grant to each of us the assurance and conviction of that woman, so we too may say: "If I only reach out and touch Him, I will be healed." Thank you Jesus for your healing touch. Amen.

ABRAHAM'S FAITH AND FULFILLMENT

Text: Genesis 15: 1-6; Hebrews 11: 8-12; John 8: 51-59.

Theme: Abraham's Faith; a Faith Unconquered.

Theme Statement: God encourages us, just as He did Abraham, not to give up or give way to fear when things look hopeless. God is always ready to hear our honest complaints, brought to Him in faith and reverence, just as He heard Abraham's complaint that, although God had promised him a son through Whom all peoples would be blessed, he remained childless.   God responded to Abraham's fear and disappointment with His word of assurance, that He, God, was Abraham's shield and very great reward, and that Abraham would certainly have that son, and through his seed all peoples on earth would certainly be blessed. And so it came to pass that Abraham, 100 years old, and Sarah his wife, 90 years old, had a son Isaac. But more, much more! When Jesus, Son of God, came to earth and took on our humanity as Son of Man to accomplish the will of the Father, which was human redemption, and through Him all peoples would be blessed, Jesus, Son of God and Son of Man, also became Son of Abraham.

Key Passage: John 8: 58. "I tell you the truth," Jesus answered, "before Abraham was born, I AM!"

God's call came to Abraham when he was 75 years old. God told Abraham: "Leave your country, your people and your father's household and go to the land I will show you. I will make you into a great nation and I will bless you; I will make your name great, and you will be a blessing. I will bless those who bless you, and whoever curses you I will curse; and all peoples on earth will be blessed through you."

The first great evidence of Abraham's faith is his obedience. We're told that he left, as the Lord had told him. Think of that! A man, 75 years old, at a time of life when one thinks of living out one's life in ease and comfort, enjoying the fruits of one's labor, told to pull up stakes and leave and go to a far off land that God would show him. You would think that God could have at least told him where he was going. Abraham believed God's promise and went out not knowing where he was going. He went wholly and completely in faith and trust, and we're told that his faith was counted to him as righteousness. When I consider such faith, my faith appears as miniscule.

In our Genesis reading, Abraham was apparently growing weary of waiting for the fulfillment of God's promise and experiencing some fear and misgiving. God had promised that through Abraham's seed all peoples on earth would be blessed. What seed? He was probably in his eighties by now and his wife Sarah, 10 years younger, well past the age of childbearing. And so, Abraham brings his complaint to God, reverently and honestly. "O Sovereign Lord, what can You give me since I remain childless…You have given me no children."

God honored Abraham's complaint, just as He is always ready to hear our honest fears, doubts, and complaints brought to Him in faith and reverence. God is a Friend whose ear is always open to His people. God responded to Abraham's fear and doubt, and encouraged and reassured him, just as He responds to our fears and doubts and encourages and reassures us when we pour out our hearts to Him. God tells Abraham, and us, "Do not be afraid, I am your shield, your very great reward." God knew Abraham's fears; He knows the fears of each of us because He knows us completely. Why should Abraham and we not be afraid? Because God is our shield. Therefore, we need not give way to fear, no matter what happens, no matter how impossible things appear. And certainly the situation appeared impossible to Abraham.

And God tells Abraham, and us, that He, God, is our very great reward. God is not only our rewarder; He is Himself our great reward - the Father Who pours out His grace on us; the Son Who purchased our salvation for us with His Body and Blood; the Holy Spirit Who brought us to saving faith and Who sustains and sanctifies us in that faith. And the rewards of a believing and obedient faith are waiting to be bestowed on us, just as the rewards of Abraham's believing and obedient faith were waiting to be bestowed on him.

God reassures Abraham and again promises him a son, and to emphasize His reassurance, God shows him the stars of the heaven and tells him, "so shall your offspring be." The Word by which God created the stars would also guarantee Abraham a son. God also promised to Abraham that He would give to his descendants the entire land of Canaan. We're told that Abraham considered Him faithful Who made the promise; he believed the Lord and the Lord credited it to him as righteousness. Abraham was declared righteousness, not by his works, but by his faith. So are we! The works were simply evidence of his faith, just as ours are of our faith. And so, the miracle happened. Abraham, 100 years old, and Sarah his wife, 90 years old, had a son Isaac, the son of promise. And from this one man, Abraham, would come descendants as numerous as the stars in the sky and as countless as the sand on the seashore. Abraham is the biological father of all Jews, of all Arabs, and the spiritual father of all Christians.

In Hebrews 11:1, we're told: "Faith is being sure of what we hope for and certain of what we do not see." This was Abraham's faith, and in this faith he lived and died. He knew that the earthly inheritance of the land would come long after his death. God had told him as much. But it probably made little difference to him since he knew God's promise would be fulfilled. And as we're told in Hebrews, he was looking forward to not only a temporal fulfillment, but even more, to an eternal fulfillment. He was looking forward to the city with foundations, whose architect and builder is God. As his spiritual descendants, we look forward to the same. And so, in God the Father's perfect timing, that other descendant promised to Abraham through Whom all peoples on earth would be blessed, was born in a stable in Bethlehem - the Son of God Who also became Son of Man and Son of Abraham, the Messiah, the Savior.

In our Gospel reading, Jesus refutes the Jewish leaders claim of Abraham as their spiritual father - biological yes, but spiritual no. Abraham's faith was counted to him as righteousness before God, whereas the Jewish leaders looked to the law and obedience thereto for righteousness. Therefore, Abraham was not their spiritual father.

Jesus had just told them: "I tell you the truth, if anyone keeps my Word, he will never see death." The Jews thought Jesus was demon possessed because of this claim. "Abraham and the Prophets had died," they said, "yet You say that if anyone keeps your Word, he will never taste death. Are You greater than our father Abraham?....Who do You think You are?"

In their blindness they had substituted physical death for eternal death. They should have known better. Jesus had often told them of eternal life of which He was now speaking. They may have known this, but in their hardness of heart, their wicked intention was to not understand or accept whatever He might say if it did not serve their purpose. "Who do You think You are?" they ask Jesus. That He is greater, infinitely greater than Abraham, the Prophets, or any mere man, they reject, no matter all the evidence of their Scriptures, the miracles, the proofs Jesus had given them in regard to His deity. There are many like them today, whose hearts are hardened and who reject God's grace poured out through His Son.

Jesus tells them that if He glorifies Himself, His glory is nothing. It is His Father Whom they claim as their God, Who glorifies Him. What a contrast with these Jewish leaders whose priority was their own glory, their own status. Jesus declares Who He is, the Son of the Heavenly Father. The Jews may dishonor Him, but God the Father not only honors Him, but glorifies Him.

Jesus tells them, "Though you do not know Him, I know Him and keep His Word." Here the Greek gives a fuller understanding of what Jesus is saying. When He says, "I know the Father," He uses the Greek word *oida* for know. This word refers to the very presence of the Son with the Father, the knowing that comes from the Oneness of the Son with the Father. When He says that the Jews do not know the Father, He uses the Greek word *ginosko* for know, which is knowing God through experience, learning, knowledge, through His Word. Jesus tells them that they do not possess even this knowing of God. Their conception of the true God was in conflict with the revelation God had given of Himself in His Word. When Jesus says, "I know Him and keep His Word," He is claiming both types of knowledge of the Father - His Presence and Oneness with the Father, and His knowledge of the Father's will and the keeping of His Word. Jesus is keeping, witnessing, and defending the Father's Word.

Jesus not only states the facts of His relationship with the Father, but then states His relation to Abraham whom they consider their spiritual and biological father. Jesus tells them, "Your father Abraham rejoiced at the thought of seeing my day; he saw it and was glad." He is telling them that Abraham's response to Him was very different from their response. The Jews answer: "You are not yet fifty years old, and You have seen Abraham!" And then Jesus gives the answer that drives them into a rage. "I tell you the truth," Jesus says with the strongest emphasis, "before Abraham was born, I AM!"

Jesus does not say, "I was," for this would infer a beginning for Jesus, just as for Abraham. Jesus says, "I AM!" which means absolute existence with no point of beginning or end - from everlasting to everlasting. Jesus declares that although His earthly existence covers less than fifty years, His existence as a Person is constant and independent of any beginning in time like that of Abraham and all humanity.

With these words, Jesus testifies to His divine, eternal, preexistence. When Moses asked God "what is your Name?" God told him "I AM is my Name" - YAHWEH. That Name was so hallowed by the Jews that they wouldn't even say it for fear of offending it. And here this Jesus of Nazareth uses the Name to refer to Himself. And in doing so, He clearly, forcefully, declares Himself to be the Son of God - God Himself. The Jews understood this, and to them it was rank blasphemy.

They took up stones to kill Him, but apparently as they went to get stones, Jesus was able to slip away from the temple grounds.

Christ, in His humanity, is the Son of Abraham. When Isaac was born to Abraham and Sarah, Abraham saw the beginning of the fulfillment of God's promise that through his seed all peoples of the earth would be blessed, that seed being the Messiah, Christ, now speaking to the Jews. Abraham was not Jesus' biological father. Jesus was conceived by the Holy Spirit and had no biological father; nevertheless, He is the Son of Abraham, just as He is the Son of David. Abraham did see Jesus' day, and was glad.

Moreover, all believers in Christ are sons and daughters of Abraham, as the Apostle Paul tells us. Christ is the Source of our faith; Abraham the human spiritual father of our faith. In Romans 4, Paul makes the faith of Abraham a standing example. He says: "Against all hope, Abraham in hope believed and so became the father of many nations. He did not waver through unbelief regarding the promise of God, but was strengthened in his faith and gave glory to God, being fully persuaded that God had power to do what He had promised. This is why 'it was credited to him as righteousness.'"

The words 'it was credited to him' were written not for him alone, but also for us, to whom God will credit righteousness - for us who believe in Him, our Father God, the Son our Savior, the Messiah, and the Holy Spirit, our Counselor Who sanctifies us in the true, saving faith, one God from everlasting to everlasting.

Martin Luther described faith as being like glue. "It glues a believer's heart to God's promises." Such was the faith of Abraham. What a faith! What a faith! God grant to each of us such a faith today and beyond as we eagerly look forward to the glorious return of Him through Whom God promised Abraham that all peoples would be blessed - Christ our Lord and Savior, Son of God and Son of Abraham. Amen.

CALL HER BLESSED

Text: Judges 4:4-9; Proverbs 31:10-11, 20, 25-31; Luke 2:34-35

Theme: The Might of Motherhood.

> Theme Sentence: The earliest shaping force in every life is a woman's - a mother's - and the love of a godly mother is a reflection of God's love and grace.

✝

It was another of those terrible periods in Israel's history when the people gave themselves over to evil. They had turned away from God and sank into the sewer of Baal-worship. And so God allowed them to fall into the hands of Jabin, a king of Canaan who cruelly oppressed them. The commander of the Canaanite army was Sisera, and he had nine hundred iron chariots at his disposal. The Israelites were terrorized; they were paralyzed with fear of Sisera and his nine hundred iron chariots. But in the hill country between Ramah and Bethel there lived a woman who had not bowed the knee to Baal, a woman who was not afraid - Deborah. Throughout the period of the judges in Israel's history, women played important roles, but Deborah was the most outstanding. She was a Wife, Mother, and Prophetess. And she was a Judge. She judged Israel, which means she was God's chosen leader of all Israel. She was undoubtedly a person sensitive to God's leading, for we are told that the Israelites came to her for decisions.

We don't know anything about her husband, Lapidoth. Who knows? Maybe he stayed home and did the cooking, the laundry, took the kids to soccer and little league. At any rate, if he had an image problem with his wife being the leader of Israel, we're not told about it. Israel desperately needed leadership, and God appointed Deborah. One might ask, "Where were the men?" The implication here is that there was a lack of qualified and/or willing men. It is interesting that when Deborah gave Barak, who was to lead the Israelite army against the Canaanites, the battle plan the Lord had given her, Barak's response was, "If you go with me, I will go, but if you don't go with me, I won't go." His response gives us a measure of Deborah's greatness. And Deborah told him, "Very well, I'll go, but because of your demand, the honor will not be yours, for the Lord will hand the enemy Sisera over to a woman." Well, God gave the Israelites a great victory which brought peace to the land for forty years. And the enemy Sisera - he was killed by Jael, another woman.

But that's not the end of the account. After the victory, Deborah sang a song of praise to God - the song of Deborah given to us in chapter 5 of the Book of Judges. And what's fascinating is that in her song she didn't refer to herself as a prophetess or a judge, or even as a great military victor. She just called herself a mother. In Judges 5:7, Deborah sings, "Village life in Israel ceased, ceased until I, Deborah arose, arose a mother in Israel." When God needed someone to do a mighty job, gender wasn't an issue. When God needed a supermom, He knew where to look. For Israel at this time, God's best man was a woman.

In a very real sense, every mother is a prophetess with a prophet's calling. The first shaping force in every life is a woman's - a mother's. And sadly, more often than not, it is the mother who has to be the spiritual instructor to her children, instead of both husband and wife filling this most important God-given responsibility. Like the men in Deborah's day, too many fathers today are timid, hesitant, faltering, when it comes to giving their children a solid, Biblical, Christ-centered foundation upon which to build their lives. I think there will be a lot of embarrassed fathers in heaven when the Lord asks them why they failed to obey His command to teach their children His Word, and then when He tells them they should be grateful that He gave them godly wives and mothers of their children who obeyed His command when they failed to. I'm thankful that I won't have to be one of those fathers because after we were married for some years, my wife pointedly told me, "You, as husband and father are appointed by God to be spiritual leader of this family. I suggest that you get with it!"

Ask any group of people where they got their first spiritual training and instruction, and I'll bet that the majority will answer, "from my mother." A man was once telling a friend about his loving memories of his mother when he stopped, hesitated a moment, then said, "You know, as a boy I received my first lesson in theology from my mother. It was when she told me, "God help you if you ever do that again."

A man who was raised by a godly mother was telling how, when he was rocked to sleep at night, his mother didn't sing to him just the little ditties and lullabies. She sang to him the hymns of faith. He remembered her singing to him "A Mighty Fortress is our God," "More Love to Thee, O Christ," "My Jesus, I love Thee," "Come, Thou Fount of Every Blessing." She sang the deep songs. And he said, "I remember, I remember those hymns. And when I got to church, I had already heard and learned many of the hymns." That godly mother made a contribution to her son's life that he would never forget.

Chief among the blessings of life is having, or having had, a godly mother. Abraham Lincoln said it well when he said, "No one is poor who had a godly mother." The grandest title ever given to woman is "mother." A mother's tender love for her children is a direct reflection of God's tender love for us. And that love is the mightiest force on earth. "Mighty is the force of motherhood" says the poet across the ages. The motherhood instinct is latent in every woman.

And it's a great thing to enlist this motherhood instinct in public service too. It was the mother's heart in Deborah that agonized over her peoples' misery. It was her motherly concern for her distressed children that stirred her to action. Deborah, as a mother in Israel, acts like the mother of Israel. One of the unfortunate mistakes, common today even in women, is to suppose that a woman must become more masculine in order to be effective in the public arena. On the contrary, what society, business, politics, desperately need are womanly women who will raise and soften and humanize the work by exercising the very gifts God gave them - the gifts that make mother the center of the home.

Deborah's public service did not lessen, but increased, her simple faith in the God of her fathers. It is a tragedy that many of the well-known, so-called, women leaders of today are conspicuous, not for their faith, but for their lack of it. The Light of the World, Jesus Christ, does not shine from their souls. And as Alfred Tennyson, the poet said, "What the sun is to the sunflower, so is Jesus Christ to a woman's soul." What this world needs is more women leaders like Deborah.

Deborah was what we would call a Proverbs 31 woman. Our reading from Proverbs is part of a poem of praise for the godly wife and mother. It might be considered unrealistically ideal; yet, it is the ideal God's Word gives us. The wife and mother described here is almost a personification of wisdom. And like wisdom, she is "worth far more than rubies." And guys, here's something for us to ponder - both the Old Testament Hebrew word for wisdom and the New Testament Greek word for wisdom are feminine nouns. The woman described in Proverbs 31 is the crown of her husband. She is a source of content, not sorrow, to him. She is a diligent and willing worker. Her day begins early to prepare food for her household. She is a good manager to organize and run the household. Tell me, does a wife and mother of young children need to be a good manager? You bet!

The woman described here is also a good investor. Her opinions are necessary to the success of the family's finances. I think that women often have a keener insight regarding finances than men do. The woman in Proverbs is efficient, spinning and weaving coverings for the bed, clothing for her family, garments to sell. She is energetic, making one tired just to read all this woman does. And I'll bet most husbands today aren't aware of many of the things their wives do to make and maintain a home. Motherhood is energy intensive, especially with little children whose demands can be all-consuming. A wife once said to her husband, "Honey, I'm sort of forgetting what our baby's face looks like, I'm spending so much time at the other end."

I think all wives and mothers often feel like the mother in a cartoon which showed a father and a three-year old boy, standing in front of the parent's bedroom door, which was shut. On the door, was a sign written by the weary wife and mother - "Closed for business. Motherhood out of order." The most important and fulfilling responsibility in this life is raising children. At the same time, it is the most difficult and frustrating job. Mothers can be forgiven for sometimes feeling like the mother of three unruly preschoolers who, when asked whether she would have children if she had it to do over again said, "Sure, just not the same three!"

The Proverbs 31 woman is a woman of mature character. And her character comes from her acknowledging God in every aspect of her life. She speaks wisely and kindly. Her talk is not empty, aimless chatter or gossip. She is not a dominating woman, but one who has the confidence of all because of her kind ways. Her love is so great that it reaches out beyond her family to include the poor and needy, and this helps her children to grow up to be unselfish and self-giving. Because of her effectiveness as a wife and mother, her husband can exercise his full powers as an elder and leader in the community. The old saying, "Behind every successful man is a woman" seems to be the emphasis here. Finally, in spite of all her hard work, she never loses her God-given feminine charm. And then, the highest praise - bestowed on her by her husband and children. Her husband tells her that "she surpasses all other women," and her children "rise up and call her blessed." Only a woman whose high character comes from a way of life that acknowledges God in every sphere of life will measure up to the picture of wife and mother given here. And only God's help, strength, and grace can make that possible. Truly, truly, such a woman deserves to be called blessed.

Jesus, during His life and ministry on earth, honored women. Women were included in His inner circle and they fulfilled essential roles in supporting His ministry. In our Gospel reading, we see Jesus' love for His mother, and His mother's love for her Son. Mary, along with the other women, was at the cross. Her love for her Son impelled her to be with Him right to the end, as horrible as it was. Isn't that just like a mother? Mary had already paid a high price for the privilege of

184

being the human mother of the Messiah. Doubtless, she had suffered much reproach and slander for what many would have considered her illegitimate child. But the worst suffering she was to experience had now come. I'm sure that Mary, devastated at the sight of her Son hanging on that cross, remembered the words of the prophet Simeon, spoken to her when she and Joseph had taken the baby Jesus to the temple to present Him to God. After Simeon prophesied concerning the Messiahship and ministry of Jesus, he told Mary, "And a sword will pierce you own soul too!" That prophecy was now being fulfilled. In remaining with her Son until He gave up His Spirit, Mary shows us a mother's love.

And Jesus shows His love for His mother. In the throes of agony, as the perfect sacrifice bearing the sins of the world - your sins and my sins - amid His indescribable, incomprehensible, personal suffering as the ransom for our redemption and salvation, amid all this, Jesus fulfills the fourth commandment - "Honor your father and mother." Even now as He dies, His mother is in His heart. In the highest love, Jesus provides for His mother in her remaining years. He chooses John, the disciple closest to Him, as a substitute son to care for His mother. John was with His mother at the cross, supporting her in her overwhelming grief. Mother-love is usually rated as the purest and strongest type of human love, but the love of Jesus for His mother, as well as for you and me and all His human creation, exceeds even mother-love.

There is a well-known painting which pictures the mother of Jesus being led gently away from the terrible scene after her Son's crucifixion. She is broken-hearted, crushed by the sights she has witnessed; yet on her countenance a strange light glows, suggesting faith. The painter was a man of insight, for he added a touch of his own. In Mary's hand, he placed the crown of thorns which had pierced the brow of Jesus, as though instinctively she had lifted the cruel thing from her Son's head. Isn't that just what a mother would do? In our own lives, wasn't it mother who pulled out the thorns, bandaged the cuts, caressed the fevered brow, wiped away the tears, bound up the wounds, whispered the words of comfort?

God in His wisdom bestowed on mothers an awesome power. Godly mothers, more than any other human beings, shape the individual. Mothers have shaped the destiny of nations. And what a great thrill and blessing it is to point to a wonderful woman and be able to say to all the world, "That's my mother!"

"If I were hanged on the highest hill,

I know whose love would follow me still.

If I were drowned in the deepest sea,

I know whose tears would come down to me.

If I were damned by body and soul,

I know whose prayers would make me whole.

Mother of mine, O Mother of mine."

(Kipling)

Mother! "Call her blessed!" Thank You God for mothers. And thank You God for the mother's love, as well as the father's love, that You poured out for us in Jesus Christ, Your Son, our Lord and Savior. Amen.

CHAPTER 7 - WARNINGS

"Unless the Lord had given me help, I would soon have dwelt in the silence of death. When I said, 'My foot is slipping,' Your love, O Lord, supported me. When anxiety was great within me, Your consolation brought joy to my soul."

Psalm 94:17-19

1 Peter 5:8
Be sober, be vigilant; because your adversary the devil, as a roaring lion, walketh about, seeking whom he may devour

THE DEADLY SILENCE

Text: Psalm 32; Romans 4: 1-12; Luke 15: 1-10.

Theme: The devastating effects of unrepentance.

Theme Statement: In this Penitential Psalm, David describes the devastating spiritual, physical, and psychological effects of his failure to repent of sin, and the blessed relief of his suffering when he came to his senses, bared his soul to God In confession and repentance of his sin and received God's pardon and cleansing of his sin, guilt, and shame. David teaches us not to keep silent as he did, the foolishness of ignoring sin or trying to hide it from God, and that when we confess and seek God's forgiveness of our sin, He instantly responds and forgives and removes that sin from us for good. The Blood of Jesus Christ just keeps on cleansing us of sin.

Key Passage: Psalm 32: 5. "Then I acknowledged my sin to You and did not cover up my iniquity. I said, 'I will confess my transgressions to the Lord' — and You forgave the guilt of my sin."

✝

Here we consider Psalm 32, a Penitential Psalm of David, entitled a Meskil. The term is generally taken as a literary or musical term to be the tune to which it was set and was to be sung. Others think the term more significant, a psalm of instruction. And there is nothing in which we have more need of instruction than in the nature of true blessedness which David speaks of, what it consists of, and what we must do to receive it.

When David prays, "Blessed is he whose transgressions are forgiven, whose sins are covered. Blessed is the man whose sin the Lord does not count against him, and in whose spirit is no deceit," he identifies the ground, the foundation of blessedness from which all other ingredients of blessedness flow. Only those who God forgives by grace for the sake of His Son have this blessedness.

Upon our confession and repentance, our sins are forgiven for Jesus' sake Who paid the full and terrible price for them on the cross. The punishment which is ours by virtue of the sentence of the law was placed on Christ hanging on the cross, and we are cleansed in His Blood. God laid upon Him the iniquity of us all and made Him to be sin for us. He robes us in Christ's righteousness to remove our guilt and shame. Sin makes us loathsome in the sight of God and utterly unfit for communion with Him. And when our conscience is awakened, when convicted by the Holy Spirit, sin makes us loathsome to ourselves also. Only the Blood of Christ can cleanse us of this loathing.

This describes David's condition which he speaks of in this Psalm. His terrible sin is not identified in the Psalm, but given the extent of his suffering, it was probably his sin of adultery with Bathsheba and then his ordering the murder of her husband Uriah. David says, "When I kept silent, my bones wasted away through my groaning all day long." Why his silence? Perhaps he was terrified of God's wrath and hot displeasure. Perhaps he was so overwhelmed with shame and guilt that he wanted to hide his sin from God. After all, he was the one who God described as "a man after my own heart." He was the one who, as a boy, had slain the Philistine giant Goliath. He was the one whom God had saved from countless dangers and threats to his life during the ten years between Samuel anointing him as King of Israel and his being placed on the throne. He was the one to whom God promised that his descendant - the Messiah - would establish a kingdom that would be an everlasting kingdom.

What does David teach us in this Psalm? First, he teaches us that keeping silent about our sin before God out of shame, guilt, or for whatever reason, only makes the condition far worse. He says, "When I kept silent, my bones wasted away through my groaning all day long." The infection of sin, if not cleansed and healed, will fester and grow intolerably loathsome and painful. Scripture tells us that he that covers his sins shall not prosper. David's stubborn silence of unconfessed sin filled his life with groaning. The pain of his unconfessed sin affected his whole being, his spiritual being, his physical being, his mental being, his emotional being. And so it is with us, if we refuse to be honest with God about our sin.

Second, David teaches us that one cannot hide from God, and it is utter folly to try. David says, "For day and night your hand was heavy upon me." The hand of divine wrath against sin was heavy on David, causing extreme anguish of his spirit and soul, and this anguish was having a terrible effect on his body. David says, "My strength was sapped as in the heat of summer." David, the mighty warrior who had slain thousands of Israel's enemies, who was feared by the other nations, was reduced to weakness and frailty because of his sin. Did God bring this spiritual, physical, and mental suffering on David as punishment for his sin? No! God intended for this suffering to bring David to the point where he would confess and repent of his sin. God's primary goal in dealing with our sin is not punishment, but our repentance so He can forgive, cleanse, and restore us.

It has been said that God is more ready to pardon our sin upon our repentance than we are to repent in order to obtain that pardon. God is eager, anxious, and ready to forgive the sins of those who sincerely confess and repent of them. Why? For two reasons: 1. Because His Son suffered the full and terrible punishment for our sins so we can be forgiven, cleansed, and reconciled to the Father, and 2. Because every child of God, including you and me, is more precious to Him than we can ever imagine. Our Gospel passage clearly shows us that.

In the Parable of the Lost Sheep, the Lost Sheep, of course, represents a lost sinner. The lost sheep strayed from the care and control of the shepherd. So the sinner strays from Jesus and is lost. The Good Shepherd leaves the ninety-nine in a safe place and goes to find the lost sheep. This pictures the inestimable value that God places upon the lost sinner. Man's attitude would be: What does one sheep matter? I still have ninety-nine. If the sheep is that dumb to stray, it deserves to be lost. The time and effort of seeking that lost sheep is too much, and then too, even with all that effort, it might not be found.

But God's attitude is: That lost sheep is precious to Me. I must find it. My Son poured out His Blood for that sheep. And so, in every case of a lost sheep, the Good Shepherd goes to find it. The climax of the parable is the joy over finding that lost sheep, a joy not only of the Shepherd and his neighbors and friends on earth, but a joy in heaven and before the angels of God. The very angels sing with delight. This sinner who has strayed and lived a long time without repentance, who is precious to God, now under the leading of the Holy Spirit and through the Good Shepherd Christ, repents and is saved and joins the ranks of the righteous. And this causes jubilation in heaven. All the mighty works of men cause no jubilation in heaven, but one miserable sinner's repentance does. It is that which causes the astounding joy. Repentance rings out in this Penitential Psalm of David, and it is that repentance which leads to the blessedness that David speaks of.

Well, David learned the lesson that one cannot hide from God. And apparently he learned it well, for in another Psalm he wrote the beautiful words, " Where can I go from your Spirit? Where can I flee from your Presence? If I go up to the heavens, you are there; if I make my bed in the depths, you are there. If I rise on the wings of the dawn; if I settle on the far side of the sea, even there your hand will guide me, your right hand will hold me fast."

Finally, David surrenders. The suffering caused by his deadly silence and his withdrawal from God had become unbearable. David says, "Then I acknowledged my sin to you, and did not cover up my iniquity. I said, I will confess my transgressions to the Lord — and you forgave the guilt of my sin." David went to the tabernacle, completely humbled himself before God and prayed that beautiful and powerful prayer of confession and repentance which we have in Psalm 51.

Acknowledgement of our sin to God is a vital component of a penitential prayer. And it requires total honesty with God, no attempt to whitewash or excuse or gloss over our sins. It is a confession of particulars, acknowledging the ugliness of our sin, the disobedience of our sin, the rebelliousness of our sin, the grievous offense to God caused by our sin. We confess our sins with shame and guilt, and with fear and trembling. Luther put it this way: "I will rebuke myself; then God will praise me. I will degrade myself; then God will honor me. I will accuse myself; then God will acquit me. I will speak against myself; then God will speak for me."

Another lesson David teaches us is that as soon as we confess our sins and repent of them, we are forgiven immediately. He says, "I will confess my transgressions to the Lord, and You forgave the guilt of my sin." Immediately he received the comfort of God's pardon and rest to his spirit, soul, and body. What an encouragement to us poor penitents, that we shall find God not only faithful and just, but gracious and kind to immediately forgive sins and remove them from us as far as the east is from the west.

David encourages us to come boldly to the throne of grace. "Therefore," he says, "let everyone who is godly pray to You," and he adds, "while You (God) may be found." David warns us not to do what he did - keep silent and expose ourselves to the suffering and pain he experienced. Instead, go speedily, immediately, to the Lord to acknowledge and confess sin and receive pardon "while He may be found," lest death cut us off, and then it will be too late to seek Him.

David assures those who are sincere and abundant in prayer that they will be safe in God's hands during times of trouble. Surely when the mighty waters rise, the waters of trouble, trial, temptation, hurt, loss, disappointment, whenever everything seems to be against us, the waters will not destroy us. The body may be destroyed, but the soul is safe in God's hands. In all the onrushing waters of affliction, Christ is our Rock of Refuge on which we stand so that they do not drown and devour us.

David professes his confidence in God. Having tasted the sweetness of divine grace to a penitent sinner, he knows that in that grace he will find both safety and joy. Safety is described in his words, "You are my hiding place; You will protect me from trouble." What greater safety is there than to be hidden in God? Joy is described in His words, "You will surround me with songs of deliverance." Wherever the child of God looks, in all situations and circumstances, he shall see occasion to rejoice and to praise God, and his brothers and sisters in Christ will join their songs of deliverance with his.

David says, "I will instruct you and teach you in the way you should go." Those best able to teach others the grace of God are those who have themselves experienced it. But in all things, it is God, through the Holy Spirit and the Word, both the Living Word - Christ - and the written Word Who will instruct us and teach us the way we should go - the way of the cross. It is He Who will counsel us and watch over us. We yield to His instruction and counsel, even when we don't understand it, especially when we don't understand it, just as Abraham did when God told him to leave his father's house, his land and his country, and go to a place God would show him. And Abraham obeyed, not knowing where he was going or what God was up to.

Paul tells us in our Epistle reading that "Abraham believed God, and it was credited to him as righteousness." Abraham is the prime Old Testament example of "justification by faith alone," and is known as the "spiritual father of all believers." All Christians are the true spiritual children of Abraham and are justified exactly as he was - through faith. And just as Abraham's good works glorified God and were evidence of his faith, so our good works glorify God and are evidence of our faith. But it is faith alone that justifies us. Faith alone, by grace alone, through Christ alone.

David gives a word of caution to us sinners. He says, "Do not be like the horse or mule that have no understanding, and must be controlled by bit and bridle. In his silence, David was like a beast before God, foolish and stubborn, and had to be controlled by God's chastening. He warns us not to be so, and we would be wise to heed his warning. Where there is renewing grace as all penitent sinners experience, there is no need of the bit and bridle of restraining grace.

David says, "Many are the woes of the wicked, but the Lord's unfailing love surrounds the man who trusts in Him." The wicked are those who rule themselves and do not want God's rule. They are surrounded by the wrath and judgment of God. Sin will have sorrow, and if not repented of, everlasting sorrow for the wicked. But those who trust in the Lord will be surrounded by the Lord's unfailing love and mercy. They shall never depart from God.

David ends the Psalm with an exhortation for us. He says, "Rejoice in the Lord and be glad you righteous; sing all you who are upright in heart." The heart that is right with God, and not wrapped up in self or in something other than God, has an abundance out of which it can rejoice, sing, praise, glory, strut and boast, but as the Apostle Paul says, " Let him who boasts, boast in the Lord."

Let them be so overwhelmed with holy joy as not to be able to contain it, and let their joy be a witness to others that a life of communion with God is the most blessed, pleasant, exciting, rewarding, fulfilling, and abundant life one can have in this world, and even far, far, greater in the next world, where we share the fullness of the Kingdom of Him Who is our all-in-all, the Son of Man, the Son of David, the Son of God - the Christ. Amen.

THOSE BIG EXCEPTS

Text: 1Kings 3: 3-14; Ephesians 5: 15-20; John 6: 51-58.

Theme: The "Excepts" that hinder us from following Christ in faith and obedience.

Theme Statement: Solomon humbled himself before God, and in answer to his prayer, God gave him wisdom and discernment greater than any other king. And God not only gave him wisdom which he asked for, but He gave him riches and wealth which he did not ask for. Yet, his life was a tragedy, mainly because of three big "excepts." 1. He loved the Lord, except he allowed and eventually participated in idolatry. 2. He loved the Lord, except he disobeyed the Lord's command and took to himself foreign wives. And 3, He loved the Lord, except he allowed the amassing of even more riches and wealth to become a priority of his rule. Those "excepts" resulted in disaster for Solomon and the people of Israel. What are the big "excepts" in our life that hinder us from following our Lord in faith and obedience?

Key Passage: 1Kings 3:3. "Solomon showed his love for the Lord by walking according to the statutes of his father David, except that he offered sacrifices and burned incense on the high places."

†

N o man has had greater potential for true greatness than Solomon. First, he had David for a father - David, God's warrior, poet, musician, military genius, who had a heart for God, and who God referred to as "a man after My own heart." Solomon had giant shoes to fill, and he knew it. He was only 20 years old when he became king. Israel was at the height of its power, and we can imagine how fearful and intimidated Solomon was over the crushing responsibility of leading this greatest of all nations and following in the footsteps of his father.

And so, when the Lord appeared to him in a dream and told him, "Ask for whatever you want Me to give you," Solomon humbled himself before God, acknowledged his own immaturity, his inexperience, and called himself a child. He prayed that God give him wisdom and a discerning heart to govern God's people and to distinguish between right and wrong, so he could lead the nation as God wanted him to lead the nation.

A discerning heart literally means "a hearing heart," a heart tuned to the voice of God through His Word. I wonder, do we have hearing hearts? In our prayer requests to God, is asking for wisdom, a "hearing heart," a priority of ours? Do we pray that our leaders have "hearing hearts" so that they lead this nation as God wants it to be led?Solomon's primary concern was not for himself, but for his people. He placed the good of God's people above his personal ambition or any desire to become a powerful and popular king. And he knew that his greatest need, the greatest gifts, were the wisdom and discernment that only God can give, and does give to those who ask.

And so, early in his reign, Solomon desired to be good more than great, and to serve God's will and honor more that to advance his own will and honor. His values were right from God's perspective. Therefore, God gave him what he requested - a wise, discerning heart and mind. So much so, that there has never been anyone so wise, except for the GodMan Jesus. And since Solomon requested what was most important - wisdom and discernment - God promised to also give him what was least important and what he did not ask for - riches and honor. Solomon had wisdom given to him because he asked for it, and wealth given to him because he did not ask for it. Long before Jesus gave His Sermon on the Mount, Solomon obeyed Jesus' commandment to "Seek first the kingdom of God and His righteousness, and all these things will be added to you."

God also promised Solomon long life upon the condition that he remain faithful to pursue the will of God and obey God's Word. Later in his reign, however, Solomon failed to meet that condition, and so, though he had riches and wealth above all others, he did not have as long a life to enjoy them as he might have had. He became king at 20 years of age and ruled for 40 years, which means that he only lived to the age of sixty.

How did Solomon fail to meet that condition? How could the train of Solomon's life, that was going straight down the track of God's will, end up a train wreck? I submit to you that it was because of the "excepts" in his life. You know what the "excepts" in life are, don't you? How often have you or I said, "I know I should do this, except…." Or, "I know I shouldn't do this, except….." We all have those "excepts" in our life. Solomon had three big "excepts" in his life which resulted in tragedy for him and for Israel. Let us consider those "excepts" and how they apply to our lives.

The first big "except" is mentioned early in our passage. "Solomon showed his love for the Lord by walking according to the statutes of his father David, except that he offered sacrifices and burned incense on the high places." Early on, the Israelites had adopted the Canaanite custom of offering sacrifices at altars on high places, hilltops and other elevations. The pagan Canaanites felt that the closer they got to heaven, the more likely their prayers and offerings would reach their pagan gods.

The Israelites were forbidden by Mosaic Law to use those Canaanite altars for worship and offerings to the Lord. They were instructed to break down, smash and burn those altars. Offering sacrifices at places other than the altar of the Tabernacle, which at the time was in Gibeon, or before the Ark of the Covenant, which was in Jerusalem, was prohibited. Why? Because God knew, and Moses had warned, that sacrifice and worship at pagan altars would lead to apostasy and syncretism. Syncretism is when you mix beliefs and practices of a pagan religion with the beliefs and practices of true religion. Those Canaanite altars had been used primarily to worship Baal, the god of fertility, and involved sexual activity with male and female prostitutes, and even occasional child sacrifice, all of which was abomination to God. And sure enough, eventually Israel started to incorporate some of the pagan

197

practices in their worship, thereby corrupting the true worship of the true God given them by God through Moses. The prophets strongly condemned this.

So, the first big "except" in Solomon's life involved idolatry. He failed to obey God's command concerning places of legitimate worship and the requirements for true worship. This failure of Solomon's brings up two questions we should each ask ourselves: 1. "Is my worship true worship, centered on Jesus Christ as Lord and Savior and on God's Word as absolute Truth?" If the answer is "yes," then my worship is accepted and blessed and anointed by God. If the answer is "no," then my worship is no better than that of those Israelites at the altars of Baal. And 2. "Am I faithful in my worship of the true God; faithful in going to the tabernacle, or today the Church, and worshipping with God's people as God's Word instructs me to do?" If my answer is "yes," then I am being faithful to my covenant with God. If my answer is "no," then I, like Solomon, am inconsistent in keeping the covenant I have with God through faith.

The second big "except" in Solomon's life was illicit pleasure, evidenced by his marriages. We're told in chapter 11, "Solomon loved many foreign women…they were from nations about which the Lord had told the Israelites, 'You must not intermarry with them because they will surely turn your hearts after their gods.' Nevertheless, Solomon held fast to them in love. He had 700 wives of royal birth from other nations and 300 concubines, and his wives led him astray. As Solomon grew old, his wives turned his heart after other gods, insisted that he join them in worshipping their idols, and his heart was not fully devoted to the Lord his God, as the heart of David his father had been. Solomon built high places for all his foreign wives who burned incense and offered sacrifices to their detestable gods."

David, Solomon's father, would have been heartbroken over this. He had commanded his son to never turn away from God and His statutes. David had committed grievous sins for which he repented, but he never, never was involved in idolatrous worship. Solomon had broken the basic demands of the covenant and undermined the covenant relationship between God and the people. His actions led to the peoples' rebellion against the absolute kingship of the Lord over them, and to the utter disaster that later befell Israel - the divided kingdom, the Assyrian captivity, the disappearance from history of the ten northern tribes, the Babylonian captivity of the two southern tribes and the destruction of Jerusalem and the temple. Solomon's unfaithfulness had catastrophic consequences. There is a crucial lesson here for our nation, its Christian heritage, and for its leaders and we citizens.

You can almost sympathize with the poor guy. Imagine having 700 wives, each nagging you for her own altar. I imagine Solomon just finally gave in out of sheer frustration and exhaustion. Nevertheless, this failure of Solomon brings up two more questions we should each ask ourselves: 1. "Do I let other people, or other influences in my life, interfere with, or even prevent me from worshipping as God wants me to?" If the answer is "yes," then I, like Solomon, am relegating God to something other than first place in my life. And 2. "Am I solidly grounded in God's Word so that I cannot be led astray by others whose beliefs, philosophies or cultural values are contrary to, and in opposition to, God's Word? If the answer is "no," then I better get solidly grounded or I will certainly be led astray like Solomon.

The third big "except" in Solomon's life concerned riches and wealth. The Lord blessed Solomon with riches and wealth, but Scripture indicates that he became proud and wanted even more. God had commanded that the king must not acquire great numbers of horses for himself, nor accumulate large amounts of silver and gold, lest he say, " My power and the strength of my hands have produced this wealth for me, and forget that it is the Lord Who gives us the ability to produce wealth." Yet, Solomon had four thousand stalls for his horses, and he amassed tons of silver and gold from the tribute he exacted from the surrounding nations. Solomon's wealth was beyond imagination.

And we get an indication of Solomon's pride when we compare the temple of God with his palace. The Lord's Temple which Solomon built was 90 ft. long, 30 ft. wide, and 45 ft. high. As truly magnificent as the Temple was, the palace Solomon built for himself was 150 ft. long, 75 ft. wide, and 45 ft. high - that is, 60 ft. longer and 45 ft. wider than the Temple. How many years did it take to build the temple? Seven! And how many years did it take to build his palace? Thirteen! Almost twice as long. I think it fair to say that Solomon's initial humility before the Lord and the wisdom God gave him were adversely affected by the wealth and riches he amassed for himself.

Martin Luther once said: "Riches are the pettiest and least worthy gifts that God can give a person. What are they compared with God's Word, yes, even with physical gifts such as beauty and health or with gifts of the mind such as understanding, skill, and wisdom? Yet people toil for riches day and night and take no rest. Therefore our Lord commonly gives riches to foolish people to whom He gives nothing else."

It's so easy for the lure of wealth and materialism to replace God and take control of our lives. I'm reminded of the story of the rich, young investment banker who was driving his new BMW on a winding mountain road. He lost control and the car went over a cliff. At the last moment, however, he flung open the door and leaped from the car. Though he escaped with his life, he suffered a terrible injury. His arm had caught on the door and was torn off at the shoulder when he jumped. A trucker saw the accident and stopped to help. He found the young man standing on the roadside looking down at his burning BMW. "My BMW! My new BMW!" the man moaned, oblivious to his injury. The trucker pointed at the man's shoulder and said, "You've got bigger problems than that car. We've got to find your arm. Maybe the surgeons can sew it back on." The man looked where his arm had been, paused a moment and groaned, "Oh no! My Rolex! My new Rolex!"

The example of Solomon and his riches and wealth brings up another two questions we should each ask ourselves: 1. "Have I allowed materialism and a desire for wealth to take priority over my following Jesus in faith, obedience to His Word and worship?" And 2. "Do I truly realize that all I have comes from God, and that God gives me material possessions so I can enjoy them, not worship them, and so that I will humbly thank Him and gratefully bring my tithes to His House so that His Church can grow and become a powerful instrument in His hands."

Idolatry, pleasure and riches were the three big "excepts" in Solomon's life that got in the way of his following God's commands as he initially set out to do. And we all face the same danger. Why? Because Satan knows that we are especially vulnerable in these areas. He will tempt us with idolatry and try to water down or destroy our faith in Jesus and God's Word through false and deceptive teachings, doctrines and values of this world. He will tempt us with illicit pleasures the world offers and which are all around us. And he will try to replace the true security our faith in Jesus gives us with the false security of riches, wealth and materialism. If the wisest man in the world failed in these areas, is that not a warning to us to be very, very careful and cling to God and His Word.

Happiness is a very high priority for people. Everyone wants to be happy. In fact, many people go to church seeking happiness and expect the pastor to give them the secret to being happy. But you know what? Our happiness is not a top priority of God's. God's priority for us is our joy. Happiness is an emotion. I can be happy this morning and down in the dumps this evening. But joy is a state of being. And the joy God wants us to have, and gives us, is the joy of our salvation in Christ; the joy of fellowship and oneness with God the Father, with our Savior Jesus and with our Counselor the Holy Spirit; the joy of our communion with our Lord's sacrifice of Body and Blood which He speaks of in our Gospel passage; the joy of our inheritance in heaven; the joy of our Lord's promise that He will never leave us or forsake us; the joy of knowing, as the Apostle Paul said, that nothing, nothing in this world or out of this world can separate us from the love of God in Christ. And when we fail and commit sins of idolatry, sins of the flesh, sins of greed, which we do because of our sinful nature, it is the joy of knowing that the Father is ready to forgive us, cleanse us in the Blood of His Son, and renew us in righteousness. Unlike happiness, which is like smoke blowing in the wind, the joy that God gives us in Christ is our constant refuge, strength and assurance during both times of happiness and times of unhappiness, sickness, poverty and loss.

Do you think Solomon was happy? After all, what man wouldn't be happy, famous for his wisdom, a man with 700 wives and unimaginable wealth? On second thought, forget being happy with 700 wives. If you read the Book of Ecclesiastes, which most scholars ascribe to Solomon since the author identifies himself as the Teacher and king over Israel in Jerusalem, you'll find that he looks back on his life and takes stock of it. His attitude is almost cynical, and his words reflect an unhappiness and sorrow, as if, in taking stock of his life, he realizes that he had misplaced his priorities. He refers to man's striving for knowledge, striving for pleasure, striving for riches and wealth as meaningless, as a chasing after the wind. What a tragedy for a person to look back on their life and realize that they had misplaced their priorities and their life had simply been a chasing after the wind.

Do you think Solomon repented before he died? Oh, I hope so, because I would like to see him in heaven. And his concluding words in Ecclesiastes gives me hope that he did. He said, "Now all has been heard; here is the conclusion of the matter: Fear God and keep His commandments, for this is the whole duty of man." That tells me that he did repent and regain the humility and wisdom he had in the beginning.

I can't give you a twelve-step program for a happy life. No pastor, psychiatrist or counselor can. Jesus said, "In this world you will have trouble, but be of good cheer (in other words, be joyful) for I have overcome the world." But I can leave you with a three-step program for a joyful life, taken from our Epistle reading: 1. Be very careful how you live - not as unwise, but as wise, remembering that wisdom comes only from God through His Word. 2. Seek to understand what the

Lord's will is for your life through His Word, prayer and worship, for that is the only true, lasting success and fulfillment in life. If you seek, you will find. And 3. Be filled with the Spirit, and sing and make music in your heart to the Lord, always giving thanks to God the Father for everything, in the Name of our Lord Jesus Christ.

And that, my friends, is the joyful life, the abundant life. It is a life that this world cannot give with all its allurements, pleasures, and riches. It is the life that only God the Holy Spirit can give through faith in Christ. It is the life that honors God, the life that makes a difference; the life that leaves a lasting legacy; and the life that finishes well. God grant such a life to each of us, for Jesus' sake. Amen.

TRUTH FALLEN IN THE STREETS

Text: Isaiah 59:14-15; 2Timothy 4:3-5; John 8:31-32, 42-47

Theme: Only God's absolute Truth in Christ brings freedom and blessedness to both individuals and nations.

Theme Sentence: Where justice is compromised and sin allowed free course, truth is soon fallen in the streets and the social fabric is ripped and becomes unraveled.

Key Passage: Isaiah 59:14-15. "So justice is driven back, and righteousness stands at a distance; truth has stumbled in the streets, honestly cannot enter. Truth is nowhere to be found, and whoever shuns evil becomes a prey."

✝

Tuth can be a bitter pill at times. All of us, I'm sure, have a few skeletons in the closet that we want to keep there, wrongs that we have done about which we would rather not have the truth be known. The only exception, of course, would be the person who has never sinned, and if you are such a person, please forgive me for including you in with the rest of us miserable sinners.

Have you ever noticed how truth often has a way of eventually becoming known, despite feverish attempts to mask it and cover it up? It's like the story of two brothers who were very rich. They were also very wicked and used their wealth to cover up the dark side of their lives. On the surface, few would have guessed it, for they were expert cover-up artists, attending church every Sunday and contributing large sums of money to church related projects. Then the church called a new pastor who preached the Gospel truth with zeal and courage. Being a man of keen insight, the pastor saw through the hypocritical lifestyle of the brothers.

And then, one of the brothers died. The day before the funeral, the surviving brother took the pastor aside and handed him an envelope.

"There is a check in there large enough to pay the entire amount needed for a new sanctuary," the brother whispered. "All I ask is one favor. Tell the people at the funeral that he was a saint." The pastor gave the brother his word that he would do what was asked. That afternoon, he deposited the check in the church's account. The next day, the pastor stood before the casket at the funeral service and said with firm conviction: "This man was an ungodly sinner, wicked to the core. He was abusive to his wife, hot-tempered with his children, ruthless in his business, and a hypocrite at church. But compared to his brother, he was a saint." Truth can be a bitter pill, and because it is, we sinners want to sugarcoat it, fudge it a bit so it's not so distasteful. But God doesn't sugarcoat or fudge the truth. And He will not accept our doing so.

God's prophets in the Old Testament would not fudge the truth, compromise the truth God gave them to speak to the people, and which the people needed to hear, but did not want to hear. And because they wouldn't fudge the truth, they suffered severe persecution and most of them paid with their lives. Isaiah was one of the greatest of these prophets. Isaiah spoke the words of our Old Testament reading at a particularly low, low point in Israel's history. Isaiah told the people that their iniquities had separated them from God, their deeds were evil, acts of violent crime had become commonplace, their feet rush into sin, their lips speak lies, they are quick to shed innocent blood, justice and righteousness were driven back, and whoever speaks out against evil becomes a prey to be hunted down and silenced. Truth had stumbled and fallen in the streets. It was bad and getting worse.

Come to think of it, it sounds like today's news in the paper and on TV. In many ways, the situation in Israel in Isaiah's day reflects the situation in our society and many societies of the world today. What Israel desperately needed was godly leaders of courage who would fill the gap and restore truth and order. But the leaders of the nation, along with the false prophets, judges, and the people alike, formed a barrier which kept truth back. Truth no longer stood in the midst of the nation. For when justice is compromised and sin is allowed free course, truth is soon stumbled and fallen in the streets and the social fabric of a society is ripped and becomes unraveled. The true prophets knew that compromising the Truth given by God was sin of the most dangerous kind. And they took sin very seriously. You know why? Because they took God's righteousness seriously. And any compromise of God's Truth is a compromise of God's righteousness because God's Word and God's nature cannot be separated.

I think the greatest problem both the Church and the nation face today is the compromise of Truth, Biblical illiteracy, and the failure to take sin seriously. In many ways, truth has stumbled and fallen in our streets. And all of history shows that when truth stumbles and falls, bad things happen to society. You've heard the statement, "Things will get worse before they get better." Well, when truth continues to be compromised, when truth continues to stumble and fall, the statement changes to "Things will get worse before they get worse."

There are those who say that there is no such thing as absolute Truth, that truth is relative, it changes with time and circumstances, and that each of us is free to establish our own truth, our own code of ethics, and live accordingly. That philosophy has proven to be disastrous to both individuals and society as a whole. For if each of us is free to establish our own truth, then there is no such thing as truth, restraints are lifted, and the door is open to sin, injustice, corruption, devastation, and destruction.

But there most certainly is such a thing as absolute Truth, unchanging Truth, and you hold that Truth in your hand when you are holding the Bible. It is the only absolute, unchanging, Truth, and it alone holds the key to salvation, wholeness, peace, and fulfillment in this life and everlasting joy in the next. And that key is Jesus Christ, Son of God and Son of Man, Who as the GodMan showed us the sinless life we should strive to live, and then went to the cross to be the pure, holy sacrifice for our sins, that we might, through faith in Him as Lord and Savior, be forgiven our sins and be restored into God's family and made heirs of the Kingdom of Heaven. Jesus Christ is the Way, the Truth, and the Life, the only Way to God the Father, the ultimate, absolute Truth, and the only source of the fulfilled Life here on earth and eternally in heaven.

But just as the people in Isaiah's day, there are today many, far too many, who deny this Truth, rebel against God and turn away from His Truth to follow their own way. Isaiah describes the people of his day as the blind groping along the wall, stumbling in broad daylight as if it were night. So it is today with so many.

Why do so many rebel against God's Truth? Why are so many misled by the philosophies of this world, like that which says there is no such thing as absolute truth? The Apostle Paul gives us the answer in our Epistle reading. He tells young Timothy, and us, that the time will come when people will not want sound doctrine or sound teaching. Instead, to suit their own desires, to get what they want, they will gather around them teachers who will say what their itching ears want to hear. They will turn their ears away from the truth, and turn to myths. Itching ears are ears that want to be scratched, scratched by hearing what they want to hear, scratched by hearing things that correspond with their own desires, the way they want to follow, scratched by hearing that God didn't really mean what He said when He condemned things that violate His good and perfect will for us, things that are in direct violation of His created order, things which are corrupting to our spirits, souls, bodies, and minds. They want to hear that times change, truth changes, and that God will understand if we fudge on His Word a bit, compromise His Truth in order to bring it up to date with modern concepts and attitudes.

Did you know that there is a very famous woman politician, whose name is familiar to everyone, who made the comment that the Bible, the Word of God, must be brought up to date to conform with modern standards. What arrogance to claim that God is too old-fashioned for modern tastes! What rubbish! She, and they of her ilk, don't want to hear that God's Truth, which is inseparable from God Himself, is the same yesterday, today, and forever. Jesus said, "Heaven and earth will pass away, but my Words shall never pass away." And Scripture tells us that he who adds to or takes away from God's Word, his name shall be taken from the Book of Life.

The Apostle Paul speaks directly of a condition of apostasy that will appear in some churches during latter times. And we have such apostasy today. Many churches, in their zeal to attract people, have forsaken solid scriptural teaching, compromising God's Word, rejecting the whole truth of God's Word, and thus turning from divine spiritual reality to falsehood. And sometimes the falsehood can be very subtle and go over peoples' heads. A man once walked into a church in the Berkeley, Calif. area. It was a great stone structure with massive doors and a vast narthex. In the narthex were huge portraits of great people - Jesus, along with Mahatma Ghandi, Socrates, and others. Above the portraits, these words were engraved in bronze: "You are all the sons of God.....," with a series of dots as shown. Those dots, or ellipses as they are called, meant that the quotation was not complete. The reference was Galatians 3:26. The man was curious, got a Bible, and looked it up. The complete verse says, "You are all sons of God through faith in Jesus Christ." They weren't all sons of God unless they were in Christ through faith. Now that is deception, and that church chose to engage in deception, to pervert God's Word, probably to appeal to as many people as possible. But God doesn't like it when we pervert or misuse His Word, regardless of the reason. And the Apostle Paul, who wrote that verse under the inspiration of the Holy Spirit, would strongly rebuke that church for giving that verse a meaning contrary to its true meaning.

Good Law and Gospel teaching and preaching both crushes and heals. It doesn't tickle itching ears. Scratching itching ears with a tickle doesn't bring about a new birth in Christ. The Law boxes those itching ears until the itch is gone and the person is brought to a true awareness of their sin and hopeless condition. The Gospel of Christ then pours in the power of grace and mercy that forgives, pardons their sins, regenerates and renews the person into a new creation - a son or daughter of the Kingdom of God. The Apostle Paul tells Timothy, and

208

us, to "keep your head," which denotes clarity of mind, sound judgment that is solidly rooted in the truth of God's Word, that is not deceived, blinded and carried away with false teaching.

In our Gospel reading, Jesus says, "If you hold to my teaching, you are really my disciples. Then you will know the truth, and the truth will set you free." The Truth - not philosophical truth, not truth designed by human intellect, desires or wishes - but the absolute and ultimate Truth that leads to salvation. And the freedom that this Truth gives is freedom from the bondage of sin, freedom from deception, freedom from death. And this truth and freedom comes to all who "hold to Jesus' teaching." Holding to Jesus' teaching means being permanently fixed, established in the true faith, in the absolute Truth of God's Word. Outside this absolute Truth of God's Word is truth fallen in the streets, and truth fallen in the streets is spiritual death. To remain fixed in Jesus' Word is true life now and forever and the very essence of discipleship.

Absolute Truth centers on Jesus Christ. In Him, we have the reality of God's grace and salvation. In Him, we have the only Truth that sets us free. And the more we realize this Truth, learn of this Truth, and grow in this Truth, the more we are set free. Jesus' words should inspire us to ever greater faith and knowledge of His Truth in order to be free from all delusion, falsehood, and spiritual bondage. The devil has no place in truth; the truth has no place in the devil. The devil wants to pervert God's Word, deceive us and tickle our ears with false teaching. Jesus says that lies and falsehood are the devil's native tongue for they originate in him - he is the father of lies. After all, the devil brought sin and death in all their destructive power upon the whole of humankind, and lying was the means by which he did it. And it took Jesus, the Son of God Himself, as Son of Man, to break the hold of that destructive power over us once and for all. The Truth of God or the lies of the devil! Everyone must choose between the two. There is no accommodation, no compromise possible between them. The power of God's Truth is eternal because the reality of that Truth - God's grace in Jesus Christ - cannot cease. The power of the devil's lies, however, is temporary because it is bound to be exposed and destroyed.

Because Jesus declared the truth, many would not believe or even hear Him. And Jesus challenged them by asking, "Who of you can prove Me guilty of sin?" Of course, no one could!Then He asked them, "If I am telling the truth, why don't you believe Me?" Good question! Many of God's servants today could ask the same question. The answer, of course, is that many of the people then, and many people today, don't want the truth. The people Jesus was addressing knew that He spoke the truth, but it stung them, and they wanted to rid themselves of it. Truth demands faith; it demands the obedience of faith. But many people then, just as many people today, are bent on having their own way, and they become bitter and resentful when they can't have it their way. Insisting on having our own way can not only separate us from God, it can also destroy human relationships. And when we insist on having our own way, especially apart from God, truth becomes a casualty, eventually trampled down and fallen in the streets.

The greatest need in society and in many of the churches today is truth, the Truth of God in Christ, the Absolute Truth. Consider yourself richly blessed if you have someone - a spouse, a friend, a pastor - to make you face that Truth, even though it can be a bitter pill to swallow, because that Truth brings forgiveness, healing, restoration, and life itself, both now and forever. Remember that closet with those skeletons in it that I mentioned earlier. Well, if you have the Truth of God in Christ, in faith and commitment to Him, you can throw the door of that closet wide open, and lo and behold, those skeletons are gone, gone because God has cleaned out that closet, gotten rid of those skeletons through His forgiving grace and power in Christ, and made it as though they were never there.

Jesus said, "The person who belongs to God hears what God says." We have the Truth of God's Word in Christ, and it is our most precious possession in life, for it is life. Don't let anyone deceive or mislead you. Don't let truth stumble and fall in the street of your life. Hold it close, treasure it, learn more and more of it, share it, and let it be the guiding light for every pathway of life. God strengthen us all to that end for Jesus' sake. Amen.

CHAPTER 8 - LAMENT AND SORROW

"Do not withhold your mercy from me, O Lord; May your love and your truth always protect me. For troubles without number surround me; My sins have overtaken me, and I cannot see, They are more than the hairs of my head, and my heart fails within me. Be pleased, O Lord, to save me; O Lord, come quickly to help me."

Psalm 40:11-13

Job and his "friends."

THE HEAVIEST BURDEN

Text: Psalm 32:1-5;   Hebrews 9:14-15;   John 8:31-36

Theme: Guilt and its devastating effects.

Theme Statement: Healing and reconciliation can never take place until guilt is dealt with by taking it to the foot of the cross and leaving it there where it was paid for in full by our Savior. I used Psalm 32 and the key passage given here in the previous chapter's narrative discussing David's deadly silence in initially failing to confess his sins of adultery and murder to the Lord, and the devastating effects this silence had on him. I repeat that discussion with the discussion here of guilt because silence and guilt go together like hand in glove and have the potential to destroy a person spiritually, physically, mentally, and emotionally.

Key Passage: Psalm 32:5.   "Then I acknowledged my sin to you and did not cover up my iniquity. I said, 'I will confess my transgressions to the Lord,' and You forgave the guilt of my sin."

✝

Sin, in one form or another, is the root cause of most unhappiness and misery. And guilt is the handmaiden of sin. Where you have one, you will have the other. Of all the burdens of this life, I would say that guilt is the heaviest burden. The guilt of sin affects virtually all areas of life, including our life of worship. When guilt is not dealt with, it is like a heavy weight we drag around, a weight that saps our energy and takes away our freedom, our security, our confidence, our joy. Guilt can result in spiritual, emotional, psychological, and yes, even physical deterioration and death. Guilt is fertile ground for Satan to wreak havoc in people's lives. Satan always strikes at our weakest point, and more often than not, that is guilt. He works on our guilt to drive a wedge between us and God. Satan uses our guilt to hold us where he wants us to be.

As previously discussed, King David was well-acquainted with the terrible effects of guilt, and he tells us about it in Psalm 32. He tells of his terrible sufferings of guilt after his sin of adultery with Bathsheba, followed by his sin of murder in having her husband Uriah killed. And he compounded his guilt by trying to cover up what he had done. It is estimated that David refused to acknowledge his sin before God for approximately a year. This great man, whom God called "a man after My own heart," foolishly tried to cover up his terrible crime. And during this time, the burden of guilt became unbearable. He tells us that when he was silent, his bones wasted away. He did not suffer merely emotional distress due to his stubborn silence, he also suffered physical affliction, illness, and pain. His strength was sapped and his life was filled with groaning day and night. His suffering from guilt was spiritually, physically, and psychologically devastating. And the misery lasted as long as he kept silence.

Why did David keep silent? Perhaps he thought his sin was too great for God's mercy and compassion. Perhaps he was too ashamed of what he had done to even admit it to God. At any rate, it's a safe bet that David would have died from guilt if God had not forced the issue and acted to save him. God sent Nathan the Prophet to confront David and force him to acknowledge and face his sin and guilt. And that is precisely what David needed. As an aside, we can take comfort from the fact that God always knows what we need, even when it is something we would rather not deal with.

Nathan told David a story, a parable, of a rich man who had many flocks of sheep and of his servant who had only one little ewe lamb that was like a member of the family. When the rich man received a visitor, instead of taking a sheep from one of his own many flocks to feed his visitor, he took the little ewe lamb of his servant, had it killed and prepared to serve himself and his visitor. David flew into a rage and said the rich man would be punished severely for his brutal, selfish crime. Nathan pointed his finger at David and said, "You are that rich man. You have many wives and concubines; yet, you took Bathsheba, Uriah's only wife and slept with her while he was out in the field with the army fighting your enemies. And then, when Bathsheba informed you that she was pregnant, you had your General arrange to have Uriah killed in battle."

David, totally humbled and devastated by the weight of God's hand applied through Nathan the Prophet, makes full confession of his sin. Then he goes to the Temple and prays that beautiful and powerful prayer of confession and repentance we read in Psalm 51. And his burden, his misery, his terrible guilt was lifted. When he would not confess and repent, he was crushed with guilt, but when he did, he found God ready to forgive, cleanse, heal, and restore completely.

There is an old saying that goes: "He who suppresses his sins without confessing them conceals an inward wound and burns with secret fire." A guilty conscience is like a bleeding wound, a raging fire. It is the heaviest burden. Shakespeare described it this way: "To be alone with my conscience is hell enough for me. Trust me, no torture that the poets feign can match the fierce, unutterable pain he feels who, night and day, devoid of rest, carries his own accuser in his breast." And someone else, I don't know who, said this: "What your conscience knows about you is more important than what your neighbors say about you."

Guilt is not all bad, however. Guilt produces a sense of our unworthiness and our need of God's grace in Christ. As David said, the hand of God was heavy upon him. God uses our guilt to our advantage, for our good, to bring us to full awareness of our sin, sorrow over our sin, contrition for our sin, and repentance of our sin. It is good that we feel guilty for our sins. Not to feel guilt for our sins is a sign of spiritual deadness. The Holy Spirit uses our guilt to reveal to us what deadliness lurks in sin, just as He led Nathan to tell that parable to David to impress upon him the deadliness of his sin. The Holy Spirit prompts us to get rid of the guilt through confession and repentance, and enjoy the blessedness of the cleansing and freedom we have in Christ Who paid the full penalty for all our sins on the cross. We can either respond to the Holy Spirit's leading and receive that blessedness, or reject the Holy Spirit's leading, grieve the Holy Spirit, and suffer the ravages of guilt.

It is a fact, however, that some people prefer to hold onto guilt. Over time, they become comfortable with it; it becomes like a defense mechanism, a crutch that allows them to stay inside their little shell and nurse their grievances and resentments. Or, what often happens, they transfer the guilt they feel onto someone else, and this allows them to avoid all responsibility for their own sin and unhappiness. It's all the other person's fault. Now, when people hold onto guilt, they frustrate the Holy Spirit's working in their lives, just as David did. Certainly, the Holy Spirit was prompting David to confess and repent all the time before Nathan was sent to force the issue. But David was frustrating those efforts through his stubbornness. When people hold onto guilt, they are denying themselves the full benefit of Christ's sacrifice for their sins, in effect saying that Christ's atonement is not sufficient to cleanse them from their guilt. And that is exactly what Satan wants us to think and believe. Because he knows that guilt, if not resolved, will keep us from the abundant life that is ours in Christ, and eventually lead to spiritual deadness.

Healing and reconciliation and wholeness can never take place until guilt is dealt with. Guilt is a burden that must be lifted off the soul in order for the heart to be renewed. Before Jesus healed, He often said to the person, "Your sins are forgiven!" He knew that, for those particular individuals, guilt was a problem, and the guilt had to be dealt with and gotten rid of before the person could be healed completely.

There is only one remedy for guilt, and that is the cleansing of the conscience by Christ's Blood shed for us on the cross. And we receive that cleansing when we confess and repent of our sin as David did. Confession must be made to God, for all sin is rebellion against Him. To Him we must answer, for only He can forgive and remove the stain of sin and guilt. It is, however, Scripturally attested to, to have a devout and trusted Christian friend through whom confession is made to God, and who then assures the confessor of God's mercy, cleansing, and forgiveness. Our confession must be a complete unburdening of the heart, frank and open without any excuses or hiding. If we do this, we will find, just as David did, that God, in His mercy and grace, receives us, forgives us, and restores us. Just as God brought David out of the darkness of sin, guilt, sickness, and depression, into the light of His glorious grace and healing, so He will do for us. We have His Word on that. Satan will try to plant doubt in our minds, trying to convince us that our sin or sins are too serious to be forgiven. Don't fall for this! Tell Satan to go to hell where he belongs.

Our loving God is the Shepherd that searches for the lost sheep until, with rejoicing, He finds it. Our God is the woman who searches for the lost coin until, with rejoicing, she finds it. Our God is the Prodigal Son's Father, Who runs to meet his lost son who has returned, embraces him, rejoices that his son, who was dead, is alive and holds a great feast to celebrate his return.

Like David, after our confession and repentance, we too can say, "I acknowledged my sin to You, and did not cover up my iniquity. I said, 'I will confess my transgressions to the Lord,' and You forgave the guilt of my sin." Selah! Selah! The Hebrew word used here and in many Psalms tells us to pause and ponder, digest, think upon what we have just heard.

In our Epistle reading, Paul tells us that the Blood of Christ cleanses our consciences from acts that lead to death. And for what reason? So that we may serve the Living God. We cannot serve God as we ought, as He would have us serve Him, with pure hearts and renewed minds and right spirits, if we are living with a guilty conscience, if guilt is a dead weight we are dragging around. Guilt makes a cheerful heart sad and crushes a cheerful spirit. But God has given us cheerful hearts and would have us serve Him with cheerful spirits. Happiness is an emotion and may well elude us, as it often does in this vale of tears, but joy and cheer is an attitude and should be a constant attitude of the Christian, for we have much to be joyful and cheerful about. A man once asked his musician friend why his church music was so cheerful. His friend answered: "I cannot make it otherwise. I write according to the thoughts I feel. When I think upon God, my heart is so full of joy that the notes dance and leap, as it were, from my pen, and since God has

216

given me a cheerful heart, I must serve Him with a cheerful spirit." A cheerful spirit and a guilty conscience are incompatible.

Paul goes on to say that Christ died as a ransom to set us free from the sins committed under the first Covenant, the Covenant of Law. Satan would like to keep us bound to that first Covenant of Law, bound to our sins against God's Law. But Christ died as a ransom to set us free from the condemnation of the Law, and through faith in Christ as our Lord and Savior, we are children of the New Covenant, the Covenant of Grace. His Blood not only washes away our sin, it also cleanses us from guilt. Guilt cannot coexist with grace; guilt must give way to grace. Jesus took not only our sins to the cross, but also our guilt. Do we really want to take it back? God forbid!

In our Gospel passage, we are told that if we hold to Christ's teaching, we will know the Truth, and the Truth will set us free. Christ is the Truth, the Ultimate Truth, the Absolute Truth. To know Christ and His Word is to know this Truth. To know this Truth is to be set free, free from sin, free from guilt. Every effort of David to help himself, to heal himself, only aggravated the pain as long as he refused to humble his heart before God. Christ is our only freedom from sin and guilt. This is not religion, philosophy, psychology, or abstraction; it is divine revelation and everlasting fact, the eternal wisdom of God, and it remains so, whether people know it, realize it, acknowledge it, accept it, or deny it. Only Christ has mediated, and continues to mediate our sins and guilt. The entire past, the entire present, the entire future, thus rests on Christ's death on Calvary and His resurrection, on the Lamb slain from the foundation of the world. When we are fixed and firm in the Word of Jesus, our freedom from sin and guilt is fixed and firm.

Satan wants to keep us enslaved, and cheat us out of our inheritance in Christ by holding our sins and guilt before us. But Truth, the eternal Truth of Christ and His Word, Christ our Ransom, our Sacrifice, our Atonement, our Living Savior and Lord, conquers the opposing and enslaving power of sin and guilt. Those who shut out this Truth forfeit this liberating power and remain enslaved to sin and guilt. Those who shut out this Truth have no tenacity, no resistance, no perseverance, no strong defense against the enslaving power of sin and guilt. Like the house built on sand in Jesus' parable, when the storms came, the winds blew, the floods raged, it crashed and was washed away because it was not built upon rock, so those whose lives are not built on the rock of eternal Truth of Christ and His Word will be lost and swept away.

In our Gospel passage, Jesus says that a slave has no permanent place in the family, but a son (or daughter) belongs to it forever. We are no longer slaves if we are in Christ by faith, because Christ has set us free from the bondage of sin and guilt, and brought us into God's family as sons and daughters of the Most High. And Jesus goes on to say that "if the Son sets you free, you will be free indeed!" Jesus is our great Liberator. Christ is our Liberty. Men have fought and died for liberty on this lower plane of life on earth; philosophers, seers, and politicians dream of it in the intellectual realm. But Jesus assures it to us on the highest plane, that of body, soul, and spirit in the new heavens and the new earth.

David's Psalm ends with rejoicing and singing. What a wondrous change from the man whose bones were wasting away, whose strength was sapped, whose days and nights were filled with groaning. The heaviest burden of sin and guilt becomes the joy of pardon and freedom. The grief of estrangement becomes the joy of reconciliation and the cheer of renewal. A heart torn with misery and full of unrest becomes a heart filled with the peace of God which passes all understanding. The terror of judgment becomes the assurance of cleansing and restoration and the love of God. And so it is with us, my brother and sister in Christ. So it is with us!

God's love is a personal love. He loves you and me and our brothers and sisters in Christ as individuals and as the Communion of Saints. It grieves Him as a Father grieves for a child when we hold onto guilt and refuse the freedom Christ gives us. Again, don't ever think for a moment that your sin and guilt is beyond God's grace. Yes, we

Christians are great sinners, but we have a greater Savior. David's terrible guilt of adultery and murder was covered by grace. The Apostle Paul's terrible sin and guilt in persecuting the Church before his conversion was covered by grace. Peter's terrible sin and guilt in denying his Lord three times, even with cursing and swearing, was covered by grace. How dare anyone think that their sin and guilt is so great that it can't be covered by grace. God forbid that we ever think so!

Triple repetition is the Hebrew way of giving maximum emphasis to something. And so, I end with saying for the third time: "Don't ever let Satan keep you enslaved by sin and guilt. Get rid of it. Take it to the cross and leave it there , where it was paid for in full by our Lord and Savior Jesus.

I knelt in tears at the feet of Christ, Carrying a heavy burden of guilt for my sin. And all that I was, or hoped, or sought, I surrendered it all unto Him! God grant that we do so, for Jesus' sake. Amen.

HOW LONG, LORD?

Text: Psalm 13: 1-6; 1Peter 4: 14-16; John 15: 20-21

Theme: Trust in the face of affliction and suffering

Theme Statement: Trouble and affliction that last long with no end in sight often leads to frustration, strained patience and waning hope. The Psalms are filled with this theme. Yet, we always see the Psalmist passing from the depths of despondency to the heights of confidence and joy. He throws himself without reservation on the mercy and care of the Lord. He pours out his complaint, his grief, before the Lord, remembering God's unfailing love and help in the past, and his faith in God's mercy, love and salvation overcomes his distress and anguish.

Key Passage: Psalm 13: 1. "How long, Lord? Will You forget me forever? How long will You hide Your face from me? ... But I trust in your unfailing love; my heart rejoices in Your salvation."

Four men went mountain climbing. One of them slipped over a cliff and landed on a ledge below. The others yelled, "Joe, are you O.K?" "Both my arms are broken," Joe answered. "We'll toss a rope down to you and pull you up," they said. After dropping one end of the rope down, they started tugging and grunting, pulling Joe to safety. When they had him half-way up, they remembered he said he had both arms broken. They yelled, "Joe, if you broke both arms, how are you hanging on?" Joe responded, "With my teeeeth!" Sometimes in the trials, suffering, sorrows and stresses of this life, we may feel like we're hanging on by our teeth.

Troubles, stress, sickness are all part of this life because we live in a fallen world. God is not the source of pain, sickness, sorrow, disasters, or even death. These are the natural consequences of man's fall into sin. And so, happiness in life is interspersed with sorrow and pain. The good news is that God can, and does, use pain, sickness, sorrow, and

221

even death, to work His good and holy purposes. C.S. Lewis said, "God whispers to us in our pleasures, speaks to us in our conscience, but shouts to us in our pain; it is His megaphone to rouse a deaf world." Donald Guthrie, another theologian, said, "Affliction brings out the glory of a Christian's faith, as lightning shines brighter in the depths of night than in the glare of day."

Yet, when we suffer serious sickness, deep sorrow and heavy stress, we find it difficult to hold on to God's promise that He will work it out to our highest good. God understands this. He tells us in His Word that He knows that we are weak; He knows we are but dust. God invites His people to bring their griefs, pour out their complaints to Him. God Himself is afflicted by the afflictions of His children, troubled by our infirmities, and His Word tells us in Hebrews 4:15,16 that "We have a High Priest - Jesus, the Son of God- Who, as the Son of Man, can sympathize with us in our temptations, sufferings and afflictions because He was tempted in every way that we are, yet was without sin, and He suffered, as the Son of Man, the ultimate pain, affliction, and suffering of the cross for our salvation, to give us eternal life free of all pain, suffering and affliction.

Psalm 13 is a prayer David prayed when he was suffering a prolonged serious illness and was close to death. At the same time, his enemies were plotting against him. They wanted him to die. So David cries out to God for deliverance. Let's consider his three petitions in this Psalm. First, he petitions God to consider his case, his suffering and anguish. He voices his complaint to God. (v. 1-2). "How long, Lord, will You forget me? How long will You hide Your face from me? How long must I wrestle with my thoughts? How long will my enemy triumph over me?" Four times David cries out, "How long, Lord?" His greatest fear was that God had forgotten him, had hidden His face from him.

Have you ever felt that God has forgotten you, that He is hiding His face from you? Have you ever wanted to cry out, "How long, Lord, must I wrestle with my sorrow, my anxieties, worries, fears and stress?"

222

"How long, Lord, will these enemies - sickness, sorrow, pain - triumph over me?" We all feel overwhelmed at times, but there are some among us who have felt sorrow and pain at a deeper level than the rest of us. In asking "How long, Lord?" David is petitioning the Lord to consider his case, see his anguish, hear his complaint. And God invites us to do the same.

(v. 3a). David's second petition is for the Lord to look on him and answer him. How often have we cried out in frustration to God to look on us now, to answer us now, rescue us now? But God has His set times for us, just as He did for David, and it is not for us to know them. We must wait for them. But God does assure us that He will never forget us or hide His face from us. He tells us, "Don't despair, don't lose hope, I will keep My Word to work all things out for your good, but in the meantime, I am using your tribulation to develop you, form and shape you, test and strengthen you, build you up in faith and prepare you for the good I have for you. And while I am working, keep on asking Me to look on you and answer you."

(v.3b-4). David's third petition is for God to give light to his eyes. David asks God to enable him to look beyond his present trouble and despair, enable him to see the infinite goodness of God that is greater than the worst distress. David asks for divine wisdom and discernment, and so should we when we are suffering spiritually or physically and God seems distant. "Give light to my eyes, O Lord, the light of faith, that I may see beyond my anguish and distress, that I may see the goodness and faithfulness of You, my Refuge and Strength, my ever-present Help in trouble."

And then, David passes from the depth of despondency to the height of confidence and joy. Just as we considered his three petitions, let us now consider three things that enabled David to pass from despair to confidence and joy. And we can express them as three "Don'ts." The first don't is: Don't think you're alone in your distress and suffering. Sickness, stress, anguish, fear can all make a person feel isolated and alone. But we're not alone. We have brothers and sisters in Christ undergoing the same kinds of affliction, even worse, but much more important, God Himself feels our affliction. Even as David was asking "How long, Lord?" he knew in his heart that God had not forgotten him or turned His face from him. Knowing this, and throwing himself without reservation on the mercy and care of the Lord, he received strength and confidence to rise above his anguish and fear.

(v.5). David tells God, "But I trust in Your unfailing love." And this trust brought him comfort and enabled him to rejoice in God's salvation. David remembered how, in former distresses, dangers and suffering, he trusted in the mercy of God and God never failed him, never left him alone. Trust was his anchor in the storm, even when no harbor was in sight. And even if he died, he would die trusting in God's unfailing love. He knew that he was not alone, that God was with him. And we should never think that we are alone in our trials.

(v.6). The second don't is: Don't think that your troubles and suffering will last always. During times of pain, suffering and sorrow, when our hearts are broken, every moment seems a lifetime, and we think it will never end. But God promises us that our sufferings and afflictions are only for a time, and He will, in His time, come to us with healing in His wings. David expresses his confidence that God would deliver him when he says, "I will sing to the Lord, I will rejoice in God's salvation." A man was once asked what was his favorite Bible verse, and he answered, "It came to pass..." When asked to explain, he said that it was comforting to him to know that no matter what sorrows and troubles this life brings, "it came to pass."

Finally, the third don't is: Don't ever think that God doesn't care. David ended his prayer with the words, "For He has been good to me." David knew that, even in his suffering, especially in his suffering, he had fellowship with God, that God cared deeply about his anguish and suffering, that God would be good to him just as God had been good to him. And it's the same today. Every sick and suffering Christian, every distressed and persecuted Christian, bears the face of Christ because He Who suffered all for our salvation identifies with His brothers and sisters who suffer.

Everyone wants to avoid suffering. But there is a suffering we should not turn away from, the suffering the Apostle Paul speaks of in our Epistle. He says, "If you suffer because you are a Christian, do not be ashamed, but praise God that you bear that name." If you are insulted because of the Name of Christ, insulted because you refuse to conform to the values, beliefs, morals and ways of this world, you are blessed because "the Spirit of glory and of God rests upon you." Dietrich Bonhoeffer, the great theologian martyred by the Nazis, believed and taught that "Suffering is the badge of true discipleship."

Jesus, in our Gospel passage, tells Christians to expect persecution. He says, "No servant is greater than His Master. If they persecuted Me, they will persecute you also, because they do not know the One Who sent Me." "Since I have chosen you as My own, called you out of the ways of this world, set you apart for Myself, the world will hate and persecute you just as it hates and persecutes Me." The world indeed talks of God, may even call Him Father, or Mother, but apart from Jesus, their God is only a figment of the mind, an idol of human invention, constructed according to the ideas and ideology of this world. And so, the more the world sees of Jesus in us, the more it turns against us. We are seeing more and more of that today.

When engineers design bridges, they must take into account three loads, or stresses. They are the dead load, which is the weight of the bridge; the live load, which is the weight of daily traffic the bridge must carry; and the wind load, which is the pressure of storms that beat on the bridge. They design bracings to enable the bridge to bear all those loads. We too need bracings to enable us to carry the dead load of self, the live load of daily stresses and pressures, and the wind load of sorrows, pain and anguish. God the Father has given us those bracings - Christ and the Holy Spirit - and just as Christ, in His sufferings and afflictions, trusted Himself to the Father, so we, in our suffering and afflictions, commit and entrust ourselves to our faithful Creator and Redeemer, and leave the outcome in His hands.

So don't let those enemies defeat you. Like David, cry out to God with your complaint, keep asking Him to look on you and answer you, keep asking Him to give light to your eyes. And don't ever think you are alone, don't ever think that your anguish will last always, and don't ever think that God doesn't care or that He has forgotten you. When we trust in God's steadfast love, remembering His past deliverance and interventions in our lives, and hope in His abounding goodness in Christ Jesus, our adversities and sufferings can bring us into a more intimate fellowship with Christ in His sufferings, bring glory to God, and bring glory to us as Christians. God's Word tells us, "If we suffer with Christ and for Christ, we shall reign with Him." God help us to do so through the leading and strength of the Holy Spirit, and grant to all of us that intimate fellowship with Christ our Lord and Savior. And when we cry out in anguish, "How Long, O Lord?" God grant that we follow the example of our Savior, Who in His anguish, prayed to the Father, "Not My will, but Yours be done!" Amen.

CHAPTER 9 - ENCOURAGEMENT AND ASSURANCE

"I am still confident of this; I will see the goodness of the Lord in the land of the living. Wait for the Lord; Be strong and take heart and wait for the Lord."

Psalm 27:13-1

THE GIFT OF CONTENTMENT

Text: Proverbs 19:20-23; Philippians 4: 10-13; John 14:1-3, 27; 16: 33.

Theme: The Source of Contentment.

Theme Statement: Christians are called upon to be content in every condition of life. The Apostle Paul had learned to be content in all circumstances, whether he was in need or whether he had plenty. Jesus tells us not to let our hearts be troubled, to trust in Him in all times and places, in all conditions and circumstances, for all provision and need; in other words, be content in Him. To be content in every condition of life is a special act of God's grace, available only to those who are His through faith in Christ, because Christ's death and resurrection is the only foundation which gives us cause and strength to be content in all conditions.

Key Passage: Proverbs 19:23: "The fear of the Lord leads to life: Then one rests content, untouched by trouble."

Contentment is defined in the dictionary as the state of being satisfied with one's possessions, status, or situation. Contentment is a great blessing. People search for it, strive for it, pray for it. But too often their attitude is: "O God, if You give me a bigger house, a better paying job, a new car, I'll be content." Yet, even if they get what they want, contentment eludes them. There's always something else they want. A Quaker once offered a piece of property to anyone who considered himself contented. When a man came to claim the property, the Quaker asked him, "If you are content, why do you want my property?"

In today's fast-paced, materialistic, society, dissatisfaction and disappointment too often turn contentment into discontent. The Puritan Thomas Watson once said: "Discontent keeps a person from enjoying what they possess. A drop or two of vinegar will sour a whole glass of wine." On the other hand, as the famous preacher Charles Spurgeon said, "A little dash of the herb called contentment put into the poorest soup will make it taste as rich as the finest turtle soup."

Contentment makes much of little; discontent makes little of much. Contentment is the poor man's riches and discontent the rich man's poverty. It isn't what we have, but what we enjoy, that makes for a rich life. The wise person understands that contentment is not having everything we want, but enjoying everything we have. One of the distinguishing marks of the Christian should be contentment.

Scripture tells us that, unless we are rightly related to God, we will never have true contentment, regardless of human relationships, wealth, position, health, or what have you. Our passage in Proverbs tells us: "The fear of the Lord leads to life: Then one rests content, untouched by trouble." Solomon, the wisest man who ever lived, apart from Jesus, sought the meaning of life, the road to true contentment. In Ecclesiastes, he tells us that he first sought meaning and contentment through knowledge and the pursuit of human wisdom. But then he said that it was all a chasing after the wind, for with much human wisdom comes much sorrow, and the more knowledge, the more grief. Solomon learned that humanistic wisdom - wisdom without God - is meaningless and hopeless and leads to grief and sorrow. Solomon learned, or relearned, what his father David had said in Psalm 111: "The fear of the Lord, reverence for the Lord, is the beginning of wisdom," because in Proverbs 2:6 he said, "The Lord gives wisdom, and from His mouth come knowledge and understanding." Without this wisdom, knowledge, and understanding, a person is spiritually ignorant and can never know true contentment.

Solomon also sought contentment through pleasure. He said, "I denied myself nothing my eyes desired; I refused my heart no pleasure." But here too he found no true contentment, only a meaninglessness, a chasing after the wind. Solomon also sought contentment through work, achievement, and wealth. He undertook great building projects throughout the land, amassed huge flocks and herds, silver and gold, the treasure of neighboring kings and provinces. Yet, when he surveyed all that he had and all he had done, he saw that it was meaningless, a chasing after the wind. It didn't bring true contentment.

Finally, Solomon gives his conclusion to the matter. He identifies the only thing that has true meaning, and brings true contentment. He says, "Fear God and keep His commandments, for this is the whole duty of man." Only in God, through Christ, does life have true and lasting meaning; only in God, through Christ, does life have true and lasting pleasure; only in God, through Christ, does life have true and lasting peace and contentment.

The Apostle Paul knew such peace and contentment. Here was a man who, as Scripture tells us, had been frequently thrown in prison, who had been severely flogged with 39 lashes on five occasions, who had been exposed to death again and again, who had been beaten with rods on three occasions, who had been stoned, who was shipwrecked three times, who had been in danger from bandits, from the Jews, from the Gentiles, who had often gone without sleep, who knew hunger and thirst, often going without food, who had been cold and naked, and who, on top of all this, faced the daily pressures of his concern for all the churches he had planted. And yet, he says, "I have learned to be content whatever the circumstances…I have learned the secret of being content in any and every situation, whether living in plenty or living in want."

Paul had learned how to adjust himself to either being in need or having plenty with equal contentment. And what was the secret of contentment Paul said he had learned? He tells us in verse 13 of our Epistle passage: "I can do everything through Him (Christ) Who gives me strength." Paul says he can do everything - whether living in poverty or in abundance; whether living with sickness or with health; whether living with persecution or in security; whether living in danger or in safety. He can do everything through Christ Who gives him strength.

Notice that he is not boasting in himself or in his own strength, but only in Christ and Christ's strength.

The Philippians had passed through hard times and would have to do so again. They would need strength to overcome discouragement and discontent. Paul wanted them to know the secret of true contentment, to know that only through the strength of Him Who empowers - Jesus - could they overcome the persecutions to come and know true contentment, because He is the only source of that strength that brings true and lasting contentment.

Some of you have passed through hard times and suffering and might have to do so again, or perhaps are doing so now. You need the strength from Him Who empowers. Just as Paul's connection with the Lord through faith and trust empowered him with the strength he needed for everything in his life and work, so you too, with your connection to the Lord Jesus Christ through faith and trust, will be empowered with the strength you need for anything and everything you will face in this life.

Christians have the best of all possible reasons to be content. Jesus makes that clear to His disciples, and to us, in our Gospel passage. Jesus says, "Do not let your hearts be troubled. Trust in God, and trust in Me." Jesus makes it clear that to trust in the Father is to trust in Him, and to trust in Him is to trust in the Father, for the Two are One. Jesus had just told His disciples that He would soon be departing from them, that He would soon complete the mission of redemption given Him by the Father, and He would return to the Father. He assures them that His physical departure was no cause for discontent or distress - on the contrary, it was cause for rejoicing. He tells them that, in His Father's house, there are many rooms, and He is going to prepare a place for them, and for us, and He will certainly come back to take us to be with Him.

This is not figurative language. It is reality. Those rooms, those dwelling places, actually exist. God the Father has provided them for us, and Jesus is preparing them for us, and for all who respond to the

Holy Spirit's call to faith in Christ as Lord and Savior. All believers will take up residence there in unimaginable glory because Jesus Himself will bring us with Him into glory. Jesus promises His disciples, and us, a glorious and eternal reunion. Therefore, He says, be comforted and content.

One of the greatest examples of contentment given to us in Scripture, I think, is the example of Jesus in Gethsemane. He was overwhelmed with sorrow to the point of death as He considered the terrible suffering and death on the cross that awaited Him. But as He prayed to the Father, and submitted His will to the Father's will, He was strengthened for the terrible ordeal. Sidney Lanier expressed it beautifully when he wrote: "When Jesus emerged from Gethsemane, He was "content with death and shame." Why was Jesus content with death and shame? Because He knew that His suffering and death would pay the ransom in full for our sins, redeem us from the condemnation of sin, death, and hell, and open the gates of heaven for us. And He could face it with contentment because He trusted His Father and knew with absolute certainty that He would be raised on the third day. Jesus' contentment as He went to the cross is the foundation for the true and lasting contentment that is ours through Him.

Jesus tells His disciples, and us, "Peace I leave with you; my peace I give you. I do not give to you as the world gives. Do not let your hearts be troubled and do not be afraid...I have told you these things so that in Me you may have peace. In this world you will have trouble. But take heart! I have overcome the world." The peace Jesus speaks of is not the worldly peace people think of. Jesus makes that clear when He says "In this world you will have trouble." Jesus defines this peace as "My peace," and a peace that can only be found "in Me." Being His peace, He can leave it as a legacy, which He did, and give it as a treasure, which He does to all who believe and trust in Him. It is the peace that passes all human understanding, an objective peace that goes far beyond a subjective feeling of peace. Even when we don't feel peace, the peace that Jesus gives is still ours because it is a peace that is centered in Him, a peace that comes from Him, and the peace that brings true and everlasting contentment in Him.

Just as Jesus knew His disciples' concerns and anxieties, so He knows your sorrows, the wounds that are bleeding you inwardly. He knows your afflictions and worries and He stands ready to strengthen you to overcome every one of them. Trust Him with the true faith that goes far beyond our limited knowledge and understanding. We don't know what is coming tomorrow - sickness or health, wealth or poverty, danger or safety, life or death - but we do have the clear knowledge and assurance given to us by God Himself in His Word, that His grace is sufficient for all things, and that Christ, Who is our All in All, will give us the strength needed to have that true and Godly contentment in any and all situations.

It's not wrong to want a bigger house, a higher salary, a new car, good health, or what have you. It only becomes wrong, becomes sin, when those wants cause discontent. It has been said that "the itch for things is a virus that drains the soul of contentment," and that "we are most content when we are grateful for what we have, satisfied with what God has given us, and generous to others in need."

1 Timothy 6:6 tells us that "godliness with contentment is great gain." God grant that we be strong in the Lord and in the power of His might, that we be strong in the grace which is in Christ Jesus, and in such strength, know and experience the true and godly contentment that lasts and overcomes. Let it be so, for Jesus' sake. Amen.

HOLDING ON

Text: Psalm 40: 1-5, 11-13, 17; 1Peter 1: 3-9;
           Matthew 11: 25-30

Theme: Life's pressures.

Theme Statement: The spiritual, physical, emotional pressures of daily
life have always been with us, but with the advances in communications,
transportation, and other technologies that impact virtually all aspects
of our lives, those pressures have increased and continue to do so. How
can we not only cope, but regain some measure of stability in our daily
lives? Our Scripture passages give us the answer.

Key Passage: Matthew 11:28-29: "Come to Me, all you who are weary
and burdened, and I will give you rest. Take My yoke upon you and
learn from Me, for I am gentle and humble in heart, and you will find
rest for your souls."

Astressed-out secretary, during a period of unusually heavy job
demands, when everything was a mad rush, told her boss:
"When this rush is over, I'm going to have a nervous
breakdown. I earned it. I deserve it, and nobody's going to take it from
me." We all have times when we can relate to that secretary, don't we?
Times when the demands of job, family, other activities and
responsibilities gang up on us and cause our stress meter to peg out.
According to a USA Today article, anxiety and stress disorders are the
number one mental health problem in the nation.

And then, in addition to the demands of job, family, and all the other
responsibilities that pile up, we have a world situation that just seems to
get worse. War, terrorism, crime, immorality, a shaky economy, job
losses, bankruptcies, and what have you. Seems like there is no end of
things to worry about, to stress over. The world's a mess. But you
know something we tend to forget? The world's always been a mess,

ever since Adam and Eve decided to eat the forbidden fruit. We like to wax nostalgic about the "good ol' days." Well, the "good ol' days" were a mess too, with all the problems that exist today, just in varying degrees. But there is one aspect of life today that is different from life in the "good ol' days." Life is much more hectic, fast-paced, and can easily get out of control. A poet captured the tone of our present age when he wrote: "This is the age of the half-read page, the quick hash and the mad dash, the restless night with the nerves up-tight, the age of the brain strain, and the heart pain, the age of the catnaps until the spring snaps - and then the fun is done." Life magazine said this about today's hectic life-style: "Whoever isn't schizophrenic these days isn't thinking clearly."

Yes, life can get wearisome at times. Some people give up. Some become cynical. Some just drop out. And some rise above it. The American evangelist Dwight L. Moody once said that "Christians must never be found living under their circumstances. They must live above them." Life's pressures can have one of two consequences. They can come between us and God, pulling us away from God, or they can press us closer and closer to God. There's a saying that goes: "Some people go through life moping. Some go through life groping. Some go through life simply coping. The Christian, however, goes through life hoping. And that hope isn't just wishful thinking or a positive attitude. It's a solid optimism and hope grounded in God's promises, an optimism and hope about both the here and now and about the future."

The Apostle Peter calls the Christian's hope a "living hope." The Apostle John has been called the Apostle of love; the Apostle Paul the Apostle of faith; and the Apostle Peter the Apostle of hope. Why does Peter call the Christian's hope a "living hope?" Because it possesses life and vitality; it has life in itself; it gives life and has the object of life. It gives life because it is a hope that looks back into the past to the resurrection of Jesus Christ from the dead, a hope grounded and sealed once and for all by that resurrection. And it has the object of life because it looks forward into the future and guarantees an inheritance promised by God to all who do not lose hope and faith - an inheritance that can never perish, spoil, or fade - kept in heaven for you and me and all who are in Christ. And that living hope is the only thing that can enable us to hold on during the storms of life that beat on us because it is a living hope that brings the strength of Christ and the power of the Holy Spirit to every aspect of our lives.

And not only that, but we're told that through faith, our living hope is shielded by God's power until the return of our Lord Jesus Christ, so that we are sure of receiving that inheritance. Peter says, "In this you greatly rejoice, even though now for awhile you may have to suffer grief in all kinds of trials." Who better to speak of rejoicing in that "living hope" than Peter, who had betrayed his Lord and lost all hope, and then was restored into that "living hope" by Christ Himself after His resurrection. Peter delights in speaking of hope overcoming despair, life overcoming death, in the believer. What greater hope is there than the assurance that God's power guards us from within, to preserve us for an inheritance of salvation and glory in Christ that will be completely revealed to us when He returns. That inheritance, that crown of glory, is yours by name, by title, if you endure through faith to the end. In 1John 5:4 we're told, "This is the victory that has overcome the world, even our faith." And it is that faith, that hope, centered in Christ, that gives us the power to hold on in all circumstances.

David knew about this "living hope." Our Old Testament reading from Psalm 40 is a prayer of David for help when he was in deep distress and overwhelmed with troubles. And his distress was compounded by the gloating of his enemies who sought to take his life and who desired his ruin. David throws himself on the Lord's mercy. He says, "I waited patiently for the Lord." Patiently indicates that the relief he sought did not come quickly, but David resolved to continue believing, hoping, and praying until it did come. He waited not only with patience, but with assurance, a living hope that enabled him to hold on because it was based on the solid promises of God. You and I have that same assurance based on the solid promises of God that enable us to hold on.

David cries out, "Do not withhold your mercy from me, O Lord; may your love and your truth always protect me. For troubles without number surround me; my sins have overtaken me, and I cannot see. They are more than the hairs of my head, and my heart fails within me." David is overwhelmed, but he is holding on, knowing that God will never forsake him, that God had a wonderful plan for his life, just as He has for your life and mine and the lives of all His children in Christ.

And then, in God's time, the answer came. David says that God turned to him and heard his cry. God lifted him out of the slimy pit, out of the mud and mire of despondency and despair. God set his feet on a rock, gave him a firm place to stand, put a new song in his mouth, a hymn of praise to God. That rock upon which God gave David a firm place to stand was Christ. And Christ is our rock, the firm place where we stand against all the storms, troubles, and distresses of this world. And we can, like David, be assured that God in Christ, and through the Holy Spirit, will deliver us out of troubles and distress in due time if we just hold on, hold on.

Faith, based on the living hope, enables believers to rejoice even when their lives are being tossed about as on a troubled sea and in danger of becoming a shipwreck, even when, as Peter says, they are called on to suffer grief in all kinds of trials if it is God's will that it should be so. It is true that some believers experience greater affliction than others. But Scripture clearly says that, for the believer, no affliction or trial comes to them but that which God allows for His purpose. We are not to lay crosses upon ourselves, but we are called upon to take up the cross which God imposes on us. And it is God alone Who decides whether our faith, more precious than the purest gold, must be put through a fiery trial so it can be proved genuine and result in praise, glory, and honor when Christ returns.

In our Gospel passage, Jesus says, "Come to Me, all you who are weary and burdened, and I will give you rest." The weary and burdened are those who are loaded down with hard toil, with cares, worries, and problems. Jesus knows what it is like to be bone-weary and heavily burdened. Throughout His ministry, His fame was such that wherever He went, multitudes would press in on Him, all of them wanting something from this remarkable prophet and healer. There were times, we're told, when the weariness got to the point that Jesus hid Himself from the crowds to relax and pray, times when He would take His disciples to an isolated place where the crowds couldn't find them so they could rest and recuperate. And then there was the ultimate weariness and burden that Jesus experienced, a weariness and burden that proved too much for even the Son of God as Son of Man in His humanity, when after a full night and morning of beatings, mockings, and scourging, He was forced to drag that heavy cross on which He would be nailed for your sins and mine and the sins of the world, down that street of Jerusalem to the hill called Calvary. Jesus' human strength gave out, and the soldiers had to pull Simon out of the crowd to carry Jesus' cross for Him.

Are you overwhelmed, stressed, discouraged, depressed? Are you at a point where you don't know if you can handle the demands, the responsibilities, bearing down on you? Are you wondering how you're going to make it through tomorrow, next week, or even today? God wants to renew your strength and restore your joy. God wants you to hold on. Jesus says, "Come to Me, and I will give you rest!" He says, "Take My yoke upon you." Bring the yoke of your weariness and burdens to Him and exchange it for His yoke. You might say, "Well, that's just exchanging one load for another." But here's the difference. Christ's yoke is a yoke that rests its bearer. Oh yes, we may have to suffer affliction, persecution, hard trials for Him, but all these are more than counterbalanced by the power, help, strength, and consolation supplied by Christ when we take His yoke upon us. Compared to the yoke the devil, this world, and our sinful flesh would place upon us, the yoke that Jesus offers, He tells us, is easy and its burden is light. By placing ourselves under His yoke and learning from Him, we find the strength to hold on and we find rest for our souls. And who better to offer us rest, to take our burdens upon Himself, than the One Who took our greatest burden, the burden of sin and death to the cross, and through His death and resurrection, relieved us of that crushing load.

Martin Luther carried a heavy burden in life. He was subject to periods of deep depression and discouragement. During one of those periods, when things appeared especially bleak and hopeless, he was seen tracing two words in the dust of a table with his fingertip -- "Vivit, Vivit!" -- "He lives, He lives!" Because Christ lives, we can live abundantly today, despite the burdens and trials we face, and we can live eternally tomorrow. In Christ, we live a life that is both forgiven and forever.

In the book "Pilgrim's Progress," John Bunyan depicts the striking scene of a Christian fleeing from the world with a large bundle, a burden, resting on his shoulders. He arrives at the base of a hill. On the top of that hill there stands a cross, and below the hill there is a grave. As the man comes to the top of the hill and approaches the cross with his heavy burden, the load is suddenly released from his shoulders, drops to the ground, rolls down the hill and disappears into the empty grave. What a striking illustration of Jesus' invitation, "Come to Me and I will give you rest!". There is a Greek motto that says, "You will break the bow if you keep it always bent."

Don't let worry, stress, the demands and burdens of life keep your bow of life bent until it breaks. God wants us to live above those stresses, burdens, and circumstances, rather than live under them. Only the joy of God's presence gives us the right perspective on life. Only God's power can enable us to look above and beyond the troubles of life that will surely come. Only Christ gives us rest of soul, peace of mind and the strength to hold on no matter what the world throws at us. Christ is our secure balance, our wholeness, not only for eternity, but for right now, the day-to-day struggle of being here. The Prince of Peace is the only Sense in this non-sense world. He is Light in the confusion of darkness; He is Truth in the midst of the lies all around us; He is Clarity in what is otherwise confusion as we travel through the fog of life. We can't step out of the fog of life, but in Him, we have the only way of navigating within it and through it. "I am the Lord, and besides Me there is no Savior," God tells us. That's more than a statement of fact. It's a promise. And in the truth of those words, every part of our life holds together.

So, how are you going to make it through tomorrow, and all your tomorrows? First of all, remember what one person described as their favorite Bible verse - "It came to pass!" No matter what this life throws at you, it will pass. Second, when you get up in the morning, start the day with praise. Stretch your arms high and say, "This is the day the Lord has made; I will rejoice and be glad in it." And third, hold on, hold on to your "living hope" and all the spiritual treasures and blessings God has given you, and continues to give you, for this life and the life hereafter.

Blessed be the God and Father of our Lord Jesus Christ, Who in His great mercy, has given us the "living hope" through the resurrection of Jesus. Holding on to Jesus, I will find rest and be thankful. Amen.

PROTECTION FROM THE THREE ENEMIES

Text: Isaiah 41: 8-14; 2Thessalonians 3: 1-5; John 17: 13-19

Theme: Jesus prays for our protection.

Theme Statement: All who are in Christ are the covenant people of God, and therefore are under His protection. Time and time again God tells us in His Word, "do not fear," "do not fear," "do not be afraid." We can be sure of His Presence and protection in both the best of times and the worst of times, certain that He will strengthen us, help us, and uphold us. And we desperately need that protection, for we Christians are in a constant state of warfare in this life - warfare against the three enemies that seek to destroy us - Satan, the world, and ourselves (that is, our sinful nature.)

Key Passage: John 17: 15. "My prayer is not that You take them out of the world, but that You protect them from the evil one."

†

P rotection and security are major issues in people's lives, and always have been - protection of our loved ones, protection of our homes, protection of jobs, protection of finances and savings, protection of health, and on and on. Let us consider another protection we desperately need, the most important protection - spiritual protection. All those other protections are temporal - they pass away - but spiritual protection brings us to the ultimate security of eternal life. Do you feel protected? You should, because God's Word assures you and I, and all His family in Christ, of His protection.

Our Old Testament passage portrays God as the Family Protector of Israel. And Israel desperately needed God's protection. They returned from exile to a land and cities devastated and ruined. To restore the land to productivity, to rebuild the cities, including Jerusalem, to rebuild the Temple, seemed a monumental , if not impossible task. Not only that, but they were surrounded by enemies.

It would have been so easy to lose faith and just give up. But in our passage, God, through His prophet Isaiah, tells them three times, "do not fear," "do not fear," "do not be afraid." He tells them, "I am with you, do not be dismayed, for I am your God. I will strengthen you, help you, uphold you with My righteous right hand."

He tells them that their enemies who oppose them, who rage against them, who wage war against them, will be ashamed and disgraced and be nothing at all. He tells them, "Do not be afraid, O worm Jacob, O little Israel." Those words "worm" and "little" refer to their feeble condition. He assures them that they may depend upon His Presence and protection as their God and Redeemer, that He is all-sufficient for them in the worst of times as well as in the best of times. These words were intended to silence their fears and encourage their faith during their distress. Those words are for us too. Are you weak? God says, "I will strengthen you!" Are you destitute? God says, "I will help you!" Are you ready to sink or fall? God says, "I will uphold you with My righteous right hand."

The Apostle Paul certainly knew the absolute need for God's protection. In our Epistle passage, Paul asks the Thessalonians to pray for him and his companions. Paul wrote this letter in Corinth, where he and his companions were experiencing severe opposition from the Jews who were determined to stop the free course of the Gospel by silencing Paul and his co-workers. Paul asks the Thessalonians to pray that the message of the Lord may spread rapidly and be honored, and that he and his companions be delivered from wicked and evil men. Paul knew that prayer unites the Body of Christ.

God did not leave Paul alone in his distress. In Acts 18: 9-10, we are told that the Lord spoke to Paul in a vision and said: "Do not be afraid; keep on speaking; do not be silent. For I am with you, and no one is going to attack and harm you, because I have many people in this city." God assured Paul of His protection.

Our Gospel passage speaks of protection. It is taken from John, chapter 17, which is known as the High Priestly Prayer of Jesus. He prayed this prayer out loud with the eleven disciples before His arrest, after Judas had left to go about his plan to betray Jesus. Jesus was about to go to the cross. As our High Priest, He would enter the heavenly sanctuary of God's Presence by His own Blood, the once for all sacrifice that obtained our eternal redemption. As our High Priest, Jesus also knew the temptations, persecutions, trials, tribulations, and dangers His disciples would face after He left this world and ascended to the Father in heaven. And so, in His prayer, He asks for the Father's protection of His disciples, and not for them only, but as we read in verse 20, "also for those who will believe in Me through their message." That's you and me and every believer.

And oh, how we need that protection. We Christians are in a constant state of warfare in this life - warfare against the three enemies that seek to separate us from our Lord and bring us to destruction. Who are these three enemies?

The first enemy is Satan. Jesus prays in verse 15: "My prayer is not that You take them out of the world, but that You protect them from the evil one." Satan's primary objective is to turn people away from God's grace in Jesus Christ, discourage, and if possible, destroy the believers' faith. He knows the final outcome when Christ returns to judge the world. He knows his final destiny - to be thrown into the lake of fire - hell - for eternity, and he wants to take as many people as he can with him. A poll was taken some time ago that showed that a great many people do not believe that Satan exists. That is deadly, and exactly what Satan wants, for it leaves those people defenseless against his temptations, lies, and deception. And he is a fiendishly clever liar and deceiver.

It has been said that Satan, like a fisherman, baits his hook according to the appetite of the fish. Satan is not omniscient, all-knowing like God. He doesn't intuitively know our weaknesses. Through temptation, he searches for our weaknesses until he finds them, and there he concentrates his attacks. Give the devil an inch and he will take it to the distance. Give in to him in one small area, and soon you will find you are giving in more and more. Ephesians 4:27 tells us: "do not give the devil a foothold." 1Peter 5 tells us: "Be self-controlled and alert. Your enemy the devil prowls around like a roaring lion looking for someone to devour. Resist him, standing firm in the faith....And the God of all grace, Who called you to His eternal glory in Christ...will Himself restore you and make you strong, firm, and steadfast."

In His High Priestly Prayer, Jesus' petitioned to the Father for all His disciples and followers - then, now, and until He returns - that the Father protect us from the evil one, make us strong, firm, and steadfast in our resistance to the evil one, and when we stumble and fall, forgive and restore us in faith, strength, firmness, and steadfastness.

The second enemy we face is the world, both its allurements and persecutions. Jesus prays to the Father: "I will remain in the world no longer, but they are still in the world, and I am coming to You. Holy Father, protect them by the power of Your Name - the Name You gave Me - so that they may be one as we are One. While I was with them, I protected them and kept them safe by that Name..." O course, Jesus' protection of the disciples while He was with them was not apart from the Father, and the Father's protection of them and us is not apart from Jesus. Jesus and the Father are One.

Jesus knew that the hostility of the world against God that had fallen on Him would now fall on the disciples, and on all who would in faith receive Christ as Lord and Savior through the preaching of the Gospel. Why this hostility against Christians? Because, as Jesus says in His prayer, "They are not of the world, even as I am not of it." Believers in Christ are sanctified by the Holy Spirit - that is, set apart to God, and set apart from the world. The world system hated the disciples and followers of Christ, and continues to do so today because we are in the world, but not of the world. We see that hate all over the world today, including in America. Compared to the Word of God and our values in Christ, the values of this world are trash and rubbish, as the Apostle Paul says in Philippians 3:8. The world hates Christians for exposing its sham values and for not conforming to them. And that hatred intensifies the more the Word of God is preached and makes further inroads upon the world. The world refuses to acknowledge that Christians are in the world for the world's sake, as Christ's ambassadors, Christ's witnesses to save the world.

Jesus knew the dangers that a sinful and malignant world with its temptations and allurements would pose to Christians. The world (God's creation) is not evil, but the ways of the world are evil since the fall. Jesus does not ask that His disciples, then and now, be kept from all conflict with the world. The Christian's conflict with the world will continue until the Lord returns. Jesus asks that the Father protect them from the world's evil ways, from the corruption of the world, protect them so that they may not be overcome by the world, that they stand strong against the world and wicked men who, not being content to reject God's Word and Gift of Grace themselves, try to force others to reject it. They are truly tools of Satan. Jesus prays that His followers be kept in oneness with Him and with each other, just as He, the Father, and the Holy Spirit are One. "Protect them," Jesus prays, "by the power of Your Name," which is the same as the power of Your Word. What a comfort it must have been for the disciples to hear Jesus commit them to the care, and protection of the Father. And what a comfort for us, knowing we are included in His prayer.

And that brings us to the third enemy, and perhaps the most dangerous enemy - ourselves - that is, our sinful nature. We Christians are at war not only with Satan and the world, but with ourselves, and desperately need the protection of God against ourselves. I am convinced that I am my own worst enemy. Why are we our own worst enemy? Because, as the Psalmist tells us, "the heart is deceitful." Woe be to the person who trusts his heart instead of God's Word. Jesus spoke of this in Mark 7: 20-22 when He said: "From within, out of men's hearts, come evil thoughts, sexual immorality, theft, murder, adultery, greed, malice, deceit, lewdness, envy, slander, arrogance, and folly." That's quite a list, and pretty much covers every sin you can think of. The Apostle Paul, in Romans chapter 7, speaks of the war within each Christian being waged between our sinful nature and the

Holy Spirit Who dwells within us. Paul also tells us not to grieve the Holy Spirit. We grieve the Holy Spirit whenever we give in to our sinful nature. Paul puts it this way: "The things I should do, I do not do. The things I should not do, I do…What a wretched man I am! Who will rescue me from this body of death?" Then he gives the answer: "Thanks be to God - through Jesus Christ our Lord!"

It is part of our sinful nature to blame someone or something else for our failings. We're often like the little boy whose mother told him, "While I'm gone, don't get into the jam." "No, mother, I won't," he promised. When she returned, she noticed jam on the boy's fingers and the corners of his mouth. "Didn't I tell you not to get into the jam," she said. "Yes, mother, you did," he answered. His mother said, "Didn't I tell you that when Satan tempts you, you should tell him to get behind you?" The boy answered, "Yes, but when he got there, he pushed me right on in."

The greatest example of playing the blame game is that of our forebears Adam and Eve, and they started it right after they fell into sin by eating the forbidden fruit. When confronted by God, Adam blamed his wife whom God had given him for giving him the fruit. Eve, on the other hand, blamed the serpent who had tempted her. Both, in their newly acquired sinful nature, tried to shift the blame, and their human progeny have been doing the same right up to the present time and beyond.

The truth is that Satan and this world can tempt us, but they cannot force us to sin. We, and no one or nothing else, are at fault. Our sinful nature works through our free-will to lead us to sin, and it is our decision, and ours alone, whether to follow our sinful nature or follow the counsel and leading of the Holy Spirit dwelling in us.

The greatest danger is when a person thinks that they can stand fast against their own sinful nature and free-will under their own power. In the account of Ulysses, we're told of an island where sirens with their beautiful songs would lure sailors to shore and then kill them. When Ulysses came near their island, he lashed himself to the mast of his ship so that when he was tempted to rush toward his ruin, he could not. That's a fictional story, but there's a real life lesson in it for us. The lesson is that we must, in faith, lash ourselves to the cross of Christ, for only in His strength can we overcome our three enemies - Satan, the world, and ourselves. Jesus told Paul, "My strength is made perfect in your weakness." And Paul said, "I can do all things through Christ Who strengthens me."

Finally, Jesus prays that His disciples, and all who are His in faith, may have the full measure of His joy within us. Following Jesus' passion, death, and resurrection, His disciples would recall His words and experience the full measure of His joy from knowing that He had conquered the evil one, conquered the world, conquered sin, death, and hell, and brought eternal life to them. And we have that same full measure of His joy, knowing that we are one with Him and the Father and the Holy Spirit, one with our brothers and sisters in Christ, knowing that we are redeemed by His Blood and sanctified by the Holy Spirit, knowing that Christ is our Protector, Christ is our Security, Christ is our Joy - for time and for eternity. Amen.

YEARS OF THE LOCUSTS

Text: Psalm 39:4-7;   Joel 2:23-26;   Luke 13:6-9

Theme: God can restore the lost blessings of wasted years.

Theme Statement: God's grace is large enough to make a life eaten up by the locusts of sin and rebellion a blessed and successful life to His praise and glory and to the highest good of the individual.

Key Passage: Joel 2:25.   "I will repay you for the years the locusts have eaten - the great locust and the young locust, the other locusts and the locust swarm - My great army that I sent among you."

✝

I t was another of those periods in Israel's history when the people had turned away from the Lord and gone their own way into sin and rebellion against God. So God sent a plague of locusts over the land as punishment for their sin, and He sent the prophet Joel to call them to repentance. Joel, in his inspired book of the Bible by his name, refers to this time as "the years the locusts have eaten," so terrible were the effects of the plague and the drought. Years of work and progress were wiped out. The land was totally devastated by the vast army of locusts, so enormous in number that they hid the sun from view and blackened the sky. They devoured every scrap of vegetation in their path. They not only ate the grain and the fruit, but also the bark off the trees. What Joel describes here is indescribable calamity, utter devastation.

Joel calls for a period of national lamentation, national repentance. As God's spokesman, he calls for the priests and ministers to put on sackcloth and wear it day and night - sackcloth, the garment of mourning that symbolized humility, sorrow, and repentance. He called for all the citizens of the land to engage in confession and contrition towards God. He called for them to open their eyes and see things clearly, for only if the meaning of the locust plague, the reason God had allowed it to come upon them, was understood and accepted, only if they learned from it, could their lamentation and repentance have any lasting significance.

The years of the locusts had been wasted years for Israel - wasted because they had failed to be the people God had created and called them to be, wasted because they turned their back on the covenant God had made with them. They were to be a light to the nations; they were to reflect the light of God's love and grace to the other nations, and by their example, draw those nations to that light so they too could experience God's love and grace and salvation. But instead, Israel went its own way. The people pursued evil, and in doing so, they exchanged the light of God's grace for years of darkness and gloom and emptiness. And so Joel, God's prophet, calls His people to repentance, for this was their only hope of averting further disaster.

But Joel did something else. He brought God's promise to the people. God tells them through Joel: "I will repay you for the years the locusts have eaten. I will send you the autumn and spring rains." In Scripture, the autumn and spring rains were an outward manifestation of spiritual and material blessings, a restored fellowship with God. God tells them that if they repent and turn back to Him, their threshing floors will be filled with grain, their vats will overflow with fresh wine and oil. God would fully restore to them the blessings and abundance lost during the years of the locusts. They would again know and experience the abiding Presence of God Himself, dwelling in their midst and leading them to the fulfillment of His good and gracious will in their lives. What a great promise - "I will repay you for the wasted years that the locusts have eaten." Only God can promise that, because only God can do that. And that promise is as much for you and me, and all our brothers and sisters in Christ, as it was for the people in Joel's time.

I don't know about you, but I've had some wasted years during my life, some "years of the locusts," so to speak. I frittered away some years with little or nothing outstanding to show for them, years of insisting on having my own way instead of letting God have His way, years of self-seeking instead of God-seeking, of putting my will ahead of God's will. Instead of saying like King David, "God, my times are in your hand," my attitude was, "God, my times are in my hand, and when I need your help, I'll call on You for it." Well, the result was mostly wasted years and emptiness. And you know something? Wasted years never start out as wasted years. Wasted years start out as wasted hours and wasted days. And they go by so quickly. I believe it was Seneca, the Roman philosopher and politician, who said, "The wheels of the chariot of time turn in only one direction - forward." The years are precious, short and swift, then they are gone.

God cares deeply about how we use our time, our hours, days, and years, because that time is a gift from Him. One of the most important questions we can ask ourselves is: "How am I treating that gift?" "Am I using God's gift of time in a manner pleasing to Him, in a way that honors Him and is useful to Him." If the people in Joel's day had asked themselves that question, perhaps they could have avoided those wasted years lost to the locusts. But they didn't. So God allowed the locusts to come in order to open their eyes to what was happening, so they could learn from it, and learning, turn their hearts back to Him. And God sometimes does the same with us, allows the locusts to come into our lives, so to speak, in order to open our eyes to our circumstances and condition, and turn to Him with hearts seeking His will and purpose.

Charles Swindoll, in his book *Moses,* says that just as Israel had its wilderness experience so God could form and shape them into the people, the nation, He wanted them to be, so each of us has his or her own wilderness cycle so God can form and shape us for His glory and our highest good. God not only wants us to endure the wilderness experiences He allows to come into our lives, He wants us to learn from them. And He has given us His Holy Spirit, through Whom we are both strengthened to endure and enabled to learn what God wants us to learn. We can either humble ourselves before God, submit to the Holy Spirit's leading and endure and learn, or we can remain proud and self-centered and refuse to learn and experience more locust years. It's our choice.

I'm sure we've all said at one time or another, "Why can't I work out this situation?" "Why can't I get past these obstacles that hold me back and drag me down?" "Why can't I move on from failure to success?" Could it be because we refuse to learn from our wilderness experience; we refuse to humble ourselves and submit to God's will? It's much easier to blame someone else or something else for our troubles, even God. When we say, "I can't do it," what we usually mean is, "I won't do it!" But our God is patient, and He knows how long to test each of us, how long the wilderness experience must be for each of us, how difficult the testing must be for each of us. He knows how many of our days, months, or years will go to the locusts before we give ourselves to Him completely.

In manufacturing communities, large fortunes are sometimes made out of what is technically called "waste." They recycle it and use it for productive purposes. Well, God is in the recycling business too. God recycles human lives, restores human lives, and only God can do that. We can't do anything about the years we wasted, years when we kept God at arms length. We can't recover those years lost to the locusts, restore those years spent in the wilderness of rebellion against God. We can't undo the past, as much as we might like to, and there are certainly portions of my past I would like to undo. But God, Who is not limited by time or circumstances, has the wonderful power of bringing the highest good out of wasted years, out of a misspent past. God's grace is large enough to take a person's life that has been blighted, eaten up by the locusts of sin and rebellion and failure, and make it a complete, blessed, and successful life to His praise and glory and the person's greatest good. The Bible and Christian history are filled to overflowing with accounts of the grand and fruitful work of restored individuals, individuals whose lives contained wasted years that the locusts had eaten.

Remember that promise God gave to Israel, that promise that is also ours: "I will repay you for the wasted years, for the years the locusts have eaten. I will restore you." This promise gives us a profound insight into the nature of God. It is in God's nature to be gracious, merciful, long-suffering, and full of love for His people. God's will is that His wrath be turned aside, and the key to having God turn aside from His wrath over our sin and rebellion is our turning away from our sin and rebellion through the power of the Holy Spirit, turning back to God in confession, repentance, and faith, and letting God take control of our lives, because only in Him can that which was lost be found and restored. Where there is true repentance on our part, God Himself will "repent" so to speak - that is, He will turn back the tide of judgment and reveal HIs mercy; He will repay for the years that the locusts have eaten.

That was the heart of God's message through Joel to His people, and to us today. Just as that army of locusts desolated the whole land of Israel, so sin desolates lives and separates us from God. But restoration and new life is ours through God's compassion and grace poured out on us through His Son Who paid the full and terrible price for our restoration and new life. Jesus Christ the Son of God, came to us as Son of Man, sacrificed His Body and Blood on the cross as ransom for our forgiveness and rose again for our restoration and new life. In Christ alone we have new life, we are made a new creation. The old life, the old creation is passed away, and with it our wasted years, our years eaten by the locusts, replaced with the success, fulfillment, and joy of the new life, the new creation Christ purchased for us.

And God wants us to have that restoration and new life. Oh, how He wants that. He wants to redeem our lives from the locusts, so to speak, from everything that drags us down and holds us back from being who and what He created us to be. The parable of the fig tree in the Gospel reading referenced is a picture of God's patience with us and Jesus interceding for us on our behalf. The fig tree represents Israel, but it also represents us. The owner of the vineyard represents God, and He expected the fig tree to produce fruit. Now that was a reasonable expectation since the fig tree was planted in very favorable soil - in a vineyard - not on some neglected ground, and it had received good care. But for three years, which symbolizes the owner's patience, an exceptionally long period more than sufficient for a fig tree, the tree produced nothing. So the owner told the caretaker "cut it down." It had wasted those years, producing nothing, and simply using up the soil. But the caretaker, representing Jesus, said, "Sir, leave it alone for another year. I'll work with it, dig around it, fertilize it, give it even more special attention. If it bears fruit next year, fine. If not, then cut it down!"

Here is the lesson we should take from this. Israel had enjoyed the richest blessings of God and the privilege of being in covenant relationship with God. God had every right to expect Israel to be fruitful and fulfill the purpose He had ordained for them - to be a light to the nations. But they wasted both the blessings and the opportunities God gave them. They were simply using up the soil, so to speak, without producing fruit. So God sent the locusts to devastate the land and Joel to call them to repentance so He could restore them. We, as Christians, have received the fruits of God's amazing grace in Christ - forgiveness, salvation, restoration, new life here and eternal life hereafter. God has every right to expect us, who are favored with the privileges and blessings of the Gospel, to be fruitful for Him, to be faithful and committed to Him, and to use our powers and talents He has given us in His service.

And our Lord Jesus, through the Holy Spirit, continually works in our lives to bring this about because He doesn't want the fig tree - that is, your life and my life cut down and lost.

The bottom line is this: Deny God and the locusts are victorious, and if a person continues to deny God's grace in Christ until they die, the desolation of that life will be final and complete. On the other hand, if a person turns to God in repentance and faith in the Lord Jesus Christ, God will restore to that person blessings lost during their wasted years, their years of the locusts, but even more than that, God will give them new life, a fruitful life as a new creation in Christ Jesus. God's concern is more with our present and our future than with our past. What a person is now and what they have the potential to be as a child of God, is more important than what they were in the past. God can take a wasted past and make a beautiful, fulfilling life out of it. I like Martin Luther's comment concerning this: "God can carve the rotten wood," in other words, make out of wasted years a thing of exquisite beauty.

Life is too short to waste any of it, to give any of it away to the locusts. As the Psalmist says, "My days are a mere handbreadth and my life is but a breath. My hope is in God." God grant that we not waste a day of time remaining to us in this life, that we remain faithful to the Lord Jesus Christ Who gave His life for us, and that we bear much fruit for Him Who is so patient and gracious to us. Amen.

WHO COULD ASK FOR MORE.

Text: Acts 20: 17-35; Revelation 7: 9-17; John 10: 22-30

Theme: Christ - Our Fulfillment, our Glory, our Security.

Theme Statement: In our reading from Acts, the Apostle Paul gives his farewell address to the elders in Ephesus. He reviews his life and ministry among them. He had served the Lord with all humility, and with tears and trials. Most precious to Paul was not his own life, but finishing the course and the ministry he received from the Lord Jesus, to testify to the Gospel of the grace of God. Paul rejoiced in his ministry, in his suffering for Christ, and in the churches Christ had established through his ministry. In Christ, Paul found total fulfillment - fulfillment in this life and the next. In our reading from Revelation, the Apostle John, in his vision given by Christ, sees the Church before the Throne of God in eternal fulfillment and glory. Multitudes which no one could number raised their voices in a crescendo of praise to God and the Lamb. The glory of John's vision is beyond mortal comprehension, and we who are Christ's through faith will fully experience that great glory. In our Gospel reading, Jesus speaks of His sheep (that's you and I and all believers). Jesus defines the relation between Him, the Shepherd, and we His sheep in four short statements: 1. "I know them." 2. "They hear My voice." 3. "They follow Me." 4. "I give them eternal life." He says that His sheep will never perish and that no one can snatch them out of His hand and the Father's hand. That's ultimate and total security. And so, in Christ, we have Fulfillment, Glory, and Security: Who could ask for more?

Key Passage: John 10:27-28. "My sheep hear My voice, and I know them, and they follow Me. I give them eternal life, and they will never perish, and no one will snatch them out of My hand."

I n one of his great writings called *Orthodoxy*, G.K. Chesterton said: "As I have studied and restudied the life of Jesus, I have discovered a great secret. That secret is Jesus' great joy. Jesus experienced heartache, loss, sorrow, and of course extreme suffering for our sake, but in spite of it all, He was, in His humanity, a Man of Joy."

People tend to confuse joy with happiness. They are quite different. Happiness is an emotion, a feeling, whereas joy is an attitude. Happiness can quickly be replaced with sorrow and deep sadness with trials and tribulations and loss in this life. But joy, especially and only for the Christian, can remain a constant, and strengthen and uphold us during those times of deep sadness. Scripture tells us that for the joy set before Him, Christ endured the cross, suffering and death for our salvation. True Christianity is a joyful Christianity. We are a forgiven, redeemed people, who belong to the faithful flock on the way to heaven. We are people with great joy which no sadness can take away. Some of our brothers and sisters in Christ are already in Heaven experiencing that ultimate, completed joy in all its fullness. But we, who are still in this world, have joy in Christ now, and one day at the Lord's calling, will also experience it in its totality and fullness. There are many aspects to our joy in Christ, and our Scripture readings give us three of those aspects - Fulfillment, Glory, and Security.

First, *Fulfillment.* In our reading from Acts, Paul addresses the elders of the church at Ephesus, and his words reflect a heart of tenderness and love for his flock. He reviews his life and work among them. He says that he served the Lord with all humility and with tears and with trials. The Greek word used here for served or servant is *doulos,* which means slave. Paul is saying that he slaved for the Lord with tears and trials.

Paul says that he did not shrink from declaring to both Jews and Gentiles repentance toward God and faith in the Lord Jesus Christ. The entire Gospel is centered in this repentance and faith. Paul never concealed or held back a single thing of God's Word, and he suffered for it. It would have been so easy for him to have kept still on some parts of God's Word that angered and offended some people, or to give those parts of God' Word a false interpretation that would have been acceptable to those people. Many preachers, teachers, church officials do that today, and consider themselves wise in doing so. God, in His Word, calls that foolishness and abominable. Paul always bore in mind the accounting for his ministry that he would have to give to his Lord at the last day. So he proclaimed all the counsel of God, every doctrine, every Truth of God, omitting, altering, toning down nothing. That is something the false teachers in the church today should keep in mind, and tremble in fear at the thought of giving an account to their Lord.

Preaching, teaching, and witnessing God's Word to others in its full truth will inevitably result in criticism, resistance, persecution, and tears. So it was with the Prophets, with Jesus, with the Apostles, with Paul, with many of the Lord's faithful servants today, and so with us. Paul warns those elders of the church in Ephesus of the coming dangers after his departure - fierce wolves, even some among their own number, who will not spare the flock, who will speak twisted things, false doctrine, to draw people after them. He exhorts those elders to pay careful attention to themselves and to all the flock - yes, all the flock - because a true shepherd loves every sheep, every lamb. What Paul exhorts those elders to do pertains to every Christian, because Christians built up in Christ, and knowledgeable of God's Word, are the Church's best defense against those fierce wolves and false teachers.

Paul knows, through the Holy Spirit, that more imprisonment and afflictions await him. He could have refused of his own will, but Paul was wholly submissive to the Holy Spirit's will. The divine will superseded his human will. Paul tells the Ephesians that they will not see his face again. A spiritual father is taking a last leave from his spiritual children. But he does one more thing before parting. He commends them to God and to the Word of His Grace. Paul did not consider his own life as most precious. Most precious to him was finishing the course and the ministry he received from the Lord Jesus, to testify to the Gospel of the grace of God. He was willing to die at any time for the Lord's Name. And he did die; he was martyred for the Lord's Name.

What do we see when we consider Paul's life? We see fulfillment, a fulfilled life. Paul would later say: "I have fought the good fight, I have finished the race, I have kept the faith. Henceforth there is laid up for me the crown of righteousness which the Lord, the righteous Judge, will award to me on that day, and not only to me, but also to all who have loved His appearing." That's true fulfillment, a truly fulfilled life. Do you want a fulfilled life? Who doesn't want a fulfilled life? Well, this world isn't going to give it to you. A fulfilled life is only a life in Christ, because Christ is the Source of that life, the Creator and Redeemer of that life. Before we were ever born, God knew each of us by name, and designed His plan, His purpose for our lives. God told Jeremiah the prophet: "Before I formed you in the womb, I knew you, and before you were born, I consecrated you; I appointed you a prophet to the nations."

The fulfilled life is a life open and submissive to the Holy Spirit leading us to God's plan and purpose for our life, a life whose highest priority is accomplishing God's plan and purpose for us by the grace of God, the leading of our Savior, and the power of the Holy Spirit. And hear this: God never takes a true and faithful servant of His out of this life until His plan and purpose for that life are accomplished. Death cannot prematurely foil God's plan and purpose for one of His saints. God is Sovereign over both life and death. We have a hard time understanding this, especially in the case of someone taken out of this life at what we consider an early age. We say, "Why Lord? He/she was young, had so much more to accomplish as husband, father, wife, mother, and servant of Your Church." But God Who establishes the plan and purpose for each of our lives, in His all-knowing wisdom, knows when His plan and purpose for the life of each of His saints is fulfilled, and God insures that the life of each of His saints is a life of fulfillment. Fulfillment is an integral part of that complete joy each saint has in God's Presence. We too have the joy of fulfillment now, but we

258

will experience it fully when we go to join our brother and sister saints in the Presence of Christ. The joy of *Fulfillment* in Christ! Who could ask for more?

Another aspect of the joy we have in Christ is that of *Glory*. In our reading from Revelation, we get an awesome picture of this glory. In the vision given him by the Lord, the Apostle John sees the Church before the Throne of God in eternal blessedness. No one could number the multitude gathered before the Throne, and the greatness of that multitude is brought out in the four part phrase - "out of every nation and tribe and people and language" - the entire Church, the glorious fruit of the Lamb's sacrifice, and only God knows the number.

This vast host cries out with a loud voice, with thunderous acclamation: "Salvation belongs to our God Who sits on the Throne, and to the Lamb." Already, here on earth, we sing salvation when we worship, but our song is weak, our voice faint, compared to this song of salvation when all saints join in one harmonious volume in the very presence of the Throne and the Lamb. Our imperfect worship in our earthly sanctuaries shall there be in supreme perfection. And perfect worship will be our highest delight. Do you feel uplifted when you worship? I hope so. Well, just wait until you get to heaven. John sees the Church with all tribulations behind it. The saints have washed their robes, made them white, in the Blood of the Lamb. Sheltered in the very Presence of God, they have no more hunger, thirst, scorching heat. Hunger, thirst, heat symbolizes all the hardships, trials, afflictions, pains, weariness, sorrow, suffering, and loss in this life, until we reach death and instantly pass into glory to heaven, our true home, where the Lamb, our Divine Shepherd, will lead us to springs of living waters and God will wipe away every tear from our eyes. Tears here in this life; eternal joys there in the life to come.

To wash our robes means that we believe in the bloody sacrifice of the Lamb for our redemption and salvation. And only that Blood, and nothing else in the universe, whitens us so that we may stand before God. Here on earth, our robes still become stained and need constant

259

cleansing through confession, repentance, and coming to the Lord's table to receive that Body crucified for us and that Blood shed for us. But in heaven, our robes remain brilliantly white in holiness forever.

The blessedness, the joy, the glory of John's vision given to him by Christ is beyond human comprehension. It is a glory that we partially see now. As Paul said: "For now we see in a mirror dimly, but then we will see face to face." Then we will see and be surrounded by the *Shekinah*, the full and indescribable glory of God, the glory that our loved ones in Christ who have gone before us see and are surrounded by. We too will have the joy of that Glory. The joy of *Glory* in Christ! Who could ask for more?

Finally, another aspect of that joy in Christ that is ours is that of *Security*. And we are told of that security by our Lord Himself in our Gospel reading. The Jews again confront Jesus, determined to force the issue of who He claims to be. And so they challenge Him: "If you are the Christ, tell us plainly!" Jesus meets their challenge squarely in His first response: "I told you, and you do not believe." He had answered their question concerning His Person and office on other occasions in the past. It's as if Jesus is saying, "Where are your ears?" And He lets them know that He knows their unbelief. Many today are like those Jews, challenging Jesus' claim because of unbelief, despite all the proofs of His claim to be the Messiah, the Christ, the Son of God, and Son of Man.

In order to settle the question once and for all, Jesus refers them to the most convincing proofs that He is the Christ - the miracles that He does in the Father's Name and which speak for Him. His miracles prove every word of His concerning His Person and office as the Christ of God. That should have removed all doubt in the minds of those Jews, and also in the minds of doubters today. The fact that He does those miracles in the Father's Name is additional proof that He is the Son of God. The cry and evidence of Jesus' miracles should have been ringing in those doubters' ears.

Jesus tells them: "You do not believe because you are not My sheep." And He goes on to say: "My sheep hear My voice, and I know them, and they follow Me." They do not listen to the voice of strangers. This analogy of Jesus is true concerning actual sheep. When a stranger calls, "Come sheep! Come sheep!" they run and flee, but when the shepherd calls, they run to him, for they know his voice. There are many strangers today, some even in churches, who are leading the Lord's sheep astray. True Christians must hear and listen to no voice but their true Shepherd's, Christ's voice which we hear in His Word, for He is the Living Word. In four short statements, Jesus defines the relationship between Him, the Shepherd, and His sheep: 1. "They hear My voice." 2. "I know them." 3. "They follow Me." 4. "I give them eternal life." Jesus chooses the path; the sheep trust and follow, and if this means the cross at times, in the power of the Spirit, they do not waver, just as the Shepherd did not waver in going to the cross for them.

Jesus says that His sheep will never perish, and that no one will snatch them out of His hand. He emphasizes this promise by adding: "My Father, Who has given them to Me, is greater than all, and no one is able to snatch them out of the Father's hand." And Jesus seals this promise with His words: "I and the Father are One!" The Father's hand and Jesus' hand. Neither satan, demon spirits, or human foes, no matter how mighty, can snatch us away from our God and Savior. Now that's Security - ultimate, total, and everlasting security. The joy of *Security* in Christ! Who could ask for more?

People seek security, strive for it, work hard for it, sacrifice for it. But if we learn anything from history, or even from 9/11, we learn that this world, government, and our institutions cannot guarantee or provide true security. The only true and certain security in this life and the next is being one of the Good Shepherd's sheep. That is the only truly secure life - the life Jesus gives. And why? Because it is the life that flows from God, is grounded in God, joins to God, and leads to God. It pulses in every believer's heart, becomes stronger as faith increases, and reaches its full flower in the glory of heaven. Temporal death merely lifts the believer from earth to heaven. And when that day of glory comes to each of us, as it did to our loved ones before us, then the life that Jesus gives will manifest itself to us in its total majesty, power, richness, and greatness, in its total fulfillment, total glory, total security, just as it is being manifested now to all the saints in heaven.

Total *Fulfillment* in Christ; Unspeakable *Glory* in Christ; Absolute *Security* in Christ. That is our joy, both in this life, and in the life to come. Who could ask for more? Amen.

THE PAST IS PAST

Text: John 21:13-19; Philippians 3:13-14; Isaiah 43:16, 18-19

Theme: Not letting sins and failures of the past determine our future.

Theme Statement: Christians are always humbled by the contrast between what they are and what they desire to be in Christ. Too often, the stumbling block to their growing more and more in Christ is something in their past that they just cannot shake off. Scripture makes it clear that Christians are not to be controlled or absorbed by past sins or failures. Just as Jesus assured Peter of total forgiveness for his denials of his Lord, and reinstated him to his high calling of apostleship, so He assures us of total forgiveness and reinstates us to our high calling of discipleship. Scripture tells us that God removes our sins from us as far as the east is from the west. When God forgives our sins, He no longer remembers them. Nor should we. The past is past!

Key Passage: Philippians 3:13-14. "Forgetting what is behind and straining toward what is ahead, I press on toward the goal to win the prize for which God has called me heavenward in Christ Jesus."

We've all done or said things in the past that we deeply regret, some things that we never thought we would do. And all too often, we allow such sins and failures to haunt us. Even, when in faith, we know with certainty that God has forgiven us for the sake of Jesus Who paid the full and terrible price for all our sins on the cross, there may be times when we just can't seem to set those sins and failures aside, be done with them, and let the past be the past. And Satan will have a field day holding those sins and failures over our head if we let him. Not letting the past be the past can seriously affect our relationship with God and with others. Not letting the past be the past can destroy friendships; it can wreak havoc in marriages; it can cause spiritual, physical, and emotional sickness, sap our energy and keep us from using the talents and gifts God has given us to be all that God wants us to be. Not letting the past be the past can destroy our future.

Simon Peter committed a sin that he never thought himself capable of committing. Impetuous and rash by nature, Peter had spoken grand statements and made grand promises. When Jesus asked His disciples, "Who do you say I am?," it was Peter who spoke up and profoundly confessed, "You are the Christ (Messiah), the Son of the Living God." When Jesus told them of His coming arrest, trial, and crucifixion, and that all of them would desert Him, it was Peter who vehemently objected and told Jesus, "Even though all of these forsake You, I will never forsake You. I will die for You!" And then, when the test came, Peter failed miserably, not once, but three times denying his Lord, denying with cursing and swearing that he even knew Jesus, or had anything to do with Him.

When Peter remembered Jesus' prophecy that he would deny Him three times, he went out and wept bitterly. Peter was absolutely devastated, broken over what he had done. He had done the unthinkable. He had thrice denied, betrayed, disowned his Lord and Master, the Son of the Living God Whom he had previously confessed. After Jesus' resurrection and His appearances to the disciples, including Peter, imagine how he must have been overwhelmed by the burden of shame and regret that the memory of those denials caused him. How Jesus dealt with this is told in our Gospel lesson, and it is one of my favorite portions of Scripture. It gives us an intimate, emotional, and loving account of how Jesus dealt with His servant who had failed Him so miserably. And it has profound lessons for us, for we too often fail to live up to our high calling in Christ.

Peter's sin, like all sin, had to be dealt with. His sin of denying his Lord caused the deepest wound to Peter, but also to Jesus. It stained Peter's office of discipleship, damaged his standing as a leader and his relationship with the others. For Peter's healing, comfort, peace, and encouragement, and for him to be able to do the great work Jesus had

264

for him, for him to become the great Apostle and leader Jesus called him to be, Jesus knew that Peter required absolute assurance of forgiveness, a renewal of his call, and reinstatement of his leadership position among the disciples. Only then, would Peter be able to let the past be the past and go forward. So Jesus lovingly and tenderly deals with a devastated and broken Peter. And He does so by addressing the crucial issue of love.

To grasp the profound nature of this exchange between Jesus and Peter, it's important to know that in the English language we have one word for love - "love," whereas in the Greek language, there are three words for describing love - "eros," which is erotic or sexual love; "phileo," the love of affection, brotherly love; and "agape," the highest love, a sacrificial love. It is these last two - phileo love and agape love - which are crucial to fully understand the passage.

Jesus asks Peter, "Simon, son of John, do you truly love Me more than these?" referring to the other disciples. The word Jesus uses for love here is "agape," the highest love, the sacrificial love. In asking this, Jesus is reminding Peter of his boasting that even if all the rest of them deserted Jesus, he, Peter, would not forsake Him; he would die for Jesus. That's "agape love." Peter answers, "Yes Lord, You know that I love You." But the word Peter uses for love is "phileo," the love of affection , brotherly love. Here we see the effect that Peter's sin and failure had had on him. We see a total humbling of Peter. We see his honesty in admitting that he cannot claim an "agape" love for Jesus as he had done in his boast. The proud boasting is gone; a deep humility bows his soul. In using the word "phileo," Peter is saying, "Yes Lord, You know that I have deep affection for You." Jesus' response is, "Feed My lambs," in effect assuring Peter that he is forgiven and reinstated as an Apostle of Christ.

But then Jesus asks a second time, "Simon, son of John, do you truly love Me?" And again, the word for love that Jesus uses is "agape," the sacrificial love. Peter again answers, "Yes Lord, you know that I love You!" And again, the word for love that Peter uses is "phileo," the love of affection. He will not presume to claim a love for Jesus that is the highest form of love. His boasting is gone. Jesus again assures Peter that he is forgiven and reinstated as His Apostle with His statement, "Take care of My sheep!"

And then, Jesus asks Peter a third time, "Simon, son of John, do you love Me?" Peter had denied Jesus three times, and apparently it was necessary that he profess his love for Jesus three times to completely remove the stain of his sin. But there is a profound difference between Jesus' third question and His previous two questions. In this third question, the word for love Jesus uses is "phileo" instead of "agape." It's as if He is asking Peter, "Are you sure you love Me even with a love of deep affection?" Peter was grieved that Jesus would question whether he had even the "phileo" love of deep affection for his Lord. But Jesus had to do that for Peter to be cleansed completely of his sin. In his denials, even common affection and regard for Jesus had been thrown to the wind. He claimed to not even know Jesus. That's hardly affection. And so Peter had to drink the cup of full and complete confession. He could not be spared the pain of it if he was to be completely freed of guilt.

Peter answers, "Lord, You know all things; You know that I love You!" Again, the word for love is "phileo," the love of affection. Peter appeals to Jesus' divine knowledge, and by doing so, he truly honors Jesus and places all his trust in his Lord. Peter is saying, "Lord, you have divine knowledge of what is in my heart. I don't know my heart as You do. I thought I did before, but my prideful heart deceived me. You show me what is in my heart. Peter makes full confession to Jesus, and full confession brings healing. Jesus responds, "Feed My sheep!," and with this third response, makes it clear that He accepts Peter where he is at, that He accepts his love, even though it may not yet be an "agape" love, the highest, sacrificial love. Jesus, in effect says, "It's o.k. Peter, I know how badly your denial of Me has hurt you and broken you. I understand that you cannot profess an "agape" love for Me yet. I forgive you and accept your "phileo" love.

Jesus grants Peter full absolution, and crowns that absolution with the authority of apostleship. Those three responses of Jesus, "Feed My lambs"; "Take care of My sheep"; "Feed My sheep" is His call to Peter to nurture, shepherd, and instruct the flock - the followers of Christ-from the small lambs to the mature sheep. He impresses upon Peter the greatness of the commission He is entrusting to his love and care. After accepting Peter's confession and profession of love, and publicly reinstating him as an apostle, Jesus prophecies what kind of death would crown Peter's apostleship - a martyr's death. It's as if Jesus is saying, "Peter, you may not yet be able to confess an "agape" love, a sacrificial love, for Me. But the day will come when you will demonstrate to the world your "agape" love for Me, when you will show the highest love for Me by dying for Me." And that's exactly what happened. After 35 years of apostolic ministry, feeding Jesus' lambs, tending His flock, shepherding them, Peter glorified God and his Savior with his death of martyrdom. Early Christian writings tell us that Peter was martyred during the time of Emperor Nero. He was crucified upside down because he said that he was unworthy to die as his Savior died. Peter's entire apostleship, as well as his death, was in obedience to his Lord's command, "Follow Me!"

So, let's consider the profound lessons for us in this account of Peter's sin, his humbling, and Jesus dealing with His beloved disciple.

1.   Peter's three-fold denial of Christ shows us that self-pride is fertile ground for Satan to lead us into sin that we would never have thought ourselves capable of. Those who boast, "I would never do that!" court disaster and leave themselves wide open for Satan to prove them wrong.

2.   Sin, left unconfessed and unrepented of, can have disastrous effects on one's spiritual, emotional, and physical well-being.

3.   There is no sin so heinous, so terrible, that it is not covered and washed clean by the blood of Christ, except the sin of rejecting Christ as Lord and Savior in this life, and dying in that unbelief.

4.   Confessing our sins, especially those sins that cripple us with extreme shame and guilt, and being cleansed of them, can be a painful process, just as it was for Peter, because it requires a complete humbling and total honesty before our Lord. In dealing with us, our Lord will go directly to the source of the problem, the sore spot so to speak, just as He did with Peter, in order to heal us completely from the inside out. And that can be devastating to our ego, our pride, our self-image, our self-confidence. But it is only such healing - healing of the heart, the spirit, the soul, that will free us completely of the burden of guilt and shame and enable us to leave the past in the past. Jesus, like a good physician, may hurt us, but He hurts in love and in order to heal and make us whole. Like Peter, Jesus wants us free of guilt and shame, healed and whole, so we can be in the place He wants us to be, doing the work He wants us to do. Jesus dealt with Peter, and He deals with us, as a true Pastor and our loving Lord and Savior.

5.   We are to let the past be the past. Like the Apostle Paul in our Epistle reading, we are "to forget what is behind and strain toward what is ahead, pressing on toward the goal to win the prize for which God has called us heavenward in Christ Jesus." Forgetting what is behind doesn't mean losing all memory of our sinful past, or else we might repeat it. But it does mean leaving it behind us as forgiven, done with, and settled. God wants us to go forward, growing in faith, love, and service to our Lord. After Jesus assured Peter that he was forgiven and reinstated, He told him, "Follow Me!" In essence, Jesus was saying, "Now Simon, the last speck of that dark cloud that has been hanging over you since that night you denied Me three times is dispelled completely. From now on, it's as if it never happened. The past is past. Leave it there and go forward with Me." And our Lord says the same thing to you and to me.

God's love for us is "agape" love, the highest love, the love of intelligence, purpose, and sacrifice. He proved that by giving His Son to be our Savior. Jesus Christ, Son of God and Son of Man, is God the Father's "agape" love. What is our love for God? How would we answer Jesus' question, "Do you love Me?" Could we say, "Lord, I love

You with an "agape" love?" Could I say that? In all honesty, I don't think I could. But I think I'm being honest when I say, "Lord, I want to be able to say that. Help me grow and mature in faith and love and commitment to You to the point where I can truly say that." That's my prayer for myself. That's my prayer for each of you, my readers. Amen.

CHAPTER 10 - TESTING AND TEMPTATION

"No temptation has seized you except what is common to man. And God is faithful; He will not let you be tempted beyond what you can bear. But when you are tempted, He will also provide a way out, so that you can stand up under it."

1 Corinthians 10:13

Every day is a spiritual battle between the Spirit within us and Satan, the world, and our sinful nature. Every day, through confession and repentance, we set aside the old man and experience renewal as the new man. Every day, in Christ, is a joyful rebirth day.

Temptation 1 - Stones to Bread

Temptation 2 - Leap from Temple

Temptation 3 - World's riches

Satan gone. Jesus ministered to by angels

VICTORY IN THE DESERT

Text: Luke 4: 1-13; Romans 10: 8b-13.

Theme: Our only defense.

Theme Summary: In His divinity, Jesus was co-equal with the Father and the Holy Spirit - One God. Yet, as a man, the Son of Man Jesus was under God, under the law of God, as we all are. In the battle against Satan's temptations in the desert, as well as in all His battles against Satan's temptations during His ministry, Jesus made no use of His divine powers. He had to vanquish Satan in His humanity, as Son of Man in order to be the sinless, perfect sacrifice for our sins. If Jesus, as a man, had given in to Satan, God's plan of redemption would have been nullified and we would still be dead in our sins and condemned by the law to hell. So, as Hebrews 4:15 tells us: "We have a Savior, a High Priest, Who can sympathize with our weaknesses, with our infirmities, Who was in all points tempted like we are, yet without sin." The Living Word (Jesus) uses the written Word to defeat Satan. We too can overcome the evil one through faith in the Living Word and use of the written Word - the Sword of the Spirit. The Living Word and the written Word are our only sure defense.

Key Passage: Luke 4: 4,8,12: "It is written: 'Man does not live on bread alone, but on every Word that comes from the mouth of God.'"

†

Have you ever had a spiritual mountaintop experience, and then shortly afterwards found yourself in a spiritual valley of suffering and depression? Charles Spurgeon, a great English preacher, said that often after a great spiritual victory, he would suffer a bout of deep depression and satanic attack. And Luther, we are told, once got so mad at Satan that he threw an inkwell at him and told him to leave him alone. I think Jesus, in His humanity, had His mountaintop and valley experiences.

273

In our Gospel reading, Jesus had just been baptized by John the Baptist. He saw the Holy Spirit descend on Him in the form of a dove and heard the Father's voice saying: "You are My Son Whom I love; with You I am well pleased." Then, right after that great affirmation, that great mountaintop experience, Jesus was led by the Spirit into the desert to be tempted by Satan to the uttermost. It was the Father's will that this mighty battle be fought now at the beginning of Jesus' ministry on earth. Jesus would face a supreme test, and the outcome of this test would determine whether Jesus would embark on the mission given Him by the Father to be the Redeemer of mankind. For in this desert battle against Satan's temptations, as well as in future battles against Satan's temptations during His ministry, Jesus could make no use of His divine powers. He had to vanquish Satan in His humanity, as Son of Man, in order to be the sinless, perfect sacrifice for our sins. If Jesus, as Son of Man, had given in to Satan at any time during His ministry on earth, right up to Gethsemane and the Cross, the Father's plan for our redemption would have been nullified, and we would still be dead in our sins and condemned to hell. But Jesus remained faithful to the Father and the mission given Him by the Father. Thank You Jesus! So as Hebrews 4:15 tells us: "We have a High Priest, a Savior, Who can sympathize with our weaknesses, our infirmities, Who has been tempted in every way just as we are - yet was without sin." That passage is of immense comfort to me, a sinner.

The devil knew that this was God's Son in His humanity as Son of Man, the Messiah, come to crush him, free humankind from his bondage, and establish the Kingdom of God among men.

Satan resolved that, just as he had defeated the first Adam in the Garden of Eden, he would defeat this second Adam before He could start His great mission of redemption. And so, the stage was set for this great confrontation, which Jesus had to endure and overcome before He started His ministry. During the entire forty days, Jesus endured temptation by the devil, finally culminating in these three recorded. He fasted the entire time and it was now, when His hunger was the greatest and His physical endurance and resistance the lowest, that Satan pulled out all the stops.

He starts by trying to raise doubt in Jesus' mind. "If you are the Son of God, tell these stones to become bread." Prove your Sonship! Satan knew that Jesus, as the Son of God, could perform this and other miracles. In his cunning, Satan wanted to take advantage of Jesus' desperately weakened human condition and cause Jesus, in His humanity, to question in His mind the Father's Word and sow the seed of doubt in Jesus' heart. "Did the Father really affirm my Sonship? Will the Father save Me from starvation in this desert? Does the Father know My physical need?"

In the Garden of Eden, Satan had used food to cause Adam and Eve to doubt and distrust God's Word. He now tries the same with Jesus, but here the temptation was much stronger. Adam and Eve weren't starving. Jesus was! If Jesus had given in to this temptation, it would have been a clear sign of distrust of the Father. After all, it was the Father's will that had brought Him to this hunger and this ordeal.

Satan tempts us in this same way, when our resistance is lowest. When we are going through a real downer, experiencing suffering, sorrow, pain, discouragement, failure, the first thing he will try to do is raise doubt in our minds, doubt in God's Word and promises. "Does God really promise to uphold me, sustain me, heal me, lead me? Why am I going through this terrible trial and tribulation? Will God bring me through it? Where are you God? Do you hear my prayers, do you see my need, do you know my condition?" Satan tempted all the great men and women of God in this way. David cried out in the Psalms: "Why have You turned from me O God? Why do You not hear my supplications?" Of course he was wrong; God never turned from him. And God never turns from those who are His in Christ. He hears our prayers, sees our need, knows our condition, and He will work out His perfect will and purpose and our highest good in all our trials and tribulations. He promised that and His promises are sure. Romans 8:28

tells us: "In all things God works for the good of those who love Him, who have been called according to His purpose."

Despite His desperate human need, Jesus defeats Satan. Instead of the doubt the devil wanted Jesus to show towards the Father, Jesus responds with perfect trust and reliance on the Father. He answers: "It is written: 'Man does not live on bread alone, but on every word that comes from the mouth of God.'" He defeated Satan, not with His divine power, but as a man trusting in God the Father and using the Word of God.

Satan takes Jesus to Jerusalem and sets Him on the pinnacle of the temple. Satan had failed to conquer Jesus in regard to His bodily needs. Now he tries to conquer Jesus on the basis of pride. "If you are the Son of God, prove it in a heroic way. Throw yourself down from this great height and show your trust in God's promise given in Psalm 91 which says: 'He will command His angels concerning you to guard you in all your ways; they will lift you up in their hands so that you will not strike your foot against a stone.'" The devil is telling Jesus that if He has real trust, He will not hesitate to do this. Then too, if Jesus does so and lives, He will prove to the people that He is the Messiah and they will worship Him.

The cunning of Satan is shown by his use of Scripture, and he is an expert in handling Scripture - wrongly. The devil's art of corrupting Scripture to achieve his evil purposes is an art practiced by many today, even by some in the Church. They attempt to use the Bible to justify a personal agenda or ideology, to make the Bible appear to say what it does not say. Even when the Bible clearly and plainly refutes what they want it to say, they will put a spin on it in order to suit their purposes.

With this temptation, the devil tries to stir up pride in Jesus and get Him to challenge the Father and use this gracious promise of God given in the Word to justify a foolhardy act. God's great promises of protection are meant for our humble trust in Him, not for our presumption. To use a promise of God to justify some foolish act would be to tempt God, and that is a sin against Him and His promise.

276

Tempting God can be dangerous. In 1929 Samuel Whitaker was convicted of having his wife killed. He cried out in court, "If I am guilty, I hope God will strike me dead before I reach my cell." The judge sentenced him to San Quentin. En route he became ill and was taken to the prison hospital. He seemed to improve but before he entered his cell, he dropped dead.

Do we ever tempt God out of pride or use Scripture wrongly as Satan did for personal motives? Do we ever read into Scripture what we want it to say instead of what it actually says? Do we ever claim a promise of God in order to justify something we want or are about to do when we know in our heart that it is probably not in God's will and that the promise we claim does not fit with our desire? Do we ever misuse Scripture in order to feed our own ego or pride? Many are doing all of that today. Scripture tells us that the heart is deceitful, and our sinful nature makes it so easy to follow our deceitful hearts instead of God's Word. We must constantly be on our guard against Satan tempting us to do that. We must ask and trust the Holy Spirit to convict us when we do that and turn us back to the Truth.

Jesus again responds with the Word. He tells Satan: "It is said: 'Do not put the Lord your God to the test'" - in other words, "You shall not tempt the Lord your God." Jesus places one Scripture passage beside another, and in doing so, explains both and eliminates any false conclusion from one passage. That is true interpretation. Scripture is primarily interpreted and explained through Scripture. Again, Jesus' use of the Word defeats the tempter and the temptation.

Finally, Satan comes out and presents himself as prince and ruler of this world. He speaks as if he were the rightful ruler of all the kingdoms of this world and as if God had given him this rule. This is a lie. Scripture says that God is Sovereign over all the kingdoms and nations, over the heavens and the earth and all they contain. Satan usurps God's authority, and for that he will eventually face God's justice.

In this third temptation, Satan no longer tempts Jesus to prove He is the Son of God. He accepts that. Now he tries a different tactic - a tactic consisting of greed and a shortcut to the Messiahship. First the greed. He shows Jesus all the glory, riches, and power of the kingdoms of the world, so alluring and magnificent, and offers it all to Jesus. All the arrogant pride of the devil who, as the archangel Lucifer first rebelled against God and was thrown out of heaven because of that pride, comes out in this offer - "All this I will give you."

His boldest stroke was in the condition attached to the offer - "if you will bow down and worship me." Satan knew that Jesus was the GodMan, fully divine and fully human, and as the Son of God, He was Sovereign over all the kingdoms of the world. So he appeals to Jesus' human nature, hoping that the Son of God as a man will succumb to the human nature's capacity for greed and the lust for power.

Not only that, but Satan sweetens the pot. He offers Jesus a shortcut to become King of kings and Lord of lords. Hebrews 12:2 tells us that: "Jesus, for the joy set before Him, endured the cross, scorning its shame, and sat down at the right hand of the throne of God." It was the Father's will that Jesus, as the GodMan, be King of kings and Lord of lords through His suffering, death, and resurrection for all humanity. That was the whole purpose for His taking on our humanity. The divine nature is immutable; the divine nature cannot be humiliated, suffer and die - only the human nature. Instead of the long, bitter road to Messiah-Kingship which the Father willed and which was necessary for our salvation, Satan offers Jesus the opportunity to avoid the bitter cup the Father wanted Him to drink, avoid the shame, pain, and agonizing death through which alone we could be redeemed. The opportunity to have the kingship without enduring the cross. In other words, the easy way out. All it would take is one little act of worship, one bowing of the knee.

Of course it was all a lie. It would be a false messiahship, false kingship, that Satan would give. The kingdoms and the authority promised to Jesus by Satan would remain Satan's. The transfer would be an illusion. By that one act of worship, Jesus would rebel against the Father, betray His Sonship and become a slave of Satan.

Satan apparently thought that even the Son of God in His humanity could not refuse his grandiose offer. After all, he had succeeded with thousands and thousands of others by appealing to their greed and lust for power, and still does so today. Have you and I ever compromised our Christian walk by succumbing to greed? Have you and I ever compromised our Christian walk by succumbing to pride and ego? Have you and I ever compromised our Christian walk by taking the easy way in our spiritual journey, taking the easy road instead of the harder road to maturity in Christ and commitment and service to Him? Have you and I ever refused to take up our cross and follow our Savior?

Jesus again defeats Satan with the Word, and His indignation and righteous anger over Satan's tempting Him to worship him instead of the Father are shown in His response: "It is written: 'Worship the Lord your God and serve Him only.'" And in Matthew we are told that at this point Jesus commanded: "Away from Me, Satan!" This command for Satan to leave Him is Jesus' announcement of victory. It was Jesus, the GodMan, Who decided when the contest was finished, and Satan had no choice but to obey. We're told that the devil left Him until an opportune time and angels came and attended Him. There would be other temptations right up to the supreme battle in Gethsemane where Jesus would also be victorious.

Satan tempted Jesus with physical gratification, pride, and worldly power, fame, riches, and glory. And he tempts us today in those same areas. Spiritual warfare is real and it rages in us and all around us and will only end when we go to be with the Lord or He returns. Victory in this most critical battle of our lives is of the first importance since our eternal state depends on it. Victory is ours if we follow Jesus' example.

Jesus defeated every temptation with a word of Scripture, the Word of God. Consider the profound nature of this. Jesus is the Living Word, the Logos (Word) made flesh. "In the beginning was the Word, and the Word was with God, and the Word was God." (John 1:1). Every word of Scripture, Old Testament and New Testament, is the Word of Jesus given through the Holy Spirit. Here, in this confrontation with the devil, we see Jesus, the Living Word, using the written Word to defeat the devil. Now if Jesus Himself, the Living Word, used the written Word to defeat Satan, what makes us think we can defeat him with anything else. Jesus gives us the example, and through the Holy Spirit indwelling us, He enables us to follow His example.

Not all the secular self-help books and programs in this world will give us victory over Satan. Not all the 5-step, 10-step, 12-step or how many steps self-help programs man invents will threaten Satan or defeat him. He laughs at them. The Word of God is the only shield and weapon he fears and which will defeat him. And that written Word is backed up by the Living Word and the Spirit Who indwells us.

As our Epistle reading tells us: "That Word is near us, in our mouths and in our hearts." The Apostle Paul refers to that Word as the "Sword of the Spirit." A sword is a weapon of war. In Psalm 144:1 David says: "Praise be to the Lord my Rock Who trains my hands for war, my fingers for battle." How are we trained for spiritual warfare? By growing in that Word, holding fast to that Word, by keeping that Word near us, in our mouths and in our hearts - in short by learning how to use that Sword of the Spirit just as Jesus used it.

And remember, a sword is both a defensive and an offensive weapon. When Satan attacks you, use that Sword of the Spirit to defend yourself, but not only that, use it to attack Satan right back, and don't stop attacking him until he flees from you. We should never take Satan lightly or joke about him, for he is our worst enemy. But we should not fear him or be timid when he attacks us. We are told in 2Timothy 1:7 that "God did not give us a spirit of timidity, but a Spirit of power…" We cannot prevent Satan from tempting us but we can prevent him from defeating us. As Luther put it, "We cannot prevent the birds from flying over our heads, but we can prevent them from building nests in our hair." Many people are walking around with nests in their hair because their attitude towards temptation is like that of the boy whose mother asked him, "Do you know what happens to boys who give in to temptation and lie?" He answered, "Yeah, they get into the movies at half price."

We all fail and fall into temptation at times because we are all sinners. But don't let Satan discourage you. Tell him: "You may have won a skirmish, but you haven't won the war. You may have hurt me and wounded me, and I may be bleeding, but I am not slain. I have a Savior Who sympathizes with me, a Savior Who defeated you, a Savior Who will lift me up, forgive me, wash me clean in His Blood, take from me the stained rags of sin and clothe me again in His righteousness. And I will again take up the Sword of the Spirit and fight you right up to the day my Lord casts you into the lake of fire and takes me and all my brothers and sisters in Christ into heavenly glory." The victory is ours in Christ. God grant that, in the power of the Holy Spirit, we hold fast to that victory. Amen.

TEMPTATION AND THE MATURE CHRISTIAN

Text: Psalm 119:153-168; Luke 7: 18-28.

Theme: Temptation as a precursor for spiritual growth and becoming equipped for God's service.

Theme Statement: Though fully God with all His divine attributes, the Christ Child, in HIs humanity as Son of Man, had to grow to spiritual maturity. For Jesus, this meant growing during His infancy, adolescence, and finally adulthood, into a greater and greater, and finally full awareness of Who He was, His oneness with the Father, and His purpose and mission as the GodMan given Him by the Father. For Jesus, the Son of Man, and for us, in our path to spiritual maturity, three essential catalysts for that growth were (and for us still are) involved. These are Prayer, Meditation, and Temptation. Prayer and meditation on God's Word for spiritual growth are crucial. Here we consider the catalyst of temptation for spiritual growth and becoming a mature Christian.

Key Passage: Psalm 119: 165. "Great peace have they who love your law, and nothing can make them stumble."

We're told that the Child Jesus grew in stature and wisdom. The Child Jesus was fully God, with all His divine attributes. Yet, in His humanity, as Son of Man, those divine attributes were, so to speak, put on hold to some extent, and Jesus had to grow to spiritual maturity and full awareness of who He was - the GodMan - and the mission given Him by the Father. Luther said that three things are necessary in becoming a theologian, which all Christians are called to be. These are Prayer, Meditation, and Temptation. Like us, Jesus' growth involved those three things. It is apparent that Prayer and Meditation are essential for spiritual growth and maturity. Here we consider Temptation and its role in spiritual growth and maturity.

Luther said that theology is an art that is learned only from life-long experience. He said that he had to search constantly deeper and deeper for it, and that his temptations did that for him. No one, he said, can understand Holy Scripture without living it, and temptations are a part of that. By temptation, Luther meant not only enticement by the devil to sin, but even more, attacks upon the Christian through persecution, suffering, opposition, loss, etc., in an attempt to destroy the Christian's faith.

Spiritual growth involves spiritual warfare, the battle between Christ and Satan in the Church, and the battle between the Spirit of Christ and Satan, this world, and our sinful nature in the individual. In combating temptation, we experience the righteousness and truth, the sweetness and loveliness, the power and strength of God's Word with our whole being, not just with our intellect or emotions. Prayer and meditation do not take place in a spiritual vacuum, in isolation from the temptations of the devil, the world, and our flesh. Struggling against temptation can strengthen and purify our faith, just as the forge strengthens and purifies steel. And God uses afflictions, trial, and temptation to drive us away from dependence on self and to dependence on Him, our Rock, Refuge, and Strength.

Our Lord, as Son of Man in His humanity, had to overcome the full power of Satan's attacks and temptations in the desert to prepare Him for HIs mission of salvation. And He did overcome through the power of the Holy Spirit and the Word. Every Christian who will share in the Lord's glory is also called to share in His sufferings, and that involves sharing in His temptations. Every Christian is to be a spiritual warrior, wielding the weapons of God's Word and the Holy Spirit's power.

Psalm 119 is a lament born out of the suffering and persecution caused by the temptations of Satan and this world and our own flesh. David knew these temptations first hand. But he also knew that those who love, remember, and keep God's Word will, through the power of the Holy Spirit, endure the trials and persecution the devil and the world and their sinful flesh bring upon them through temptation. Psalm 119 serves as an instruction book for the Christian to overcome temptation. David's adversaries were many and mighty, and he was apparently in great danger. He prays: "Look upon my suffering and deliver me; redeem me and preserve my life." And he reminds the Lord, "I have not forgotten your law; I have not turned from your statutes; see how I love your precepts." David knew, and we must remember, that God is always mindful of His peoples' afflictions and needs, and that He constantly invites us to bring our case before Him and leave it to His compassionate consideration to do that which, in His wisdom, will be to His glory and to our highest good, and to do it in His perfect time and way.

David prays: "Defend my cause; many are the foes who pursue me." David had a just cause - as the Lord's anointed king, to bring all Israel under the Lordship of God's law and God's will. He knew that God will be the Advocate, the Mediator, the Defender of all whose cause is just, according to His holy will. That includes our just causes. David says that "salvation is far from the wicked because they do not seek out God's decrees." He says that he looks on the faithless with loathing, for they do not obey God's Word. David was astonished by the attitude of the wicked towards God's law because, to him, God's law, God's Word, was life itself, more precious than all riches, and "sweeter than honey from the honeycomb."

Like David, we too should look on the wickedness of the wicked and their rejection of God's Word with loathing, but also with sorrow and mercy. But wait a minute! How about our own wickedness and sin? Yes! We should loathe that even more, for we are God's children. Like David, after his terrible sin of adultery with Bathsheba, and his murder of her husband Uriah, we should say: "My guilt has overwhelmed me like a burden too heavy to bear; my wounds fester and are loathsome because of my sinful folly." David was grieved over the sins of the wicked and his own sins, and so should we be grieved. And like David, we flee to God in confession and repentance. We flee to the cross for cleansing, for on the cross, the Son of God as Son of Man paid the full and terrible price for our sins that we might be forgiven and cleansed.

David prays: "See how I love your precepts." Notice he does not say, "see how I fulfill your precepts, your Word." David was quite conscious of his own failures and shortcomings. Again he prays: "Preserve my life, O Lord, according to your love." David knew that he was totally dependent on God's love, and so are we. Our obedience is pleasing to God, but only when it comes from the principle of love. David knew, and we must know, that we are to be reflections of God's love to this world. Matthew 22: 37, 38 tells us: "You shall love the Lord your God with all your heart and with all your soul, and with all your mind"..."You shall love your neighbor as yourself." And 1Corinthians 13:13 tells us: "And now these three remain: faith, hope, and love. But the greatest of these is love." You know why love is the greatest? Because only through genuine love, a love that reflects God's love, can there be a living faith, and only through a living faith, can there be a living hope. David's love for God's Word, so strongly expressed in Psalm 119, was the basis for his living faith and his living hope. And so our love for God's Word is the basis for our living faith and our living hope.

David prays: "All your words are true; all your righteous laws are eternal." David's comfort and strength stemmed from the faithfulness of God's Word, and that is the source of our comfort and strength. And that faithfulness of God's Word endures forever, to all eternity. Jesus said: "Heaven and earth will pass away, but My Word will never pass away." David says: "Great peace have they who love your law, and nothing can make them stumble." God's Word only is the source of our peace, the peace that passes all understanding, and God's Word only is the source of the strength that arms us against all the temptations and persecutions of Satan and this world. David says, "My heart trembles at your Word." So should our hearts tremble.

David says, "I rejoice in your promise like one who finds great spoil." He took pleasure in God's Word, pleasure in reading it, hearing it, meditating on it. The more reverence we have for the Word of God, the more joy we shall find in it. David says, "Seven times a day I praise You for your righteous laws." Praising God is a righteous duty which, like David, we should abound in. 1Thessalonians 5:18 tells us to "give thanks in all circumstances," even for our afflictions, for God, in His grace and wisdom, will bring good through them, for His honor and for our highest good.

Finally, David says, "I obey your statutes for I love them greatly. I obey your precepts and your statutes for all my ways are known to you." Here is the whole duty of man - to keep our eyes on Christ and His Word as our rule in life. To seek the Lord's will in all things and do it. That's the answer Solomon came up with in Ecclesiastes when he set out to discover the meaning of life. Solomon's conclusion was: "Fear God and keep His commandments, for this is the whole duty of man." And David's prayer: "All my ways are known to You," should serve not only as a gentle warning, but as a loving word of comfort and assurance that the child of God is never alone. As David said in another Psalm: "My father and mother may forsake me, but God will never forsake me." He is always there to take my hand, enfold me in His arms, comfort me, strengthen me, preserve and protect me, lead me to my highest good in this life, and finally take me into glory.

Our Gospel passage gives us another example of a servant of God who loved God's Word and stood steadfast against the temptations and persecutions of Satan and the worldly authorities - the Prophet John the Baptist. John had been cast into prison by King Herod for condemning Herod's action in taking his brother's wife, Herodias, to be his own wife. While in prison, we're told that John sent two of his disciples to Jesus to ask Him: "Are you the one to come, or should we expect someone else?"

Was John expressing any hint of doubt as to who Jesus was? Absolutely not! God had clearly identified Jesus as the Messiah to John, and he had seen the Holy Spirit in the form of a dove descending on Jesus when he baptized Him. But his question does indicate that John was perplexed. With the coming of the Messiah, John expected to see the great Messianic works of both grace and judgment. But Jesus' Messianic ministry seemed to be only grace without the judgement. John wondered if another one would follow who would perform those works of judgment? It's important to remember that, throughout the Old Testament Messianic prophecies, the interval of time between the first coming of the suffering Messiah, bringing grace and redemption, and the second coming of the victorious Messiah, bringing judgment, was left unrevealed by God in HIs wisdom. So John's question was not far from the facts. There would not be another Messiah, but there would be another coming of this Messiah, Jesus the Christ.

Jesus told the messengers to tell John what they had just seen and heard - great miracles of grace and the good news preached - all prophesied of the Messiah. John had not seen any of this - he was in prison.

Then Jesus pronounces His great estimate of John. John was more than a prophet because he not only prophesied Christ's coming, but he actually prepared the way before Him. Then Jesus, with the voice of authority, says: "I tell you, among those born of women, there is no one greater than John." Then He adds, "Yet the one who is least in the kingdom of God is greater than he." How is he greater? In his prison, John could not see the great miracles Jesus was doing. He would soon be martyred and would not see the consummation of Jesus' work, His death and resurrection, the fulfillment of the Messiah's works of grace. All those who witnessed these things were therefore in a sense greater than John, not in person, but in revelation. John was in prison because he would not compromise God's law, one of God's commandments. Certainly Satan attacked him, tempted him through his suffering to save himself. Just compromise a little bit on God's Word and accept Herod's marriage to his brother's wife. It's no big deal. But John would not budge an inch. He loved God's Word too much, and his love for God's Word and his faithfulness to his calling as the Messiah's messenger, gave him the strength to resist Satan's temptations. And so, he was beheaded in that prison.

There are many modern day examples of those who, although severely tempted, refuse to compromise their faith, and in the power of the Holy Spirit are strengthened through temptation and stand fast with their Lord. I'll close with just two examples. There's the American pastor Saeed Abedini who languished in an Iranian prison for years, tortured and wasting away with sickness because he would not renounce his faith in Christ. He stood fast and finally his release was secured. Then there is the American three-star army General, General Haines, a devout Christian, who, while on a DOD official trip to Los Angeles, was invited one night to attend a Christian event in a nearby town. He accepted. A congressman heard of his attending that Christian event while on an official trip and made an issue of it. General Haines was called before a congressional committee where this congressman berated him, trying to get him to admit to wrongdoing. No taxpayer money was spent. The General rented a car to travel to that meeting at his own expense. General Haines was being considered for a fourth star at the time, and everyone in DOD considered him a shoo-in for promotion. That congressman informed General Haines that attending that Christian event just might jeopardize his getting his fourth star if he did not admit to wrongdoing. General Haines had enough. He told that congressman: "Congressman, I would rather be a doorkeeper in the house of my God, than be an Army four-star general." General Haines didn't get his fourth-star and he retired shortly thereafter.

May we stand steadfast when under attack by Satan and this world and our sinful nature. When we are tempted to compromise our faith and God's Word, even if only a little, may we stand steadfast with our Messiah Who came to us as a Babe, Who withstood the severest temptations for us, Who took upon Himself our sins and iniquities and steadfastly took them to the cross. And to paraphrase General Haines, may our response to temptation be: "I would rather be a doorkeeper in the house of my God than have all the riches and power and pleasure that Satan and this world can offer." Grant that to us, Lord Jesus, for your sake. Amen.

CHAPTER 11 - DISCERNMENT

"Show me your ways, O Lord, teach me your paths; Guide me in your Truth and teach me, for You are God, my Savior, and my hope is in You all day long."

Psalm 25:4-5

Be shrewd as serpent. Be innocent as doves. Don't emphasize the gnats. Don't swallow the camels.

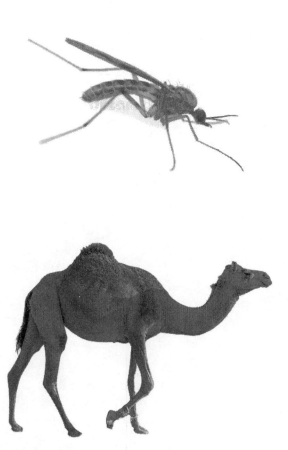

SNAKES AND DOVES

Text: Proverbs 14:12, 34;   Titus 2:11-14;   Matthew 10:16

Theme: Discernment essential to wisdom and godly living.

Theme Statement: The ways of this world and its values seem right to those who are worldly, but in the end they lead to destruction. Satan's strategy is to make us more worldly because that will lead us away from God. Therefore, Christians must do as Jesus said, "Be shrewd as snakes" - that is, exercise discernment and awareness concerning spiritual and physical danger, and "Be innocent as doves" - that is, be harmless to others and live self-controlled, upright and godly lives in this present age.

Key Passage: Matthew 10:16. "I am sending you out like sheep among wolves. Therefore, be shrewd as snakes and as innocent as doves."

A man was asked the question, "Are you a Christian?" "Yes, I am," he replied. He was then asked, "Are you a believing Christian?" Again he replied, "Yes, I am!" At first, he thought it strange that he was asked that second question. After all, there can be no such thing as an unbelieving Christian. It's a contradiction of terms. But then he realized that the man who asked him that question had discernment because he knew that there were those who merely wear the label of Christian, as opposed to those who genuinely believed, those who were in fact Christians.

Discernment is the ability to recognize the difference between simply rhetoric and real conviction, the ability to differentiate between right and wrong, truth and falsehood, the genuine and the phony. It's the ability to recognize the moral and ethical qualities, or lack thereof, underlying the words and actions of individuals and groups. In short, discernment is the ability to view things as God sees them. Without discernment, there is no wisdom, because discernment, godly

293

discernment, leads to wisdom. I believe that godly discernment is the most critical need in Church, government, our educational and cultural institutions, and society today because true and godly discernment, and standing firm in such discernment, gives stability and confidence to people and nations, whereas a lack of godly discernment leads to an "anything goes" environment and eventual confusion and chaos.

Life is more hurried and hectic today than probably any other time in history. Along with this frantic pace of life, there has been a drastic decline in the morals and ethics of a multitude of people in our society, government, business, schools, and even the church. Biblical illiteracy has increased exponentially, and along with it, the ability for godly discernment. Too many people simply go along with the crowd, accepting what was unacceptable in the past, either because they don't know better or its the easiest thing to do.

When Jesus told His disciples to be shrewd as snakes and innocent as doves. He was essentially telling them to use godly discernment. His message is for us today also, for we too are His followers and godly discernment is available to us if we will only use it. Jesus used the term wolves to characterize the world as vicious and hostile to Him and His followers, because the world is filled with sin and wickedness and His disciples, including us, are like defenseless sheep, vulnerable to the hostility and attacks of the wolves of this world. Therefore, they must be shrewd as snakes.

The word "shrewd" does not imply cunning or trickery. It means having a keen awareness and ability to recognize and avoid danger when possible, just like a snake has. In the disciples' case, and in ours, it means recognizing and avoiding things that will cause spiritual or physical harm. Being shrewd is being prudent and insightful, having a keen awareness of the pitfalls all around us, the common sense to avoid them when possible, and the wisdom to speak and conduct ourselves as God would want us to. In other words, shrewdness is equated with godly discernment. Jesus Himself, on occasions, demonstrated shrewdness when He discerned the wicked motives of His enemies and countered their arguments in such a way that left them dumbfounded while He escaped out of their hands. The book of Acts tells us of occasions when the Apostle Paul used shrewdness to confound or escape from his enemies.

How about us? Are we shrewd as serpents in our discernment of what is happening around us, shrewd and wise enough to discern right from wrong when all around us people are calling wrong right, and right wrong? Are we shrewd and wise enough to discern, even when others cannot or will not, the logical outcome of the decline of morals and ethics in society and our institutions, which is increased confusion, chaos, and disaster? Are we shrewd and wise enough to discern that some things are just not negotiable with God, including His moral law, plan, and purpose? Are we shrewd and wise enough to recognize the danger of not depending on God's Word as our ultimate guide for faith and conduct in all aspects of our lives, and reject all that is contrary to that Word. All of us, Christian or not, are called to exercise godly discernment, to be shrewd as serpents as we live in a world of wolves.

Jesus also told His disciples, and us, to be innocent as doves. Just as the snake is an example of shrewdness, so the dove is an example of innocence. Being innocent as doves means to be harmless to others, innocent of giving offense to others insofar as possible, innocent of saying or doing anything that might damage our credibility as witnesses for Christ, bring scandal on the Church, or blaspheme the Word of God. Being innocent as doves means living lives of self-control, uprightness, and godliness while we wait for the glorious return of our Lord and Savior. In other words, lives of faith and obedience. A Christian who truly loves Christ and looks forward to His return will zealously want to bring his/her life into conformity with God's will, and will earnestly seek and pray for the discernment necessary to do this.

Discernment brings understanding of what God has done for us in Christ and leads to godly living - that is, being innocent as doves. The Apostle Paul, in our Epistle reference, reminds us of the grace of God and salvation purchased and won for us by Jesus through His sacrifice of Body and Blood on the cross. This salvation, he says, changes us, "teaches us to say no to ungodliness and worldly passions." How does it teach us to say "no?" By the discernment given to us by the Holy Spirit when we embrace the Word of God in faith.

As our knowledge and wisdom in the Word of God grows, our power of discernment grows, the discernment to be shrewd as snakes and innocent as doves. We become more expert in differentiating between truth and falsehood, the godly and the ungodly, that which comes from God and that which comes from Satan or man. The ungodly or worldly person's desires are focused only on life in this world, and they seek satisfaction in nothing higher. But God's saving grace in Christ, His Word of Truth, and the leading of the Holy Spirit Who indwells every believer, saves the child of God from the grip of this ungodliness and its terrible ultimate effects. It provides cleansing in the Blood of Christ for us whenever we fall. Our minds become balanced by grace, discernment and wisdom. We live in communion with God and grow in this communion. We are educated and trained for the new life in Christ. Our love for Christ and our assurance and expectation of His Second Coming moves us, motivates us not to live for self or this world, but to live for Him.

The passage from Proverbs tells us: "There is a way that seems right to a man, but in the end it leads to death." It is referring to the ways of the world, the values of the world, which are sinful, and in the end they lead to destruction. We're also told that "Righteousness exalts a nation, but sin is a disgrace to any people." A primary objective of Satan is to make people and nations more sinful so he can lead them away from God. And how does he make people and nations more sinful? By making them more worldly, committed to their own ways and ignoring God's ways.

And it would appear that Satan is succeeding in this. Consider the state of our society and culture today compared to what it was five or six decades ago. Consider how God has been removed from many of our public institutions, including our schools. Consider what people accept today in movies, television, music, and other venues of entertainment that they would have been appalled at back then and fiercely protested against. And the excuse people give, "Well, it's just the times we live in," is evidence that they have surrendered to the culture of worldliness, allowed it to redirect their focus from God and His ways to the world and its ways. Such worldliness is nothing short of idolatry.The sin of worldliness, people and nations giving priority to their own ways and the world's ways, reflects a lack of discernment and wisdom and eventually destroys both individuals and nations. History clearly shows this. People and nations cannot get away with sin and wickedness indefinitely. Ultimately, if they don't repent, judgment will come. Our Founders understood this clearly. Thomas Jefferson expressed the common feeling when he said: "When I consider the fact that God is just and that His justice cannot be delayed indefinitely, I tremble for my country."

Unrepented sin puts disgrace on a nation and removes the favor of God. Righteousness, however, exalts a nation because it elevates people's minds, promotes virtue, makes them thankful to God, and brings the favor of God. When Israel was faithful to their covenant with God, they achieved greatness. Virtue, goodness, and prosperity filled the land and they were the envy of all the nations around them. But when they forsook God, wickedness, corruption, and idolatry filled the land, and it brought total disaster upon them. They had lost their discernment of God's Word and God's will and insisted on going their own way. People today in the western nations, including the United States, are losing their discernment of God's will and God's ways because of a decades long decrease in the knowledge of God's Word. They are going their own way rather than God's way, and like Old Testament Israel, the result will be utter disaster unless they get their focus back on God and HIs Word and repent.

Don't let Satan use worldliness and the world's values to undermine your godly discernment. Don't let him get you away from God's Word which alone gives one the ability to see things with godly discernment and wisdom. Be like the Psalmist who prayed, "Give discernment to me, your servant; then I will understand your Word." Be like Athanasius, a great hero of the early Church, who said, "If the world goes against the truth (of God's Word), then Athanasius goes against the world." Live a life filled with a zeal guided by knowledge of God's Truth, motivated by love, and directed to the glory of God, a zeal founded on faith, wisdom, and godly discernment so that nothing or no one will be able to deceive you. God grant that we all follow Jesus' advice and be shrewd as serpents and innocent as doves, for His Name's sake. Amen.

GNATS AND CAMELS

Text: Micah 6:6-8; Colossians 2:20-23; Matthew 23:13-24

Theme: Human ignorance versus spiritual reality and truth.

Theme Statement: Like the Pharisees, today's culture, to a great extent, substitutes ritual, feelings, and emotions for reality, formality for faith, appearance for genuineness, and thus slides further and further into mediocrity.

Key Passage: Matthew 23:24. "You blind guides! You strain out a gnat, but swallow a camel."

A pastor was describing a lady in his congregation to another pastor. He said, "She constantly argues about the little things - for example, the use of lipstick. She thinks it is awful and that a woman should not use it, justifying her opinion with 1Peter 3:3 which says, 'A woman's beauty should not come from outward adornment, but instead from the inner self, the unfading beauty of a gentle and quiet spirit which is of great worth in God's sight.' And so she condemns the use of lipstick. And yet, she has the meanest tongue in the congregation, a tongue that is harsh and critical, a tongue that is quick to engage in gossip and slander." That woman didn't see anything wrong in that, conveniently ignoring the Scripture passages that condemn gossip. The poor woman failed to realize that the paint of gossip on the tongue is lots worse than a little paint on the lips. She gave full attention to straining out the little gnat of lipstick, while at the same time swallowing the huge camel of gossip.

There are lots of people like that woman - those who make so much of little things while turning a blind eye to things of far greater importance, people who put great emphasis on the externals - the gnats - but refuse to deal with what is inside - the camels - the sins that lurk in the heart. They strain at gnats and swallow camels. Many of them are in the church, appearing nice and pious on the outside, but refusing to deal with, or even acknowledge, sin on the inside. Perhaps even you and I do that on occasion.

In our Gospel passage, Jesus talks about gnats and camels. He strongly criticizes the Pharisees and Scribes for their spiritual blindness, their obsession with the gnats while ignoring the camels. This section of Scripture contains some of the harshest words in the New Testament - perhaps in the entire Bible - and they were spoken by Jesus to the religious elite of the day. He calls them hypocrites, bling guides, blind fools, snakes, vipers and sons of hell. It's difficult to imagine language that could be more harsh than that. What prompted Jesus to issue such strong condemnation of those religious leaders? What stirred up His righteous anger to such a degree? The answer is that those religious leaders had failed in their God-given responsibility to shepherd the people of God faithfully and according to God's Word. They exalted themselves in word and action instead of humbling themselves before God and being faithful servants to both God and the people. And Jesus accuses them of straining out gnats while swallowing camels. What did He mean?

The significance of the terms "gnat" and "camel" was that both were considered unclean according to the Jewish Law - the gnat the smallest and the camel one of the largest of the unclean animals. Thus, to swallow a gnat or eat camel flesh would render one ritually unclean. The strict Pharisee would meticulously strain his drinking water through a cloth to insure he did not accidentally swallow a gnat and thus become unclean. Notice that Jesus did not specifically condemn this practice. What He condemned was that while they took the greatest care to avoid gnats, the smallest of the unclean, they were figuratively swallowing camels, the largest of the unclean. The Lord was not saying to ignore the little things. He criticized them for ignoring more important things, for being scrupulous in small things and extremely unscrupulous in great things, for not placing the weightier things first. How had they failed in this; in what ways were they straining gnats and swallowing camels?

First, Jesus accuses them of shutting the Kingdom of Heaven in men's faces. How were they doing this? By false teaching and their unfaithfulness to God's Word. Their emphasis was on strict obedience to the multitude of rules and rituals, many of which they themselves established as the way to salvation. They substituted works righteousness for the grace of God. In other words, you earn your way to heaven by keeping all the rules, regulations, rituals of the law. They were guilty of hiding the grace of God from the people, thereby shutting out the Kingdom of Heaven in their faces. Their teachings prevented both themselves and those they taught from entering the Kingdom of Heaven because it fostered a false sense of security and a pride that led them to reject Christ as their Messiah and the grace of God He was offering. Jesus did not criticize their observance of the rules, rituals, and regulations contained in the Word of God. He criticized their elevating the works of law above God's grace as the means of salvation. They carefully attended to the gnats, but in rejecting Christ, they swallowed the camel of unbelief to their own destruction, and encouraged others to do the same.

There are churches today that strain at gnats and swallow camels, churches that, for the sake of a misguided diversity and tolerance, minimize or downplay the Gospel of Jesus Christ, churches that emphasize good works, living lives of love, generosity, and kindness, instead of emphasizing the cross and the empty tomb - that is, Christ crucified and risen, as the core doctrines of the Christian faith. There are churches that hesitate to boldly confess Jesus Christ as Lord and Savior and the only way to heaven, for fear of offending someone. In doing so, they contradict the very one they purport to worship - Jesus Christ - Who boldly and clearly stated in John 14:6: "I am the way and the truth and the life. No one comes to the Father except through Me." Their emphasis on works of righteousness is not wrong since such works are to flow from our faith in Christ, but they are not the means of salvation. In their hesitancy to boldly proclaim Christ crucified and risen as the only means of salvation, these churches, like the religious leaders Jesus criticized, shut the Kingdom of Heaven up in men's faces. Their primary concern is the gnats, not the camels.

Second, Jesus accuses the Pharisees and the Scribes of elevating the material value of a thing above its spiritual value. He uses the example of the gold of the Sanctuary. The Pharisees said that if a person swore an oath by the Temple, if they said "I swear by the Temple of God......" they weren't bound by that oath. But if they swore an oath, made a promise, by the gold of the Temple, they were bound by that oath. And Jesus says to them: "You blind fools! Which is greater, the gold or the Temple that makes the gold sacred?" And the same is true for the altar and the gift on the altar, He says. Jesus criticized them for giving greater importance to the material value of things than to their spiritual significance, for concentrating on gnats while swallowing the camels of hypocrisy and greed.

There are churches today that do that. They place greater importance on their finances, the size of the collection, and the size of the congregation than on whether or not the Word of God is being proclaimed and taught truthfully and faithfully, whether or not the church is a true witness for Jesus Christ. Now don't get me wrong! The church certainly needs resources and faithful giving of time, talents, and money by the people if it is to accomplish God's work. Certainly we as individual children of God need to provide that time, those talents, and that money, if we are to grow in faith, in our likeness to Christ, and in our fellowship with our God and Savior and our brothers and sisters in Christ. But God grant that we never elevate the material above the spiritual. By the way, Jesus made it clear that he who swears by heaven swears by God's throne and by the One Who sits on it. This should cause those people who have the habit of saying, "I swear to God," or "I swear to heaven," to stop and think about what they are saying. They may think it's a gnat, but it's really a camel. They don't realize the spiritual significance of their words. I cringe when I hear a person say, "I swear to God."

Thirdly, Jesus says to those Pharisees and Scribes that, although they were meticulous in their tithing, they were neglecting the more important matters of the law - justice, mercy, and righteousness. He criticizes them for not practicing the latter without neglecting the former. Then Jesus describes their spiritual blindness with the words, "You strain out a gnat but swallow a camel." The Pharisees and Scribes were rigorists when it came to the easy features of the law code, but when it came to the heavenly virtues which were the heart of the law - justice, mercy, faithfulness and righteousness - when it came to the hard part of living out the moral, spiritual parts of God's Word, of loving God with all their heart, mind, body, and soul, and loving their neighbor as themselves, they disregarded those virtues with not a qualm, not a thought. And in doing so, those custodians of the Law missed the consummation of the Law, God's answer to man's inability to keep the Law, Jesus, their Messiah and Savior Who fulfilled the Law perfectly and without sin for them and for us before going to the cross to suffer the terrible penalty for theirs and our failure to fulfill the Law. Their strict legalism and pride, their concern for the gnats, those less important requirements of the law, not to mention the other more than 600 rules and regulations that over time they had come up with on their own which were not in the Torah, the Law, but which they considered as law, blinded them to the Truth and caused them to swallow the camel of unbelief.

What was really tragic about it was that the uncleanness associated with those gnats was easily remedied by ceremonial cleansing. But swallowing that camel of unbelief was disastrous. They rejected the One Whom they should have recognized, the One of whom all those prophets and prophecies of the Old Testament had foretold, the Messiah, the Son of God and Son of Man Who came to fulfill God's Law completely and be the perfect sacrifice for humanity's sins on the cross, the King of kings and Lord of lords. The irony is that they knew of those prophets and prophecies; as Pharisees and Scribes they were educated in the Law, experts in the Law. If anyone should have recognized the coming of the Messiah, the fulfillment of those prophecies, it should have been them. But they didn't recognize Him. Their concern for the gnats blinded them to the greatest visitation in human history.

There are so-called religious leaders like that today who are spiritually blind. They have replaced the Biblical Christ with a Christ that is a figment of their imagination. Their theology, in the words of one renowned scholar, is nothing more than human philosophy dressed up in ecclesiastical robes. It may sound like wisdom, but when you turn the powerful searchlight of Scripture on it, it evaporates in a puff of mist. There are so-called religious leaders today who can spout humanistic philosophy all day, but who are woefully ignorant of what the Bible, God's Word, says. They are like a liberal preacher in California that Vernon McGee told about, who was shown this section of Scripture containing Jesus' harsh criticism of the religious leaders . That liberal preacher didn't know it was in the Bible; in fact, he had never read the Bible. God save us from such spiritual blindness.

A mark of the wisdom of Christ is that He saw the just proportion of things. He clearly distinguished between the gnats and the camels. We need to do the same because we are surrounded by so-called gnats and camels every day, and Satan will always try to get us so caught up with the gnats that we will swallow camels without even noticing it. We see evidence of that all around us, in society and in individuals, including even ourselves at times. Consider a few examples. People demonstrate loudly and strongly for animal rights and condemn cruelty to animals, and rightly so, for animals are God's creatures. Yet, at the same time, those same people demonstrate loudly for the right to abortion, which over the past 47 years has resulted in the cruel, barbarous murder of more than 63 million babies in the womb, and some out of the womb. They swallow that enormous camel without hardly a thought.

Or how about the view of Jesus many have today, a Jesus whose great love for us would never allow Him to condemn someone to hell for eternity. Thus, they say, everyone will eventually be saved, whether they accept Christ as Lord of their life or not. Now that's a camel that

304

Satan will try by every means to get people to swallow, because all who do belong to him. Unfortunately, many do swallow that camel because there is great misunderstanding among many as to who Jesus Christ really is, a misunderstanding contributed to by many liberal preachers. Much of liberal theology is touchy-feely, giving people the impression that all Jesus talked about was love. Now it is certainly true that the dominant characteristic of His ministry was love, that He loves sinners with a love we cannot fully comprehend, a love so great that it took Him to the cross to suffer the penalty for our sins. Jesus Christ is our Savior, our only Savior, but Jesus Christ is also Judge, something which the radical liberal view of Jesus chooses to ignore. But God's Word is clear. God the Father has put all things under the authority of Jesus Christ, Son of God and Son of Man. Receive Jesus Christ as Lord and Savior through faith and live. On the other hand, reject Jesus Christ through unbelief, and He becomes your Judge when He returns in glory at the end of time to judge both the living and the dead. Those who receive Him in faith go with Him into eternal glory in heaven. Those who reject Him go to eternal punishment in hell. Savior or Judge! It's every person's choice. As a matter of fact, God doesn't condemn anyone to hell. Those who reject God's grace by rejecting Christ condemn themselves.

Or how about the person who comes to church, who sings heartily, who joins in the responsive readings, who is attentive to the message, who joins in the prayers, and yet who leaves worship still harboring hatred and anger in their heart towards another person, who insists on swallowing that camel of hatred and anger rather than take it to God in confession and repentance and be forgiven and cleansed of that camel for the sake of Jesus Who paid the price for that sin also on the cross. That person may even be sincere in their worship, but if they leave worship harboring that hatred in their heart, their worship was not honoring to God because of that camel they swallowed and their refusal to turn it over to God and be rid of it.

It has been said that society is descending into mediocrity. Technical progress, advances in science and technology, have been astounding.

But it has been accompanied by sharp spiritual decline. Society overall is becoming less and less able to differentiate between the gnats and the camels, so to speak, between the things of greater importance and the things of lesser importance, between the things temporal and the things eternal. And the overall result is the decline into mediocrity that we see occurring in education, values, entertainment and other aspects of life.

It is crucially important to our spiritual health and maturity, as well as our physical health, to be able to separate the gnats from the camels, the things of lesser importance from the things of greater importance. And there are two ways we can do that. The first way is through knowing God's Word, becoming more and more proficient in God's Word, thus becoming more and more wise and discerning. If those religious leaders had spent the time searching the Torah, the Old Testament, and becoming expert in the prophets and prophecies concerning the coming Messiah, the Christ, that they spent on all the little rules and regulations of the law, they might have recognized their Messiah when He came on the scene. If we are faithful in the study of God's Word, keeping our eyes on Christ, the Holy Spirit will help us grow in wisdom , and Satan's efforts to deceive us will be frustrated.

The second way is through prayer, going to God in prayer and asking Him to give us that wisdom and discernment, asking the Holy Spirit to guide us and lead us to His will and purpose He ordained for us from the foundation of the world, avoiding the gnats and camels Satan would use to divert us from that purpose.

And lastly, when we do fall, when we become obsessed with a gnat or swallow a camel, so to speak, as it is probable that we will do on occasion because of our sinful nature, ask God to forgive us for Jesus' sake, take away the frustrating gnat and remove the obnoxious camel, and grant us the wisdom and discernment to put first things first and all things in their proper order and to watch out for the camels. Amen.

CHAPTER 12 - TRUE BEAUTY AND VALUE

"Your beauty should not come from outward adornment. Instead, it should be that of your inner self, the unfolding beauty of a gentle and quiet spirit, which is of great worth in God's sight."

1Peter 3:3-4

BEAUTY THAT LASTS

Text: Matthew 23:25-28; 1Peter 3:3-4;   Psalm 27:4-6

Theme: The world's standards for beauty involve a temporary, fading outward beauty.

> Theme Statement: God estimates beauty by the state of the heart and a person's character, for true beauty begins inwardly in the heart. It is a fruit of the heart and springs from our relationship to God.

Key Passage: 1Peter 3:3-4.   "Your beauty should not come from outward adornment, such as braided hair and the wearing of gold jewelry and fine clothes. Instead it should be that of your inner self, the unfading beauty of a gentle and quiet spirit, which is of great worth in God's sight.

✝

It was a traumatic experience for me when I discovered that I was going bald. My first reaction, as is normally the case when faced with an unpleasant fact of life, was denial. I wasn't really losing my hair; it was only thinning a bit and new hair would soon replace it. But it didn't and before long denial was no longer possible. So, I moved to the second reaction, which was action to stop the loss of hair. My aunt was a beautician, and she gave me a lotion reputed to stop hair loss. I used that lotion for quite some time, rubbing it into my scalp so hard its amazing I didn't scramble my brains. I know, some of you are thinking, "Darrell, you did scramble your brains." Well, after a time, it became evident that the lotion was failing to do what it was advertised to do. And so I moved to the third and final reaction - acceptance. I was going to be bald. Live with it. Remember, these were times when baldness was a stigma. Today, it is considered to a large extent attractive.

Along the way, I discovered that there were people, even some my friends, who apparently thought it their duty to remind me of my dilemma. They would ask me, "Darrell, do you know that you are getting bald?" And their question would usually reflect a patronizing attitude , as if the fact that they had a full head of hair and I didn't was evidence of some sort of superiority on their part. I felt like answering, "Why no! I didn't know that, but thank you for telling me." Actually, that's not what I wanted to tell them. I won't say what I wanted to tell them. As the hair got thinner and thinner, I recognized the truth in what a fellow fighter pilot in Germany, who was completely bald, told me. He said, "Darrell, you will find that as the hair gets thinner and thinner, the placement of each one becomes more and more critical."

And then one day, during my reading through the Old Testament, I came across the story of Elisha, a great prophet and successor to Elijah. Elisha was apparently bald. After Elisha experienced seeing his master and mentor Elijah taken up to heaven in a fiery chariot, and while he was walking along the road back to Bethel, a group of hecklers surrounded him and ridiculed him saying, "Go on up, you old baldhead! Go on up, you baldhead!" We're told that two bears came out of the woods and mauled forty-two of those hecklers. I really like that passage.

This world and our society places great priority and emphasis on outward appearance. Its standards and criteria for beauty concentrate mainly on the exterior, and frankly, I don't measure up to those standards. Perhaps you feel the same. If you're bald, or if you're carrying some extra pounds, or if you are in some way marred in physical appearance, or have some other type of defect, this would have you believe that you have missed the mark. And that can be devastating to a person, especially to our young people, who face tremendous peer pressure to conform to this world's standards for beauty and worth. We are inundated with the world's standards for beauty - in advertising, commercials, television programs, movies, music, and on and on. And it's easy to become convinced that the world is right and sub-consciously buy into those standards.

Even Samuel, one of the greatest prophets of the Old Testament and the last Judge of Israel, showed this attitude when God sent him to anoint one of Jesse's sons as King of Israel. As Samuel looked at the eldest son, at his height and appearance, his handsomeness, he thought to himself, "Surely this is the Lord's anointed." But God said "No," and told Samuel, "Do not consider his appearance or his height. I do not look at the things man looks at. Man looks at the outward appearance, but the Lord looks at the heart." Seven of Jesse's sons stood before Samuel, but the Lord did not select any one of them. Upon learning that Jesse had an eighth son, the youngest who was out tending sheep, since the youngest always got the most menial job, he directed Jesse to send for him. Upon his arrival, the Lord told Samuel, "Rise, and anoint him; he is the one I have chosen." God looks for character, and He estimates character by the state of the heart, for true beauty is a fruit of the heart. Men judge by appearance. God never judges by appearance. God would describe David, whom Samuel had anointed, as "a man after my own heart." I can think of no higher complement that God could give to a man.

In the Epistle referenced, Peter is making the point that outward adornment or appearance is not what counts in the sight of God. Peter is not saying that braided hair or jewelry or fine clothes are sinful or evil. Rather, he is contrasting outward adornment and beauty which is temporary and fading with the inward adornment and beauty of a humble, gentle, and quiet spirit which is an unfading beauty and a beauty of great worth in God's sight. A person's inward personality is to shine with spiritual beauty, the only beauty that lasts. In 2 Corinthians 4:16, the Apostle Paul tells us, "Though outwardly we are wasting away, yet inwardly we are being renewed day by day." We are renewed by the Spirit of Christ Who dwells within us; renewed with an increasing beauty that is everlasting. You see, both Peter and Paul, as well as our Lord Himself, drew a sharp contrast between what human society values and what God values, what human society considers beautiful and what God considers beautiful.

The writer of Ecclesiastes, King Solomon, in his search for the meaning of life, and after experiencing all that this world holds beautiful and important - acquiring great knowledge and riches, advancement and prestige - and after experiencing all the pleasures of the body, had this to say. "Vanity of vanities, it is all vanity." The Hebrew word can also be translated as "smoke." "Smoke, smoke, it is all smoke." Smoke that disappears and is no more. His final comment, however, shows that he had found the answer to the meaning of life. He said, "Now all has been heard; here is the conclusion of the matter. Fear God and keep His commandments, for this is the whole duty of man." He had discovered the meaning of true beauty, the inward beauty. For if beauty is only on the outside, it is unreliable, fades, and has no permanency. But the inward beauty that springs from a heart devoted to God is a permanent beauty, lasting for this life and for the life eternal.

And so, much of what is considered beautiful by this world is merely a beauty that is here today and gone tomorrow, an outward beauty that conceals corruption and death within, a beauty that is hollow. And God despises hollowness. In the Gospel passage referenced, Jesus describes the hollowness of the Pharisees and the teachers of the law. He severely criticizes their overriding concern for outward cleanness and appearance, while ignoring inner cleanness. Outward cleanness referred to their zealous adherence to ritual and religious show; yet, on the inside, they were full of greed and self-indulgence. He tells them that they should clean the inside and then the outside will also be truly clean. If you want to have your food pure, you clean the inside of the vessel more carefully than the outside. So it is with the human vessel. The attitude of the heart within will determine one's character and the quality of one's words and action. And if one's heart belongs to God, it will shine forth like sunshine in that person's life.

Jesus then likens the Pharisees and teachers of the law to whitewashed tombs. The tombs were often whitewashed in order to make them conspicuous so that Jews might not accidentally come into contact with them, and thereby become ceremonially unclean for seven days. The result was that the tombs outwardly appeared beautiful, clean and pure, yet on the inside were filled with bones of the dead and all sorts of uncleanness. Like those tombs, the religious leaders outwardly appeared righteous. But inwardly, as Jesus pointed out to them, they were filled with hypocrisy and wickedness. They appeared to be what they were not. Outward appearance meant everything to them. Of all the sins that Jesus encountered among people, none aroused His fiery indignation more than hypocrisy. And in our society today, there is every bit as much, and even more, hypocrisy than when Jesus walked this earth.

Jesus, in this passage, is not condemning them because they sin. After all, we are all sinners and fall short of God's standards of holiness. No, what Jesus is condemning is their attitude of the heart, an egotistical, self-inflated attitude, a heart bent on hypocrisy and wickedness. They pretended on the outside to be shepherds of the people, but on the inside, they despised the outcasts, the poor, the downtrodden, the diseased, the oppressed - the very ones Jesus came to minister to. Their god was their belly, the riches they gained from their position, the prestige they enjoyed and the self-pride stemming from their reputation as being zealous keepers of the law. The outside was beautiful according to worldly standards; the inside was filled with rot. In speaking of cleanness, Jesus told His disciples: "What comes out of a man makes him unclean. For from within, out of men's hearts, come evil thoughts, sexual immorality, theft, murder, adultery, greed, malice, deceit, lewdness, envy, slander, arrogance, and folly. All these evils come from inside and make a man unclean." All this applied to those Pharisees and teachers of the law.

It might even be said that those religious leaders' outward appearance of exceptional cleanness and purity was a warning sign of internal corruption, a sign pointing to hidden defilement. With their attitude of superiority, they did not accept the fact that they were miserable sinners just like those that they looked upon with contempt, and that, like them, they too were totally dependent on the grace of God. There is a lesson here. Beware of shows of exceptional holiness, purity, and beauty. Often, they are marks of destructive pride and self-righteousness. Dr. Donald Guthrie, a renowned theologian, in contrasting outward appearance and inward reality, put it this way: "The grass grows green upon the sides of a mountain that holds a volcano in its bowels."

When I consider the priority, the emphasis that this world and our society places on outward appearance and beauty, I am humbled by the inspired words of the prophet Isaiah in chapter 53, verses 2 and 3, where he is speaking of the Messiah, the Christ, and says, "He had no beauty or majesty to attract us to Him, nothing in His appearance that we should desire Him. He was despised and rejected by men, a man of sorrows, and familiar with suffering. Like one from whom men hide their faces, He was despised, and we esteemed Him not." Have you ever felt unattractive, rejected, undesired, despised? Jesus knows exactly how you feel. He felt the same, and even more.

Now, according to human standards, one would think that when the Son of God, God Himself, took on human flesh and became fully human as the Son of Man, He would have been the most handsome, strikingly beautiful person on the face of the earth, and one who would have made His entry into our world with the greatest pomp and fanfare, with riches unheard of. But no, the Son of God chose to have a body and appearance of a common person, a person like you and me, entering this world in a stable, laying in a manger, and living a life of poverty, rejection, suffering, and finally death on a cross, for you and me and all His human creation.

And consider this! There was nothing outwardly beautiful about the cross. It was a bloody, gory, humiliating, and agonizing experience for our Lord. According to society's standards, crucifixion was the outward sign of the curse of God and the curse of men. Yet, what was happening behind the scene, the inward reality, was priceless and beautiful beyond description. The grace of God the Father was being poured out for all mankind, with His only begotten Son, as Son of Man, becoming a curse for us, taking all mankind's sin upon Himself, and paying the terrible price for those sins that we could not pay, so that we can have the forgiveness of sins, direct access to the throne of God through Christ, and eternal life with Him in glory. The priceless, indescribably beautiful inward reality of our redemption, restoration to God, and eternal glory was purchased for us through the Blood of our Savior Jesus, whose outward appearance on that cross was of a brutally beaten, scourged, ravaged, and bloody sacrifice as payment for that inward beauty. All praise be to God for His profound and unspeakable grace.

Meekness of spirit in Scripture signifies humility, courage, strength of character and steadfastness in the Lord. It is the true beauty, a beauty that lasts, not one that is put on, not an earthly, bodily, outward thing, but a beauty of the soul. And it shines forth to the glory of God, giving a foretaste of the indescribable beauty that will be ours when we meet our Savior face-to-face. There was once a distinguished painter whose life's purpose was to produce on canvas a picture of the Christ. He worked diligently to paint his conception of Christ. When he had finished, he called a little girl into his studio, showed her the painting, and asked, "Little girl, tell me who that is." She looked intently, and then said, "It looks like some good man, but I don't know who it is."

The artist was deeply disappointed and said, "I fear I don't know Christ." He went to the New Testament and began to prayerfully study Christ. He soon became convicted of sin and saw the need of accepting Jesus Christ as his Savior. The joy of salvation came into his heart, giving it a beauty that had not been there before, and he began his work anew. When the second painting was finished, he asked the same little girl to look at it. Instantly, she recited the words of Jesus - "Let the little children come to Me, and forbid them not." With tears of joy, the artist exclaimed, "Thank God, now I can present Christ so that a little child can recognize Him." He had found true beauty, the beauty that lasts, the beauty that only comes from a heart that belongs to Christ, and that beauty was reflected in his work. Do we reflect that beauty to those around us, in our words, our actions, our work, our play?

Jesus tells us that all thoughts and acts spring from the heart. A person's heart is who that person is, at the deepest and most private level. The heart is the place where one's allegiances are formed, and for

Christians, the place where their allegiance to Jesus Christ as Lord and Savior is firmly rooted. And such allegiance is the wellspring of true beauty - the beauty that lasts.

Well, I'm never going to measure up to the world's and society's standards for beauty. And probably neither will many of you. The world and its followers may cast us aside because of our appearance or because they consider us useless for their agenda. But who cares? God never casts a child of His aside; nor does He ever consider our usefulness to Him ended. We never reach a point in this life or the next where God can't use us for His glory and some great work in His Kingdom.

In Christ, every Christian has both an outward beauty and an inward beauty that is infinitely greater than any this world can conceive of. And don't you dare let this world convince you otherwise. Amen.

PRICELESS POTATO PEELINGS

Text: Ecclesiastes 3:12-14;   Hebrews 11:24-26;   Luke 16:19-31

Theme: Changing value systems.

> Theme Statement: A person's value system can radically change when the circumstances of life are radically altered. The simple blessings of life, which God gives us and which are so often taken for granted in the quest for material riches, become of primary value when we risk losing them.

Key Passage: Ecclesiastes 3:12-14. "I know that there is nothing better for men than to be happy and do good while they live. That everyone may eat and drink, and find satisfaction In all his toil - this is the gift of God."

Some years ago, when I was taking graduate courses in business, the Professor of Macroeconomics, on the first night of the class, gave us a three hour strategic survey of the world from an economic perspective. It was fascinating, and when it was ended, we all wondered where the three hours had gone. He taught us many important economic concepts, one being that circumstances often determine value, that that which is considered worthless under most circumstances, may become priceless under certain circumstances, and vice versa. He was an elderly man at the time, originally from Holland, and had served on President Eisenhower's Council of Economic Advisers.

He was a young man when the Nazis invaded Holland and began a brutal occupation that lasted five years. He fought with the Dutch resistance forces until he was captured by the Nazis and taken to the Dachau concentration camp, one of the Nazi's death camps. Those who were able to work were kept alive as slave labor; the others were exterminated. He explained to the class how, under those circumstances, one's value system underwent drastic change, and he used potato peelings as an example. Potato peelings, which under normal conditions, one would throw away, became the most precious commodity to the prisoners. Potato peelings were food, nutrition; they were life to the starving prisoners. People fought over them, would kill for them. Those who had somehow managed to hide valuable items from the guards, such as wedding rings, gold, diamonds, jewelry, other precious stones, or even cash, tried desperately to exchange them for a handful of potato peelings, but to no avail. In the economy of Dachau concentration camp, gold and diamonds were worthless, and potato peelings were priceless.

In the course of our daily lives, I think we all have a tendency to take for granted many of the blessings of life which God graciously bestows on us, the simple blessings of life that are like those common potato peelings. We're too busy to give them our attention, too busy striving, competing, seeking, acquiring what we consider more valuable - wealth, material goods, status, prestige, etc.- too busy conforming to this world's value system which says more is better, get all the wealth, fame, power you can while you can, and let no one or nothing stand in your way of getting it. And in the process of all that striving and acquiring, we tend to ignore, or if not ignore, put on the sidelines, those blessings which give life much of its meaning. That is, until we lose them, or risk losing them. Then they become like those potato peelings at Dachau - priceless.

What are some of the priceless potato peelings in our lives, so to speak, those blessings which are too often given a back seat in our emotions, feelings, activities, and goals, but which give flavor, substance, and quality to our lives. The list is endless, but I'll mention just a few. How about the touch of a loved one, a tender touch that communicates love and says, "You're very special to me!" The right touch at the right time, an arm around the shoulder, a friendly hug are simple gestures, but they can be like those precious potato peelings to someone who needs assurance, comfort, and encouragement. Jesus, during His life on earth, was a person who touched others. In His healings, He seemed most often to make a point of touching the person, even lepers and others considered unclean, which was absolutely forbidden by society and which rendered the person doing the touching ceremonially unclean. The loving, compassionate touch was crucial to many of the persons He healed, and it remains so today, with us His followers.

How about a child's hugs and kisses? Or the time we spend with children, which too often, when other things are crowding In for our attention, we sometimes think of as a demand or even a nuisance. But take away those hugs and kisses and time with children, and they become like priceless potato peelings. Jesus knew how priceless time with children was, and He didn't let anything interfere with His spending time with them. In Matthew 19:13-14, when the disciples tried to stop people from bothering Jesus by bringing their little children to Jesus for Him to place His hands on them and pray for them, He rebuked His disciples saying, "Let the little children come to Me, and do not hinder them, for the Kingdom of Heaven belongs to such as these." And He laid His hands on them and blessed them.

How about the company of close friends? Friends who accept you and love you for who you are. Friends who share your joys and sorrows and to whom you can bare your heart. We sometimes take friends for granted, but what priceless potato peelings they are! Jesus put a high value on friendship, and He made a point of referring to His followers (and that includes us) as His friends. He accepts us as we are and loves us for who we are. But He doesn't leave us as we are. He constantly intercedes for us with the Father, and works through the Holy Spirit to lead us to our highest good in Him. He shares our joys and sorrows and He invites us to bare our hearts to Him. He bared His heart to us - and more - He gave His Body to be broken and His Blood to be shed for us on the cross to pay the penalty for our sins and restore us to God's family as children of the Most High.

Jesus, one might say, lived a potato peeling life. A life of poverty and hardship. He once said that foxes have dens and birds have nests, yet the Son of Man had no place to lay His head. And even though Jesus knew that the terrible suffering and agony of the cross was in His future, He still enjoyed life and the simple things of life, eating with friends, times of prayer and meditation, walking along the roads sharing fellowship with His disciples and other followers. And He especially enjoyed ministering to and healing the sick, crippled, the possessed, the outcast, and the downtrodden. He enjoyed the blessings of everyday life that come from God, and He thanked His Father for them. He knew how priceless the potato peelings of life were.

The writer of Ecclesiastes, King Solomon, the wisest man who ever lived with the exception of Jesus, learned how important the simple blessings of life are. He had experienced all the things this world values - wealth far beyond one's imagination, far greater than anyone had before or has had since; wisdom and knowledge unequaled before or since, except for Jesus; pleasure which no man has had the likes of before or since; and power and prestige that extended throughout the known world. Yet, in Ecclesiastes, he tells us that it was all a chasing after the wind, and that there is nothing better than being happy, or content, with what God has given us, doing good, eating and drinking, and finding satisfaction in all our toil. It is all a gift from God, and we find meaning in life when we cheerfully and gratefully accept it from the hand of God. Our culture says, "Think big!" However, as King Solomon learned, happiness and satisfaction, more often than not, comes when we think small, when we savor and enjoy those priceless potato peelings in our life.

Moses also had a keen awareness for things of true and lasting value, the priceless potato peelings in life. In our reading from Hebrews, we are told that Moses chose to be mistreated along with the people of God rather than to enjoy the riches and pleasures of sin for a short time as a member of Pharaoh's household. He regarded disgrace for the sake of God's people, and therefore for the sake of the Messiah, the Christ, as of infinitely greater value than the treasures of Egypt because he was looking ahead to his reward God had for him. He chose to join himself to God's people through whom the hope of the Messiah was to be realized, even though they were in slavery at the time. His choice was in direct contradiction to the world's value system. But Moses kept his eyes on the things not seen. He understood, as the Apostle Paul later stated in 1Corinthians 4:18, that "things seen are for a season only, but the things not seen are eternal."

Do we regard disgrace for the sake of Christ as of infinitely greater value than the treasures of this world? Are we willing to undergo disgrace for Christ? Is disgrace for Christ a priceless potato peeling in our lives? Are our eyes fixed on the treasures and pleasures of this world, or are they fixed on the things eternal? The glory of the Pharaohs and Egypt lie in ruins, but the glory and treasure of Moses' reward, and our reward in Christ, lasts for eternity.

And then we have Jesus' parable of the rich man and Lazarus in our Gospel reference. The rich man certainly had his eyes fixed on the things of this world. The emphasis in the parable is not on being rich, but on our attitude towards riches and our use of the riches God blesses us with. As one author put it: "Affluence in not inherently evil, but it is inherently dangerous." The rich man was oblivious to the needs of his neighbor, the beggar Lazarus, who lay at his gate covered with sores and longing only for the scraps that fell from the rich man's table, the potato peelings, so to speak. And by ignoring Lazarus' needs, the rich man was ignoring the basic demands of the law and the prophets, God's Word in the Torah, to share with those in need, to help the sick and oppressed, to lift up the downtrodden.

But when they both died, the situation was totally reversed. The rich man, in the torment of hell, looked up and saw Abraham far away with Lazarus by his side in the joy and bliss of the blessedness reserved for God's people. And he asked that Lazarus dip his finger in cold water and come and cool his tongue. The rich man, who had lived a self-serving, self-satisfied life, who could have been a benefactor to Lazarus and others in need, but instead was focused on his own riches and enjoyment of the so-called good things of life, was now in a place where all his riches were worthless, and a drop of cold water, was priceless.

Just a little water, which he undoubtedly took for granted and didn't give a second thought to during his earthly life, suddenly became that which was most valuable. A little water to the rich man was like those priceless potato peelings to the prisoners at Dachau concentration camp. Well, his request was not possible. He was informed by Abraham that, between where he was and where Abraham and Lazarus were, a great gulf existed which could not be crossed.

And consider this! The rich man is not described as being consciously or deliberately cruel. He was only totally and hopelessly indifferent. His ruin was not so much inhumanity as much as indifference. It may have been that so much claimed the rich man's attention, so much business to be conducted, so many responsibilities, that he had no time to consider Lazarus' need, or to fix his eyes on what is most important, what is eternal. So it is with us at times. The cares and responsibilities of daily life have a way of taking priority with our time, and we can become inattentive or indifferent to the needs of others, even to those most important in our lives. I have certainly been guilty of that, and perhaps you have also. The point is that when we, through our thoughtlessness or selfishness, diminish or hurt others by our inattention or indifference, particularly those persons and things most important in our lives, those priceless potato peelings so to speak, we diminish and hurt ourselves.

Well, the rich man realized that his value system during his life on earth had been all wrong. Like those potato peelings, what he considered of no value and not worthy of his attention, he now realized was priceless, of value beyond measure. And he thought of his brothers, who apparently had the same value system. He was confident that a visitor from the dead would produce repentance in his brothers. Wrong! Abraham told him that if they reject God's Word, they won't pay attention to someone who returns from the dead. And isn't that the truth? After all, when Jesus later raised another man named Lazarus from the dead, and that Lazarus was there for all to see, it did not produce repentance in the religious leaders. It only made them more determined to kill Jesus. And when Jesus Himself was raised from the dead, a resurrection witnessed by many and for which the evidence was and is absolutely overwhelming and irrefutable, it didn't produce repentance and faith in the majority of the people and their leaders, and the same is true with many people today. But thank God that you and I, and our brothers and sisters in Christ around the world know the crucified and resurrected Christ as Lord and Savior, and that in faith we shall one day take our place in the Presence of His inexpressible glory and majesty.

The arrogant of this world look on Christ and His Church as common potato peelings, as it were. They are totally caught up in the pursuits of this world and have no room or time in their lives for God. They don't realize that death makes us all bankrupt as far as worldly goods are concerned, and that we cannot gain even a drop of cold water in the next life by living only for this world in this life. The fact that earthly greatness, apart from faith in God and His Christ, is absolutely meaningless as far as heavenly greatness is concerned is plainly seen in the parable. Those who are despised and unhonored in this life for the sake of Christ will be honored and glorified in the heavenly life.

The day will come when the heavens roll back, the trumpet sounds, and Christ returns with all power and glory, and the arrogant of this world, who like the rich man, live for themselves, will, like that rich man, recognize the priceless treasure of what they treated indifferently, like common potato peelings, and would give anything and everything for what they had arrogantly ignored and refused. The good news is that, while they live, it is not too late to acknowledge and receive in faith that priceless treasure of salvation God offers through His Son. The bad news is that, like that rich man in the parable, once a person closes their eyes in death, it will be too late.

God's Word to us is, "Do not ignore or be indifferent to the priceless potato peelings in our lives." Thank God for them and take time to appreciate them. And let us strive to live a priceless potato peeling life, one with our priorities ordered as God would have us order them, a life in which we clearly focus on the things that are most important, with

Christ first and foremost. If Christ is first, everything else will assume its proper place. Why? Because the Father has so ordered it that Christ is the Source of all things and Christ is the Consummation of all things. Therefore, all things have their meaning, purpose, and destiny in Christ.

Then too, if Christ is first in our life, the Holy Spirit will increase love in our hearts, love for God and love for each other. And that love will enable us to see beyond the veil, to see the unseen as it were, and discern the things that really matter in this life and beyond.

God grant us such love and discernment, for Jesus' sake. Amen.

CHAPTER 13 - MUCH FROM LITTLE

"So there was food every day for Elijah, and for the woman and her family. For the jar of flour was not used up and the jug of oil did not run dry, in keeping with the Word of the Lord spoken by Elijah."

1Kings 17:15-16

"Taking the five loaves and the two fish and looking up to heaven, He gave thanks and broke the loaves. Then He gave them to His disciples to set before the people. He also divided the two fish among them all. They all ate and were satisfied, and the disciples picked up twelve basketfuls of broken pieces of bread and fish. The number of men who had eaten was five thousand."

Mark 6:41-44

A WIDOW'S OFFERING; A BOY'S LUNCH

Text: 1Kings 17:7-16;   2Corinthians 4:5-7;   Mark 6:30-44

Theme: How God can take our little, and make of it more than we could imagine.

Theme Statement: When we offer to God our time, talent, and treasure, no matter how little or insufficient they may seem, God, with His all-surpassing power and total sufficiency, will bring much from our little to glorify His Name and build His Kingdom.

Key Passage:1Kings 17:16. For the jar of flour was not used up and the jug of oil did not run dry, in keeping with the Word of the Lord spoken by Elijah. Mark 6:42-44. They all ate and were satisfied, and the disciples picked up twelve basketfuls of broken pieces of bread and fish. The number of the men who had eaten was five thousand.

✝

One night in Paris the great violinist, Paganini, was tuning up his violin prior to performing before a great audience. One of the strings broke. Disappointment swept over the audience. Paganini paid no attention to it and began to play with the three remaining strings. Then another string snapped, and the audience groaned, but Paganini continued to play until a third string snapped and hung down upon his arm. The audience was now plainly disgusted, believing he had a defective violin. Quietly stepping to the front, Paganini said, "Ladies and gentlemen, you will now hear one string and Paganini." He began to bring such wonderful music out of that one string that the audience leaned forward in their seats and strained their necks that they might hear it all. Paganini sat down as the entire house wildly applauded because he had brought so much out of so little. Paganini needed only one string to bring forth music indescribably beautiful.

God delights in bringing forth much from little. When we offer to God even a little of our time, talents, and treasure, no matter how insufficient they may seem, God, with His all-surpassing power and total sufficiency, will bring much from our little to glorify His Name and build His Kingdom. But just as that audience felt that a violin with only one string offered little through which Paganini could work, so we may feel that we can offer little through which the Holy Spirit can work. But God does great things with humble material surrendered to His touch. One soul surrendered to God can change, and has changed, the entire course of history. As the saying goes, God and one person make a majority.

Scripture is filled with examples of God bringing forth much from little. Our Old Testament reference gives one account. A terrible drought had come upon Israel, prophesied by God through His prophet Elijah, in an attempt to bring the Israelites to repentance. God told Elijah to go to Zarephath, where He had prepared for a widow to supply food for His prophet. Elijah found the woman and her son reduced to the point just prior to starvation. She had only a handful of flour and a little oil, and was going to prepare a last meal for her son and herself, and then die of starvation. What does Elijah do? He tells her not to be afraid, to make a cake of bread for him first out of what she had and bring it to him, and then make something for herself and her son out of whatever was left. He tells her: "This is what the Lord, the God of Israel says, 'The jar of flour will not be used up and the jug of oil will not run dry until the day the Lord gives rain on the land.'" Did you notice that she was to serve God's prophet Elijah first out of the little she had, and then use the rest for her son and herself?

I wonder what you and I would have done. She had so little - only a handful of flour and a little oil, and then starvation. And here is this foreign man, a prophet of a foreign God, since Zarephath was not in Israel, asking her to provide for him first out of the little she had and then use the rest for her son and herself. I probably would have told Elijah to get a grip on reality.

What a demand upon the faith of this woman! What a big, big risk she was asked to take. How did she know Elijah wouldn't eat and run? At the very least, it would have been reasonable for her to ask for proof that what Elijah promised would be so. But she didn't! The woman had a truly generous spirit. And she demonstrated a faith of a true sort - a heroic faith - a faith that asks no questions or demands no proof. God sometimes tests our faith, and He asks the same response from us as this woman's. He wants us to trust Him, trust and obey, without a lot of questioning.

God miraculously provided for this non-Israelite woman and her son, who, in an act of faith in the Lord's Word through Elijah, laid her and her son's lives on the line. The woman offered her little to God's prophet. And God took that little handful of flour and little container of oil and made much of it, more than she could ever have imagined. God kept on making much from the little she had for the entire three years of the drought. The container of flour never emptied, and the container of oil never failed.

God delights in making much from little, in taking that which is insignificant, woefully inadequate, weak and of little value in human eyes, and making much of it, so much that the human eye gazes in awe and wonder at what God has done. Our Gospel reference gives another startling account of this in the feeding of the five thousand.

A huge crowd from the surrounding towns had followed Jesus and His disciples as they sought a quiet and solitary place to get some rest. And Jesus had compassion for the multitude, so instead of resting, He began teaching and healing the sick, entirely unconcerned about the passing of time. And the disciples get worried. They come to Jesus and remind Him that it's getting late and they are in a remote place. They tell Him to send the people away so they can go to the surrounding villages and get something to eat. The disciples couldn't understand why Jesus would keep the people in that remote place so long. Apparently they felt that they must act if Jesus doesn't.

Have you ever been in a remote place - physically, spiritually, emotionally - with time slipping away? Have you ever wondered why God was keeping you in a remote place so long? Have you ever been frustrated over God's timing? Have you ever felt that you must act according to your own timetable because you are tired of waiting for God to act? If so, you probably have some idea of how those disciples felt. And what is the disciples' solution? Send the people away and let them fend for themselves to find something to eat. And what is Jesus' response to them? "You give them something to eat!"

Jesus' response really set them aback. Jesus was testing HIs disciples. He knew what He would do. He was trying to lead them to think of His almighty power, which they had seen demonstrated in previous miracles. He wanted them to place their reliance on Him, on His wisdom and care. He wanted a response of faith from them. But they failed to take the hint. What did the disciples do? Exactly what we so often do! They saw the problem, were overwhelmed by it, and immediately scrambled to find a human solution to it. They didn't think to place it in Jesus' hands Who alone could solve it. They didn't remember the wedding at Cana where Jesus turned water into wine. They didn't remember the miracles that followed that first one. They immediately considered what it would cost to procure food for so many people. And that would hardly be enough to buy even a little for each person. Besides, it being very late, how could they hope to procure so much food? Five thousand men, besides women and children had to be fed.

The minds of the disciples were dense. They didn't remember Jesus' great workings in the past, and saw only the impossibilities of the present situation. They didn't comprehend that these impossibilities were meant to make them think of Jesus, and that all things are possible to Him. And we, too often, react to problems we encounter that seem impossible in exactly the same way. Like the disciples, we forget that God can bring much from little. Time and time again, Scripture tells us to remember, remember, God's mighty works in the past.

Remembering God's mercies, God's mighty works in the past, strengthens us to overcome today's problems, today's impossibilities.

Jesus' question concerning how much food they had on hand must have really mystified them. And when they told Him, "five loaves and two fish," they probably thought that Jesus would now see the impossibility of the situation and send the people away. We should not, by the way, think of these loaves as our modern thick loaves of bread. These were small flat cakes of bread as they were baked at the time. What the disciples thought when Jesus commanded them to have the multitude sit down in groups we can only imagine. In effect, He was asking thousands to get ready to dine on five small bread cakes and two fish. Had He taken leave of His senses? Utterly ridiculous from a human standpoint. Grouping them in hundreds and fifties not only made it easier to serve them, but easier to count. Picture it in your mind. Thousands arranged in groups ready to dine and only a handful of food to set before them. Jesus blesses the five loaves and two fish and gives thanks. What would our prayer be in a similar situation? Would we say, "God, is this all? It's not near enough! It's way too little!"

Why do you suppose Jesus had the disciples distribute the food? It would have been simpler to just have the people file past and receive their portion. Perhaps Jesus wanted to impress upon them not to be overwhelmed by what seems impossible, and that with Him - the Christ - all things are possible. For as Jesus broke the five bread cakes and divided the two fish and gave them to the disciples to distribute, there were always more pieces to break off. The bread and fish multiplied in Jesus' hands.

There is another hero, in my opinion, in this great miraculous event, along with Jesus that is. In the Apostle John's account of the miracle, he tells us that the five loaves and two fish was the lunch of a small boy in the crowd. It was his meal, and he was certainly as hungry as the rest of them. Nevertheless, this small boy willingly offered his lunch to Jesus to use, to his Lord Who would make so much from so little. In doing so, the boy sets an example for us. Jesus wants us to do the same.

No matter how little, no matter how insignificant, our gift of time, talent, or treasure appears, when we offer it to our Savior, Jesus will make much of it, more than we can possibly imagine. I pray that none of us, when we get to heaven, will hear our Lord say, "I gave you a gift, a talent, and I was waiting for you to offer it to Me so I could make much of it and do great things with it. But you didn't! Why didn't you?". The three keys to a successful life, the blessed life, the abundant life, are remembering, discovering, and offering. Remembering God's powerful deeds in the past; discovering the Holy Spirit's unique gifts and talents given to each of us by asking Him to reveal them to us; and then offering those gifts and talents to our Lord in faith and service in His Kingdom. Remember, Discover, and Offer.

Well, the entire multitude ate. How much? Our passage says they were all satisfied. The Greek word used here, however, denotes being filled. They ate until they were full. And as usual, some people took too much and couldn't eat all of it. There were twelve baskets of leftovers. And they were not to be thrown away. None of Jesus' gifts are to be wasted. Twelve baskets! Interesting! One for each of the twelve disciples. Yet, not a basket for Jesus. Consider this, however. He Who created this bounty, so much from so little, furnished the opportunity for the twelve disciples to share their portions with Him. So it is with us. From the bounty He gives us, we are privileged to give a portion back to Him. God delights in making much from little. After all, He created the entire universe out of nothing by the power of His Word. And He sent His Son to this earth as a little Baby, Who as a man - the GodMan - would go to the cross as the sacrifice for the sins of the whole world. One solitary Man Who paid the price for the sins of the whole world, including your sins and my sins. One Man whose death and resurrection defeated sin, death, Satan, and all the powers of hell and this world, and opened the way to eternal life for all who receive Him as Lord and Savior.

And speaking of much from little, consider the disciples. Most of them were illiterate, and they were the commonest of common folk, insignificant in the world's eyes. Yet after Pentecost, and reception of the Holy Spirit, they shook this world like it had never been shaken before. God built His Church through them, and those that followed them, a Church that within a few hundred years, an exceptionally short time in historical terms, took the Gospel throughout Europe as far west as Spain and England, and in Asia as far east as India and China, and it continues to take the Gospel to every corner of the world today. So much from so little.

Then too, consider our own nation. Think of that small group of this country's founders, the vast majority of whom were devout Christians, who placed their lives, their fortunes, and their sacred honor on the line because they felt led by God to establish a free nation, one nation under God with liberty and justice for all, and a government of the people, by the people, and for the people. And from those small beginnings, God built the most powerful, the most affluent, the most envied, and I might add the most generous and benevolent nation in the history of the world. Talk about much from little!

Ephesians 2:10 tells us: "For we are God's workmanship, created in Christ Jesus to do good works, which God prepared in advance for us to do." In advance of what? Before He created the heavens and the earth, God, Who is not bound by time or space, knew every human being He would create until the end of time, and in His sovereign will, purpose, and plan, prepared far in advance of their conception and birth the works He would ordain for them (including us) to accomplish for His glory and their highest good. It is God's loving purpose for each of us that we experience the joy of seeing much come from little in the works He ordained for us.

God has made each of us in a unique way, and given each of us a unique gift or gifts to serve Him. Our efforts, our talents, may not seem significant to others, or even to ourselves, but God can use them mightily for His glory and the building of His Church. Christianity is not a spectator sport. God's will for us is that everyone use his or her talents and gifts to help accomplish His purposes on this earth and for eternity, and thus glorify our Savior. And no gift or talent, although small in our eyes, is small in God's eyes. In our Epistle reference, the Apostle Paul tells us that we have a priceless treasure in jars of clay. The priceless treasure is God's own presence and power through the Holy Spirit, shining in our hearts through faith, filling us with His glorious grace in Christ Jesus. The jar of clay is our own human frailty, weakness, and unworthiness. Think of it! So much, more than we can intellectually comprehend, contained in so little.

Our lives are God's gift to us; what we do with our lives is our gift to God. What gift, what talent, what treasure, has God given you that you can offer to Him. Don't hide it. Don't let it waste away. Don't be content with letting it remain little. Offer it to Jesus! Here Lord is my little loaf, my little fish. It's such a humble, little thing, but through your all-surpassing power, You can make so much out of something so little, to the glory of your Name. Amen.

Chapter 14 - Commitment

"Jesus replied, "Love the Lord your God with all your heart and with all your soul and with all your mind. This is the first and greatest commandment. And the second is like it: 'Love your neighbor as yourself.' All the Law and the Prophets hang on these two commandments."

Matthew 22:37-40

"Then He said to them all: "If anyone would come after Me, he must deny himself and take up his cross daily and follow Me."

Luke 9:23

LEAVE, CLEAVE, AND WEAVE

Text: Genesis 2:22-24;   Ephesians 5:33;   Matthew 19:3-6

Theme: The second most important relationship in one's life.

Theme Statement: Marriage, as instituted by God, is the beginning of a new and beautiful phase of life. In marriage, a man and a woman break free from their cocoon of self and aloneness, and together become one in the sight of God. And as one, they are to soar together on wings of beauty and love into their new life that God has prepared for them as husband and wife.

Key Passage: Genesis 2:22-24. Then the Lord made a woman from the rib He had taken out of the man, and He brought her to the man. The man said, "This is now bone of my bones and flesh of my flesh; she shall be called 'woman' for she was taken out of man." For this reason, a man will leave his father and mother and be united to his wife, and they will become one flesh."

✝

The most important commitment a person makes in their lifetime is their commitment in faith to their Lord and Savior Jesus Christ. The second most important commitment a person makes in their lifetime is to their spouse on their wedding day and beyond. In the beginning, God instituted and blessed marriage as the holy union of one man and one woman for the primary purpose of procreation and establishment of the family structure - husband, wife, children - as the bedrock of society. God Himself was the officiant at the first marriage ceremony in history, and also the first Father of the bride, since He gave the bride (Eve), whom He had created, to her husband (Adam), whom He had created.

The one flesh unity between husband and wife that Adam, and later Jesus, spoke of in our Scripture passages, is stronger than any other human kinships that exist. The Hebrew word for wife has the connotation of completer. Scripture tells us that man was incomplete on his own without a helpmate, and that the two together - male and female - as one, make a complete man. The oneness of this relationship is emphasized by Jesus in our Gospel passage when He said, "What therefore God has joined together, let man not separate!"

One might ask, "What about those in Scripture for whom it was God's will that they remain single - for example, Jeremiah, John the Baptist, the Apostle Paul, and others? It is true that God called and ordained certain individuals for a specific purpose and ministry, required them to remain unmarried, and gave them the gift of celibacy to better enable them to fulfill God's purpose. However, this was rare. The vast majority of the priests, pastors, and prophets in Scripture were married. The universal human condition instituted by God was marriage.

Marriage is often referred to as a contract between husband and wife. This is wrong. Contracts can be easily broken or dissolved, which unfortunately is the case today with a majority of marriages. However, marriage as instituted by God, is a holy estate that goes beyond contract. Marriage is a covenant between husband and wife, with those promises to love, honor, etc., in sickness or in health, in poverty or in riches, till death do us part made to one's spouse before God. Thus covenants, as opposed to contracts, are binding relationships and agreements not to be broken. In the case of marriage, the covenant bond is not to be broken or cut off by divorce for any cause except adultery or desertion by one of the partners.

When the Pharisees reminded Jesus that Moses had allowed the people to divorce, Jesus told them that Moses had permitted divorce because of the hardness of their hearts. He then reminded them that it was not that way in the beginning, and emphasized the oneness and covenant aspects of marriage and the only valid cause for divorce.

Yes, divorce is sin according to Scripture. But like all sin, it can be forgiven. Jesus paid the full and terrible price for all sin, including divorce, with His sacrifice of Body and Blood on the cross. If the divorcee's attitude is one of sorrow and regret over the failed marriage, followed by confession and repentance of sin, the person can be sure of God's forgiveness, healing, and renewal.

Scripture is very clear on the wife's duties to her husband, and the husband's duties to his wife. Ephesians 5:22-33 is one of these passages. I find it very interesting that the Apostle Paul, writing this under the inspiration of the Holy Spirit, devotes three verses to the duties of the wife to her husband, while devoting nine verses to the duties of the husband to his wife. And in the duties of the husband, the concept of sacrifice is emphasized, while it is not emphasized in the duties of the wife.

Marriage, from a Scriptural standpoint, can be described in three words. Those words are Leave, Cleave, and Weave. Let's consider each of these. First, Leave. When a man and a woman are bound together in holy marriage, there is a real sense in which they are leaving their father and mother as Scripture says. They don't leave in terms of love, or closeness, or communication. That continues. But they do leave in terms of authority and priority. Next to their relationship with God, the primary relationship in their lives shifts from the parent/son/daughter relationship to the husband/wife relationship.

This is symbolized by the act of the father giving his daughter to the groom. When the pastor asks, "Who gives this woman to be married to this man?" the father answers, "I do!" thus witnessing before God and all present that the father/daughter relationship is superseded by the husband/wife relationship.

There is also a sense in which the husband and wife leave their independence behind. 1Corinthians 11 makes that clear. "In the Lord, woman is not independent of man, nor is man independent of woman. For as woman came from man, so also man is born of woman, and all things originate from God." When husband and wife give their vows, each of them is agreeing to give up their independence. From that time forward, they are dependent on each other, and that dependence on each other is grounded in their dependence on God and their Lord and Savior Jesus Christ.

The second word that describes marriage is Cleave. A man is to cleave to his wife; the wife is to cleave to her husband. That's a perfect description of devotion and commitment, and without such devotion and commitment, without such cleaving, there can be no true oneness in the marriage relationship. The highest form of human intimacy is the intimacy that a husband-and-wife share. It is, or must be, an intimacy of spirit, mind, and body. This does not mean that they think alike in everything, but that they share the same principles, standards, morals, and virtues. Their intimacy is a gift of God and a reflection of the spiritual intimacy that believers have with their Lord and Savior Jesus Christ. Just as they must cleave to their Lord in all circumstances, so they must also cleave to each other in all circumstances without reservations or conditions.

If husband and wife cleave to each other, their love will not grow lukewarm or cold. If they cleave together, they will be strengthened for the difficult and challenging times every marriage goes through. If they cleave to each other, they will know the full joys and blessings of marriage that the Lord wants them to have. If they cleave to their Lord God and to each other through the thick and thin, through the good and through the not-so-good, their marriage will withstand all the storms of life, and their life together will be enriched in ways they cannot imagine.

The third word that describes marriage is Weave. Scripture tells us that husband and wife become one flesh. Their lives are to be inseparable; thus in their oneness their lives are woven together into a magnificent tapestry of great beauty and strength. It only takes thirty minutes or so to conduct a wedding, but it takes a lifetime of oneness to weave that great tapestry of love, commitment, sacrifice, joys, experiences, memories, adventures, intimacies, and yes, sorrows. As husbands and wives give themselves to each other in total love and commitment, as they weave the tapestry of their life together, each of them will complete the other and truly be one flesh.

There is an old saying that goes: "Before marriage, keep both eyes open, and after marriage, keep one eye shut." In other words, we are to be wise, with both eyes open in selecting our life's helpmate, and afterward, keep one eye shut to our mate's faults and idiosyncrasies, remembering that our mate is not perfect, just as we are not perfect. A lovely marriage tapestry will be filled with threads of kindness and compassion and forgiveness of each other, just as in Christ, God forgives us.

Proverbs 18:22 tells us, "He who finds a wife finds a good thing, and he obtains favor from the Lord." Husbands are to return that favor by loving that wife God gives him with a sacrificial love, as Christ loved His Bride, the Church, and gave Himself for her. He is to nurture his wife, encourage her, build her up, protect her, be her friend and lover. He is to be the spiritual leader of his family and a godly example to his wife and the children God will give them. In loving his wife with such love, the husband loves himself too, for the two of them are one.

The wife is to love her husband and give him her respect. She is to nurture him, build him up, and encourage him in his role as spiritual leader of the family. She is to be his wise counselor, his friend and lover. Her love and respect for her husband should be an example for the children. In loving her husband with such love, the wife loves herself too, for the two of them are one.

Finally, for that tapestry of their married life to be truly beautiful, strong, and magnificent, the central thread of that tapestry, the thread that binds the entire tapestry together, must be Jesus Christ their Lord and Savior. If husband and wife grow in faith and commitment to Him, if they keep Him at the very center of their tapestry of life, then His protective and loving Presence will cover them. He will safely guide and lead them through anything and everything they are faced with in this life. He will always be there with them and for them, to rejoice with them, to cry with them, to strengthen them, to comfort them and bear them up.

And so, if husband and wife weave the tapestry of their marriage and life together with the central thread being the Rock of Salvation, Jesus Christ, they will glorify their Creator and Redeemer, and certainly know the joys, fulfillment, and rewards of holy marriage - a marriage of Leaving, Cleaving, and Weaving.

I would like to close with a few Biblical quotations on marriage that I think the reader will enjoy. I've used these quotations in a previous book. First, a quotation from Deuteronomy 24:5, which I imagine all wives would heartily agree with.

"If a man has recently married, he must not be sent to war or have any other duty laid on him. For one year he is to be free to stay at home and bring happiness to the wife he has married,"

Then there is Proverbs 5:18-19 which celebrates marital love. "Fountain" refers to the wife and "Doe," "Deer," is descriptive of the wife, perhaps because of the delicate beauty of the doe's limbs.

"May your fountain be blessed, and may you rejoice in the wife of your youth. A loving doe, a graceful deer – may her breasts satisfy you always, may you ever be captivated by her love."

"A wife of noble character who can find? She is worth far more than rubies." Proverbs 31:10.

The next passage is from Song of Songs, also known as Song of Solomon in some Bibles. In it, the husband describes his wife and her charms. The word "sister" is used generically and not biologically.

"How delightful is your love, my sister, my bride! How much more pleasing is your love than wine, and the fragrance of your perfume than any spice! Your lips drop sweetness as the honeycomb, my bride; milk and honey are under your tongue." Song of Songs 4:10-11.

The next, and final passage, is also from Song of Songs, and in it the wife describes her husband and his charms. "My lover is radiant and ruddy, outstanding among ten thousand. His head is purest gold; his hair is wavy and black as a raven. His eyes are like doves by the water streams, washed in milk, mounted like jewels. His cheeks are like beds of spice yielding perfume.

His lips are like lilies dripping with myrrh. His arms are rods of gold set with chrysolite. His body is like polished ivory decorated with sapphires. His legs are pillars of marble set on bases of pure gold. His appearance is like Lebanon, choice as its cedars. His mouth is sweetness itself; he is altogether lovely. This is my lover, this my friend, O daughters of Jerusalem" Song of Songs 5:10-16

My final comment is a suggestion that every married couple should read the Song of Songs together as encouragement to enjoy fully the gift of sexual intimacy God has given to husband and wife.

CHAPTER 15 - THANKSGIVING

"Do not be anxious about anything, but in everything, by prayer and petition, with thanksgiving, present your requests to God."

Philippians 4:6

Gratitude makes sense of our past, brings peace for the present, and creates a vision for tomorrow. Praise and gratitude are inseparable. Gratitude creates hope. Hope brings joy, and it is in joy, not fear, that we find strength and give praise.

GRATITUDE - THE ROOT OF FAITH

Text: Deuteronomy 8: 1-10; Philippians 4: 6-20;
          Luke 17: 11-19

Theme: God's all-surpassing grace despite our ingratitude.

Theme Statement: Ingratitude is one of the most common of vices, whereas gratitude is a central aspect of the true faith. Too often, those helped in their needs by a merciful God are inclined to forget the God Who helped them. Too often, when beset with troubles and tribulation, we bring our prayers and petitions to God as the Apostle Paul encourages us to do, but we neglect the thanksgiving he urges us to include in our prayers. Yet, it is prayer with thanksgiving that brings the blessed "peace of God," the condition of shalom (peace). Only the thankful heart is a joyful heart. All true prayer has at its heart thanksgiving.

Key Passage: Luke 17: 18. "Was no one found to return and give praise to God except this foreigner?"

†

Next to unbelief, ingratitude is perhaps the deadliest of sins and the most common of vices. An old legend tells of two angels sent to earth, each with a basket, the one to gather up the petitions and requests of the people, and the other to gather up the praises and thanksgivings of the people. When they finished, they were grieved to find that the first basket was filled to overflowing with petitions and requests, while the second basket was nearly empty of praises and thanksgivings.

I imagine our Lord felt such grief after His encounter with the ten lepers. In this encounter, we see in the nine lepers a striking example of the thankless heart. They had faith enough for prayer, evidenced by their petition: "Jesus, Master, have pity on us!" But they didn't have faith enough for praise and thanksgiving. All of them were healed, and what joy they must have felt to discover they were healed. Were they grateful? Probably! But they just couldn't be bothered to return to Jesus and express that gratitude. Only one of the ten felt compelled to do so. Perhaps the nine were in a hurry to get home. Perhaps they thought, "We're grateful, but He will never miss us if we don't return and express our gratitude."

But along with the example of the ingratitude of those nine lepers, we have the example of the gratitude of the one leper whose priority was to return and thank his deliverer and healer Jesus. And we see the intensity of his gratitude - "he came back, praising God in a loud voice, throwing himself at Jesus' feet (an act of worship) and thanking Him." And Jesus blessed him when He said: "Rise and go; your faith has made you well." The other nine lepers had received physical healing also, but this leper, through his praise and thanksgiving, received more. He received both physical healing and spiritual healing. The ingratitude of those nine lepers wounded our Lord and disappointed Him. He said: "Were not all ten cleansed? Where are the other nine? Was no one found to return and give praise to God except this foreigner?" His words express His hurt.

Have you ever, in Christian love, sacrificed time, finances, effort, to meet the needs of another person and been met with ingratitude, not receiving even a "thank-you?" If so, you know how Jesus felt and you stand with your Lord. But just as Jesus did not let the ingratitude of those nine stop Him from helping, healing, and ministering to others, so we should not allow the ingratitude of others towards us stop our kindness and help towards those who reach out to us in need. Remember, if someone we help does not bless us for our kindness, Christ our Lord will.

But there is another question to consider which is: "How often have you and I wounded our Lord through ingratitude?" Those nine lepers, having received the great gift of deliverance from a living death, failed to recognize their obligation of thanksgiving to Him Who had delivered them. How tragic it is that so many today fail to recognize their obligation of thanksgiving to the Savior Who went to the cross to deliver them from that which is immeasurably worse than the condition of those lepers - the condition of sin, hell, and eternal damnation.

It is significant that the one who returned to give thanks was a Samaritan - a foreigner. The foreigner was more overcome with gratitude for the great gift given to him by Christ than were the other nine, who apparently were Jews, the chosen, the children of privilege. Here we have a warning for today - that the children of privilege, the called, we Christians, may become so complacent in our faith and towards God's grace in Christ that our minds become dulled to the surpassing greatness of that grace that the Author of our faith and salvation has poured out on us through His suffering and death on the cross, and continues to pour out on us through His resurrection and the Holy Spirit He has given us. How often do we let other things in this life, career, ambition, materialism, shove the cross of Christ into the background?

That one leper understood the profound significance of what Christ had done for him. Do we, as sinners saved by grace at the terrible cost to our Lord, and made co-heirs with Christ, understand the profound significance of what our God and Savior has done for us, and continues to do? Do we, as individuals and as a nation, understand the profound significance of what God did through our Founding Fathers, establishing one nation of the people, by the people, for the people, founded upon the Christian teachings, morals, and standards given in Holy Scripture, one nation under God, with liberty and justice for all? Do we understand and recognize God's profound blessings on our nation throughout its history, making it the most powerful, affluent, benevolent, and generous nation in history? Such recognition and understanding should lead to praise and thanksgiving to our gracious, awesome God. Our Founders and many of their successors clearly understood this. Tragically, too many of our leaders and people today do not.

Like those nine lepers, we too are more often ready to petition God than to praise and thank God, more disposed to ask God for what we do not have than to thank Him for what we do have. Too often, our attitude is like the grandmother who took her little grandson to the beach one day. In an unguarded moment, the little boy waded into the water and the tide carried him out toward certain death. The grandmother prayed for a miracle. A gigantic wave splashed across the beach, broke in front of her, and deposited the boy safe and sound at her feet. Lifting her eyes toward heaven, the grandmother yelled: "OK God, You brought my grandson back to me, but where is the cap that he was wearing?"

Too often, those helped in their needs by a merciful God are inclined to forget God Who helped them when their needs are met. As Billy Sunday, the evangelist once phrased it, they in effect say to God: "I'll see You later." Tragically, for many who say to God: "I'll see You later, I can't be bothered now," later never comes in this lifetime, and they are lost for eternity.

In our Old Testament reading, Moses exhorts the people, telling them: "When you have eaten and are satisfied, praise the Lord your God for the good land He has given you....Remember how the Lord your God led you all the way in the desert these forty years..." We're told that the Lord disciplined Israel during those years in the wilderness by making them depend on Him for everything - food, water, clothes, protection - everything. Failure to praise and thank God for His manifold blessings leads eventually to forgetting God and disobeying His commands. Failure to praise and thank God leads to a proud heart and forgetting that we are totally dependent on Him for all things.

In our Epistle reading, the Apostle Paul tells us: "Do not be anxious about anything, but in everything, by prayer and petition, with thanksgiving, present your requests to God" (emphasis mine). In Greek, that word anxious, or worry, means "to be of a divided mind," frantically seeking this way and that way out of our troubles. The Christian is not to worry this way about anything. Well, what about our troubles in daily life, some of them painful and depressing? The Holy Spirit, through Paul, tells us not to worry, but in prayer, with thanksgiving, bring our needs before God. It is interesting to note that Paul, when he wrote this, was in prison. If anyone was subject to worry and anxiousness, it was Paul.

Can you and I set aside worry and anxious thoughts and feelings of panic during times of trouble? Not in our own strength can we do that! We're too weak, just as Paul was. But as Jesus told Paul, He also tells us: "My strength is made perfect in your weakness." In His strength, we can overcome worry and panic when our world is collapsing around us. Can we thank God in the midst of trouble and suffering? Not in our own strength! But in the strength of our Savior and the power of the Holy Spirit we can, because we have the assurance of Christ Himself in Matthew 6:8 that the Father knows our troubles, knows our needs, even before we bring them to Him. And we have God's promise in Romans 8:28 that He will work all things out, including our troubles and crisis, to our greatest good.

God assures us that He will attend to all that we ask, either giving us what we ask for, or giving us something better and above what we ask or think. Peter, in his first Epistle, tells us: "Cast all your worry on Him, seeing that He is taking care of you." In what better hands can any troubles of ours rest than in God's hands.

Paul goes on to say that the blessed result of leaving everything in God's hands through prayer, with thanksgiving, is the "peace of God," the condition of shalom. Our hearts and minds are constantly subject to assaults, distress, harassment, and worry. In our human strength, we bravely try to hold fast against these assaults, but our human strength is a poor guard and protector. Only in the strength of our Savior and the peace of God which transcends all understanding and which is only in Christ Jesus can we stand steadfast against the troubles we face in this life.

1 Thessalonians 5: 16-18 tells us: "Be joyful always, pray continually, give thanks in all circumstances, for this is God's will for you in Christ

Jesus." As the old praise song says, "The joy of the Lord is my strength!" Happiness is an emotion which comes and goes. Joy is an attitude of the heart. We can be desperately unhappy with our troubles, while at the same time have that joy in the Lord which comes through faith, prayer, and thanksgiving. Only the thankful heart is a joyful heart. And all true prayer has at its heart thanksgiving for God's grace and blessings.

A National Day of Thanksgiving has been common throughout our history, beginning with the Pilgrims and proclaimed by our presidents beginning with George Washington. However, our current annual National Day of Thanksgiving was established by formal proclamation by Abraham Lincoln on October 3, 1863, in the midst of the Civil War, and passed by an act of Congress. In his proclamation, President Lincoln humbly acknowledged God's sovereignty over the nation and stated: "No human counsel hath devised, nor hath any mortal hand, worked out these great things. They are the gracious gifts of the most high God, Who, while dealing with us in anger for our sins, hath nevertheless remembered mercy...I do, therefore, invite my fellow citizens in every part of the United States, and those who are sojourning in foreign lands, to set apart and observe the last Thursday of November next as a day of thanksgiving and praise to our beneficent Father Who dwelleth in the heavens...It is announced in the Holy Scriptures and proven by all history, that those nations are blessed whose God is the Lord...It has seemed to me fit and proper that God should be solemnly, reverently, and gratefully acknowledged, as with one heart and one voice, by the whole American people."

True thanksgiving to God is total commitment to our Lord and Savior. Gratitude is a central aspect of true faith. And the secret of a grateful heart is a deep sense of our sinfulness and unworthiness, daily recognizing our debt to God's amazing grace, and daily, with awe and wonder, bless and praise God with thanksgiving for His salvation given to us in Christ and our adoption as His sons and daughters.

Thanksgiving blossoms from the root of faith and humility. May such thanksgiving blossom more and more in your heart and in mine, and in the hearts of all our fellowmen this day and every day to come, to the honor and glory of our great Lord and Savior. Amen.

EPILOGUE

Jesus walked the Via Dolorosa to Golgotha on Mount Calvary because of love.

He suffered His head bloody from a crown of thorns because of love.

He suffered His Body torn, ripped open with deep bloody wounds, from being scourged to near death because of love.

He suffered the soldiers nailing Him to a cross with great nails through hands and feet because of love.

He suffered the mocking, vile insults, and curses hurled at Him by the crowd and their leaders in hatred deep because of love.

Hanging on the cross, in agony, drenched with blood and sweat, He asks the Father, "Forgive them, for they know not what they do," because of love.

They know not it is the Son of God as Son of Man they mock, curse, hate and crucify, The Son of God Who, for theirs and our salvation, came to earth to become also Son of Man, conceived by the Holy Spirit, born of the Virgin Mary, in all respects human, but without sin, both fully divine and fully human as the GodMan, because of love. Why this

353

profound act of love and grace by the Father in the giving of His Son? Why this profound act of love and grace of the Son of God in agreeing to the humiliation of joining the human race as Son of Man?

Why this profound act of love and grace of the Son of God as Son of Man in agreeing to become the perfect sacrifice necessary to pay humanity's debt, yours and mine, for our sin and rebellion?

Why this profound love and grace? To forgive us for our sins, to wash us clean of sin and guilt in His Precious Blood, in order to restore our intimate fellowship with God which is His highest desire and our highest good?

Why? Because your God and mine loves us and all His human creations with a Divine, unconditional, unchanging, everlasting love so magnificently profound that the human mind cannot conceive of it.

Jesus comes today to the modern Calvary, our cities, streets, and homes because of that profound love. Offering to those who have not yet received Him in faith the forgiveness, cleansing, and fellowship purchased with His Blood.

But many, so many, just pass Him by, ignoring His love and grace, and the eternal life He gives. Oh, they would never hurt or harm Him, or nail Him to a cross like those of the earlier Calvary.

They just walk by His outstretched arms, ignoring the theology lane of life He gives, and taking the worldly lane of death.

Their apathy and indifference, like those thorns, nails, and spear of the earlier Calvary, pierce Jesus through and through.

But still Jesus, head bowed and weeping in sorrow for this modern Calvary, cries out as in the earlier Calvary, "Father, forgive them, for they know not what they do."

Darrell

Made in the USA
Columbia, SC
28 September 2023

23507303R00212